RUTH
BLAU

PERSPECTIVES ON ISRAEL STUDIES
S. Ilan Troen, Natan Aridan, Donna Divine, David Ellenson,
Arieh Saposnik, and Jonathan Sarna, editors
Sponsored by the Ben-Gurion Research Institute for the
Study of Israel and Zionism of the Ben-Gurion
University of the Negev and the Schusterman
Center for Israel Studies of Brandeis University

Seal of BGU   Seal of Brandeis

RUTH
BLAU

A Life of Paradox and Purpose

—⁂—

Motti Inbari

INDIANA UNIVERSITY PRESS

This book is a publication of

Indiana University Press
Office of Scholarly Publishing
Herman B Wells Library 350
1320 East 10th Street
Bloomington, Indiana 47405 USA

iupress.org

Manufactured in the United States of America
First printing 2023

Library of Congress Cataloging-in-Publication Data

Names: Inbari, Motti, author.
Title: Ruth Blau : a life of paradox and purpose / Motti Inbari.
Description: Bloomington, Indiana : Indiana University Press, [2023] | Series: Perspectives on Israel studies | Includes bibliographical references and index.
Identifiers: LCCN 2022060926 (print) | LCCN 2022060927 (ebook) | ISBN 9780253065957 (hardback) | ISBN 9780253065964 (paperback) | ISBN 9780253065971 (ebook)
Subjects: LCSH: Blau, Ruth. | Jewish converts from Christianity—France—Biography. | Ultra-Orthodox Jewish women—Israel—Biography. | Rabbis' spouses—Israel—Biography. | Orthodox Judaism—Relations—Nontraditional Jews. | Naṭore karta—Biography.
Classification: LCC BM755.B584 I36 2023 (print) | LCC BM755.B584 (ebook) | DDC 296.7/14—dc23/eng/20230213
LC record available at https://lccn.loc.gov/2022060926
LC ebook record available at https://lccn.loc.gov/2022060927

CONTENTS

To Shani

ACKNOWLEDGMENTS

ON A COLD MORNING IN 2008, while I was a postdoctoral fellow at the Schusterman Center for Israel Studies at Brandeis University, I received an email from my academic supervisor, Dr. Ilan Troen. His message contained the exciting news that Boston University acquired the personal archive of Rabbi Amram Blau, head of the Neturei Karta movement in Jerusalem. I went to check out this archive, and I found it to be a historical treasure; I am so glad to compose two books on the Blau family partly based on this archive. In my book *Jewish Radical Ultra-Orthodoxy Confronts Modernity, Zionism and Women's Equality* (2016), I explore the biography of Rabbi Blau. In this book that you are holding now, I tell the fascinating story of his wife, Ruth.

I am grateful to many people who assisted me in the publication of this book, and I first want to thank Nechama Davidson, Ruth's granddaughter. Nechama and I spent tens of hours talking about Ruth, as Nechama is also writing a manuscript on her grandmother's biography. Nechama shared hundreds of documents from Ruth's archive stored at her parents' house, and she also invited me to interview them. Her brother, Itzhak Davidson, was also very helpful and sent me many documents in his possession. Finally, I want to thank Joel Rappel for facilitating the transfer of the Blau Archive to Boston University, even though the archive is no longer there (Itzhak Davidson owns it now). Without the support of the Davidson family, this research could not have been so rich with details and nuance.

Dr. Ilan Troen introduced me to the archive, and I am so happy to close the circle with him since he is also the acquisition editor at Indiana University Press. The publication of this book is an excellent opportunity to thank Ilan for his support and care for so many years.

I owe a special thanks to Dr. Menachem Keren-Kratz, a leading scholar on ultra-Orthodox history. Menachem read the draft manuscript and gave me such precious advice. He also translated for me Ruth's letters from Yiddish. I thank him dearly for his friendship and collegiality.

Dr. Olivier Wieviorka explained how to navigate the French archives and even was gracious to help me find Ruth's file at the Service Historique de la Defense, France's military archives. Virginie Rumsch assisted me with translating the French documents.

My trips to Israel and France were partly sponsored by grants from the University of North Carolina at Pembroke. Dr. David Nikkel, chair of the Department of Philosophy and Religion at UNC–Pembroke, has been a great leader and always supportive. He ensured I always had time and funds to conduct my research. My gratitude also goes to Dr. Brian Stratton, my colleague from the department, who read sections of the manuscript.

This manuscript won two awards: The Hadassah—Brandeis Institute Research Award, and the Fanya Gottesfeld Heller Center for the Study of Women in Judaism, Bar Ilan University, book prize.

I want to send special thanks to Yuval Jobani, Maxine Carr, Margalit Shilo, and the anonymous readers of the manuscript for making excellent comments and suggestions. I am also glad to continue working with Shaul Vardi, who copyedited the manuscript, as he has done for all my previous books.

It is a pleasure to thank friends and colleagues for their ongoing support, including Yaakov Ariel, David Ellenson, Robert Eisen, and Mitu Ashraf.

Lastly, working on this book has been a family project. We traveled together to France to find documents in Paris, and I wrote the manuscript during the extended lockdowns during the COVID-19 pandemic, often discussing my research around the family table. Aliza, my dear wife, read the manuscript and helped me think about the findings and interpret them. Finally, I am dedicating this book to my older daughter, Shani. As Shani finishes high school and goes to college, I hope this book will serve as an inspiration for her.

In my previous book, *The Making of Modern Jewish Identity* (2019), I devoted a chapter to the life of Ruth Blau, and this book is an expansion of the previous research. Sections of this chapter are reproduced with the permission of Routledge through PLSclear.

RUTH
BLAU

INTRODUCTION

ISSER HAREL, HEAD OF THE Mossad, Israel's spying agency, landed in Tel Aviv in mid-March 1962, returning from a work-related trip, to find an urgent message waiting for him: "David Ben-Gurion wants to speak with you." Harel was one of Israel's fiercest and most sophisticated spymasters. The Mossad under his leadership had become the fear of ex-Nazis and Arab plotters. Two years earlier, Harel's team had caught Adolf Eichmann in Buenos Aires, Argentina, smuggling the Nazi officer responsible for the murder of half a million Hungarian Jews during the Holocaust to Israel and bringing him to justice.

Ben-Gurion, Israel's first prime minister and one of the most outstanding leaders of the Zionist movement, was waiting for Harel; it was almost 10:00 p.m. The two spoke on various subjects, but Harel felt that Ben-Gurion had not yet touched on the real reason he had been summoned. It was almost midnight when the meeting came to an end. Only at the doorstep, as he wished Harel goodnight, did Ben-Gurion finally say what was on his mind: "Can you find the boy?"

Harel instantly knew that Ben-Gurion was referring to Yossele Schumacher, who had been kidnapped by his ultra-Orthodox grandfather and whose whereabouts remained unknown. The kidnapping of Yossele was tearing Israeli society apart, creating an unresolved saga of a religiously motivated ideological crime. Therefore, Harel accepted the mission and modestly declared: "I will try."

It took the Mossad three months to solve the case, finding the boy hidden under a false identity in New York. The Mossad forwarded the information to the FBI, locating the boy and bringing him back to his parents. In retrospect, Harel said that solving the Yossele case was one of the most challenging and complicated operations he ever conducted.

Many people were responsible for kidnapping, smuggling, and hiding Yossele, but the person responsible for orchestrating the complex campaign was a virtually unknown woman: an outsider and French convert to Judaism called Ruth Ben David. As soon as Harel accepted the mission, Ruth became a fugitive. Harel had no idea how complex the chase would be, for Ruth herself had been a spy and gained extensive experience in undercover operations. Two great minds were playing a game of chess against each other.

This episode was not the first time an espionage agency had been on Ben David's tail. When Harel was eventually able to trick and catch her after a fleeting act of negligence on her part, it was not the first time she found herself in an interrogation room. Harel admits that she was tough to break; it took him fourteen days to get her to confess, and he almost gave up. Clearly, she had been trained to withstand questioning. Above all, this was neither the first nor the last time she put her life in danger while fighting for things she believed in, placing herself in the most precarious of situations.

"Who are you, Ruth Ben David?" was the question Harel famously asked as he tried to get under her skin—a difficult question to answer, indeed.

Very few people of the twentieth century had a life story as thrilling as Ruth Ben David/Blau. She was born in northern France in 1920 as Madeleine Lucette Ferraille, but while she was still a toddler, her family moved to Paris. She was the only girl of a disintegrating family with a sick mother and philandering father. She was born Roman Catholic, but as a young woman, she decided to renounce her birth religion. Instead, she embarked on a spiritual quest, beginning with Seventh-day Adventists but eventually finding herself in the heart of the Jewish ultra-Orthodox enclave in Jerusalem. Along the way, she passed through several stages. First, she was active in the French Resistance. Later, she embarked on an educational journey in philosophy as a doctoral candidate at the Sorbonne during the 1950s, which influenced her immensely. Next, she tried her luck in business but ended up in prison for several months due to tax evasion. Finally, she converted to Judaism in 1952 and moved to Israel in 1960 after a failed love affair. Afterward, from 1960 to 1962, she helped hide Yossele Schumacher, whose ultra-Orthodox grandfather abducted him as part of a militant conflict between ultra-Orthodoxy and secular Jews in Israel. In 1965, despite a sensational scandal, she married Amram Blau, head of the anti-Zionist ultra-Orthodox Neturei Karta faction. After the death of her husband in 1973, she took it on herself to travel to the Arab world to help the Jewish communities in Lebanon and Iran, meeting with Yasser Arafat, head of the Palestinian Liberation Organization, and his deputy Abu Jihad. But it was in Iran that she made her most significant connections. In 1979, she met with the leader of the Iranian revolution, Ayatollah Khomeini, to discuss the conditions of Iranian Jews. Her name is even connected in a convoluted way to the Iran-Contra scandal, when the United States, with the support of the Mossad, sold arms to Iran through a third party in the early 1980s.

Ruth Blau was a woman of contradictions: a lapsed Catholic who became a Haredi Jew; a free-thinking and promiscuous French woman who closed herself off in an environment that oppresses women; a devoted mother to an only son who caused immeasurable suffering to other parents who also had a son;

a businesswoman in search of spirituality; a beautiful young woman who married an elderly and infertile man; someone who ostensibly found her placed in the traditional world of Meah Shearim yet rebelled against the limited role of the submissive wife, fought to get what she wanted, and ultimately became a proximate leader in her own right. How can we explain all these twists and turns?

A LIAR?

It was the winter of 2008 when I began to develop an interest in the biography of Ruth Blau. At first I assumed that studying her life story would be an easy project: she had published an autobiography, other scholars had written about her, and she had been a media figure who regularly featured in the news. When I met someone who knew her in person, he asked me to tell him what I knew; I responded, and he started laughing. He said, "You know nothing." I insisted: "But she wrote an autobiography." He replied: "Don't believe a word she said. She was a liar."

I took this recommendation to heart. Starting from assuming that I could not trust any of the facts she mentions in her autobiography and the interviews she gave, I had to fact-check her claims by checking additional outside sources rigorously. For that purpose, I traveled to Paris, Boston, and Jerusalem to collect information, investigate archive materials, and conduct interviews with people who knew her. Sometimes my task almost felt like detective work, piecing together clues and hints from her past. After investigating Ruth's life for so many years, I can confidently state that she was not a liar. Much of what she said has been confirmed as correct. However, she did not tell us the whole story, and she sometimes distorted the historical narrative of her life. My research revealed some astonishing discoveries she had never mentioned to anyone. One can only guess why she omitted sections of her past from her narrative, especially parts of her early years before converting to Judaism.

The comment that Ruth was a liar illustrates the deep public sentiments toward her. Ruth was a person people loved to hate, an antihero, a villain. While the majority of the Jewish people were Zionists who strongly supported the newly created, struggling State of Israel, Ruth was an anti-Zionist. When Jewish secularity triumphed, she became ultra-Orthodox. She was perceived as a child snatcher and even a child abuser. For Yossele, she had the face of the devil. In an interview in 2020, fifty-eight years after his abduction, Yossi Schumacher said that he had made peace with his past, and he forgives almost all the participants in his kidnapping, with one exception: Ruth Blau.[1] Her bad reputation in Israeli public opinion included unflattering pictures in the Israeli newspapers, although everyone knew she was beautiful. Although Jewish tradition states that one must never remind a convert of their conversion, in the Israeli press, she always was described as "the convert." She had been married since 1965, but the press always referred to her by her maiden name after conversion: Ruth Ben David. Reminding the readers of her conversion and not calling her by her correct last name was a subtle way of shaming and annoying her.

Her image changed during the scandal surrounding her engagement to Rabbi Amram Blau, when it was revealed that the Haredi community opposed their marriage solely because Ben David was a convert and hence an unworthy match for a great rabbi. Many found such discrimination unacceptable, and after the protest was published in the secular newspapers, the couple received many letters of support at their home. Their love story, coming from behind the walls of the most conservative Jewish movement, touched the hearts of many as a tale of passion against all odds.

The discoveries of her past highlight some positive aspects of her life. She fought the Nazi invaders without fear, using her charm and beauty in the service of the Resistance. She helped Jews escape the Nazis. She traveled to Arab lands to help Jews in distress. The silver lining of her personality is that she always aspired to make a difference and do good things. Unfortunately, however, her moral compass sometimes sent her to dark places.

Ruth died in 2000 and is buried in Jerusalem. She was a colorful figure, well-known in Israel, with the Israeli press covering her constantly. Besides being eccentric and different, she has been an important figure in many ways. We can learn many aspects of modern Jewish and Israeli history through her biography.

METHODOLOGY AND SOURCES

To study Ruth's biography, I visited French archives in Paris to learn Ruth/Lucette's past before her conversion to Judaism. I collected information from various French libraries regarding her education, time in prison, and, most significantly, military service during the Second World War, which continued even after the war ended when she enlisted in 1945 to the French secret service.

I also traveled to Jerusalem to meet her surviving family members and close friends. I am fortunate that her grandchildren were supportive and gave me full access to hundreds of documents Ruth kept in her archive. Their memories and insights were very precious.

The archives of Boston University used to house the personal archive of Amram Blau, Ruth's husband and the leader of the Neturei Karta movement. There are eighty pages in Yiddish of personal correspondence Ruth made with prominent ultra-Orthodox rabbis regarding her marriage scandal in that archive.

From these pages and other sources, I was able to construct the dramatic events that led to her wedding. However, this archive is no longer available at Boston University. It is currently available through Ruth's grandson, Itzhak Davidson, who owns a personal collection that also includes Ruth and Amram Blau's documents.

Other sources are her unpublished autobiography from 1963 and her published book *Guardians of the City* (1979), printed in Hebrew and French, although the two narratives are not identical. These are censored versions of her autobiography, but they still provided updated information regarding her life as the wife of Amram Blau. In addition, Isser Harel, head of the Mossad, wrote his response to her narrative, titled *The Yossele Campaign* (1982), which added important information on the kidnapping of Yossele Schumacher and the ultimate resolution of this affair. Shlomo Cohen-Sidon, the lawyer who represented the Schumacher family during the abduction period, also published an important book called *Where's Yossele? The Story of Yossele Schumacher* (1963). The final primary sources are the Israeli and French presses, which reported on Ruth's activities.

THE BOOK'S STRUCTURE

The first chapter describes Lucette's upbringing, relationship with her parents, and childhood. In this chapter, I quote several letters written by her father, where he described an incident in the family when she was a teenager. His letters help the reader understand the collapse of her parent's marriage and Ruth's strong feelings against her father.

The second chapter examines Lucette's life during World War II. It starts with a general discussion of France during the war, the creation of the Vichy regime, the formation of the French Resistance, and the fate of Jews under the regime. Lucette's activities during the war are presented mainly from the materials found in French archives in Paris. She helped save Jews during the war, even before being officially recruited to the Alliance resistant movement. In 1944, she became a secret agent at the headquarters of the Gestapo in the Toulouse area. After the war, Lucette joined the French secret service, and the chapter details her mission to Morocco in 1946.

The following two chapters describe Lucette's spiritual journey. The third chapter describes Lucette's search in several different avenues, including the occult, Greek philosophy, and Seventh-day Adventism, before finding her spirituality port with the Hebrew Bible. It then describes several psychological theories on what motivates people to change their religion as a general phenomenon.

The fourth chapter outlines her conversion process. In 1951, Lucette fell in love with an Israeli student at the Sorbonne, which led her to convert to Judaism with a Reform rabbi to marry. Following her conversion, she changed her name to Ruth Ben David. After this relationship ended, she fell in love with an Orthodox rabbi and received a second conversion, this time to Orthodoxy. The couple got engaged, but eventually, the wedding was canceled. After this disappointment, Ruth joined the ultra-Orthodox community in France and Belgium. The chapter puts Ruth's conversion story in a larger context of a wave of converts (primarily women) to Judaism after World War II.

Chapters 5 and 6 tell the story of the Yossele Schumacher affair. The fifth chapter describes the family dispute over Yossele's education that led to his grandfather abducting his seven-year-old grandson in 1960. Later, the anti-Zionist ultra-Orthodox Neturei Karta got into the picture. Rabbi Avraham Elijah Maizes, who helped Ruth with her Orthodox conversion in Paris, dragged her to the affair. Under his request, she smuggled the boy to Europe and afterward to the United States. The chapter details the kidnapping trail.

In 1962, David Ben-Gurion ordered the Mossad to find the boy after two years of fruitless police investigations and while tension was brewing in Israel between Orthodox and secular Jews. The Mossad was able to connect Ruth with the boy's disappearance, and by the orders of Isser Harel, head of the Mossad, his agents kidnapped Ruth in Paris for interrogations. After fourteen days, Ruth gave the boy's location in return for immunity. The sixth chapter details how Yossele was eventually found and continues by describing the affair's impact on the young State of Israel and Orthodox-secular relations.

On September 2, 1965, Ruth Ben David and Rabbi Amram Blau, head of the Neturei Karta movement, got married in what was supposed to be a secret wedding; however, the news leaked, and the press widely reported about it. This marriage affair had all the ingredients to make it a melodrama: love, sex, manipulations, and power. At the end of the day, the marriage brought the downfall of Amram Blau as a leader and the weakening of Neturei Karta as a movement. The seventh chapter is about the marriage affair.

There is a set of social requirements expected of an ultra-Orthodox woman, and additional ones expected of a rabbi's wife, a rebbetzin. The eighth chapter discusses the institution of the rebbetzin in general terms and sees how it was applied to Ruth's life. Finally, the chapter explains Ruth's roles in the leadership of Neturei Karta as the wife of Rabbi Amram, with a particular focus on her roles in fundraising, matchmaking, and institution building.

From 1974, there is a record that Ruth traveled to Muslim countries to help Jews in distress. The ninth chapter discusses the two meetings Ruth had with the leader of the Iranian revolution, Ayatollah Khomeini (in 1979 and 1980); the reasons for these meetings; and their resolutions. In addition, the chapter describes her attempt to gain pardon for Albert Danielpour, a prominent member of the Iranian Jewish community. He was charged as a Mossad and CIA agent in 1980 in Teheran and sentenced to death by the Revolutionary Guard. In 1985, the Organization of the

Oppressed on Earth, the pseudonym of Hezbollah, kidnapped six Jewish community members in Lebanon. After Ruth's interference, the kidnappers offered to trade the hostages for Shiite prisoners in Israeli jails. Ruth also had a small part in trying to find information on the three Israeli missing soldiers after the Battle of Sultan Yacoub in Lebanon in 1982.

The tenth chapter puts Ruth's case in a larger context. Comparing Ruth's case to that of Jacob-Israël de Haan (1881–1924), the so-called foreign minister of the Ashkenazi City Council, the main religious and political organization of the Old Yishuv, shows in what special circumstances the ultra-Orthodox community allows unique outsiders to get leadership roles. Comparing Ruth to Alta Faige Teitelbaum, the wife of the Yoel Teitelbaum, the Satmar Rebbe, shows the circumstances that allow women to break the traditional role of housewife. The chapter continues to discuss how Ruth's case teaches us the place of physical attraction in ultra-Orthodox marriages and ends with a discussion of how her case explains the secular Israeli public's view of the ultra-Orthodox community.

—⟋⟍—

Was Ruth Satan, or was she a saint? I am aware that this book rehabilitates her image, and I acknowledge that some may resent this, especially Yossele and his family. I leave you, the readers, to judge.

A note about her name: she was born Madeleine Lucette, and sometimes in the Israeli press, you can see references to her by her first name, Madeleine. The current research revealed that her name before changing to Ruth was Lucette. After her conversion, she changed her name to Ruth Ben David, and this last name stuck with her. After marrying Rabbi Blau, she took his last name, which she used until her death. In this book, I refer to her according to the name she used at the time in question, be it Lucette, Ruth, Ben David, or Blau.

ONE

CHILDHOOD

MADELEINE LUCETTE FERRAILLE WAS AN only child, born in her grandmother's home in Calais in northern France on June 22, 1920. Her father, Octave, was originally from Geneva, Switzerland. Her mother, Jeanne Catherine Isaert, was from nearby Belgium, but the family also had some Spanish roots. During the Second World War, Calais was at the heart of one of the bloodiest battles, the Battle of Dunkirk, the humiliating defeat of the French and British forces by Nazi Germany. But the family moved when Lucette was three and settled in the Latin Quarter, the bustling heart of Paris.

The family lived in a small apartment on the Rue de Canettes, a home Lucette described as very pretty. The space included a bedroom for the parents, a small living room, a kitchen with a chimney, and a niche for the girl. Later, the grandmother from Calais moved in with them and shared the space with Lucette. Once a year, Ruth tells us in her unpublished manuscript, Père Noël (Santa Claus) would come through the chimney to give her presents on Christmas.

At the time (and still today), the Latin Quarter of Paris was the bohemian part of the city, home to Paris's most famous universities, including the Sorbonne. It is also an iconic tourist spot in the city. The Rue de Canettes is a charming little street; today, it has many cafés, restaurants, and boutique stores. The street connects to a beautiful plaza with a large fountain, outside the Church of Saint-Sulpice, the second-largest church in Paris, after Notre Dame, which is itself within walking distance. Saint-Sulpice is known for its magnificent organ, and its weekly concerts draw a large crowd.

Lucette attended the Lycée Fenoelon, a middle and high school for girls near her home, where many of the intellectual elite of France had studied, such as the feminist philosopher Simone de Beauvoir, who attended the school a decade before Lucette. I tried to trace Lucette's footsteps and consider how it must have been for her growing up in this setting. Walking from her home to her high school, you cross the Luxemburg Gardens and continue through narrow streets, home to students and university professors, passing some of Paris's most famous landscapes, such as the Pantheon and the Sorbonne. Lucette tells us that the family indeed enjoyed the beauty of the city, and over the weekends, they took long walks along Paris's boulevards.

Although Lucette's childhood passed in one of the most desirable and famous tourist locations in the world, her childhood memories were not so positive. As an adult, she easily left the city behind.

In her unpublished English manuscript, but not in the other published ones in Hebrew and French, she discussed her family and household.

Ruth (when she wrote the manuscript, her name was Ruth) opens her discussion with some early childhood memories; she recalls herself in a dark room crying nonstop while in another room, a woman is handing her over to her mother. In later years, her mother explained these memories to her: After birth, her mother became seriously anemic, and on medical advice, Lucette was entrusted to a nurse for several months. Baby Lucette rejected the separation from her mother and refused all food, and accordingly, she was returned home. From this she concluded that nothing could stand against her will.[1] The mother-child theme would resurface in Ruth's life many years later when she helped conceal a boy from his parents and saw no wrong in her actions.

When describing her parents, Ruth emphasized the difference between their two characters. Her mother was deeply spiritual, though not a churchgoer, while her father was agnostic. Her mother was kind and patient, while her father was stormy and impetuous; her mother modest, her father arrogant; her heart was pure, while his was divided.

Her father was taller, but since he was obese, he actually looked smaller than his wife. He had thick black hair, bushy eyebrows that met in the middle, and deep black eyes—features that, according to Ruth, made him look neither handsome nor ugly but gave him a certain charm. Ruth remembers her father as having the ability to mimic the comedian Charlie Chaplin, whose fame was then at its height.

In terms of personality, Ruth could find nothing positive to say about her father. Although he was intelligent and strong, he lacked faith and was very materialistic. The good things in life were his only realities, she observed, and he devoted all of his powers to obtaining them. However, I must question this description. After all, in her unpublished autobiography, Ruth herself tells us that her father fought in the Resistance, and after the war, he even received a medal for his service. This fact alone suggests that he was not concerned solely for material gain; had this been the case, it would have made more sense for him to collaborate with the Nazis.

Ruth disliked her father because he was abusive and mistreated her mother; as a result, their relationship was never peaceful. The reality was more complex. However, she admits that as a young child, she used to observe her father to understand him better so that she would not turn out like him one day. She said that after more than twenty years, "a feeling of pity for him surpassed all the bitterness in my heart."[2] An interesting observation I can add is that while looking at the family's old photo albums, it is very clear to see that Ruth cut out her father's image from all the family pictures. Another example of how she cut him out of her life appears in the affidavits she gave to the French police (discussed later in this chapter), in which she stated that her father remarried after the war but added that she had ceased all contact with him.

Ruth expresses much warmer feelings toward her mother, whom she loved and regarded as her most powerful influence. Ruth describes her mother as tall, slim, blond, and very attractive: "She looked like an angel."[3]

Ruth's mother died at the age of fifty-four, and her life was never easy. She was the eldest of eleven children from a low-income family. She began work at the age of twelve and after marrying, worked as a salesgirl in a large store. Ruth described her parents' twenty-year marriage as unhappy. Her mother was a great cook, but her father never liked her food. She suffered in silence, never rebelling, never dropping a hint of accusation against him, quiet and smiling, bearing all her troubles with dignity.

Her parents agreed on Lucette's education, and both prioritized discipline and endurance. Ruth says her father imposed these Spartan principles, and she described her upbringing as far from pleasant. Ruth offers a horrible example. When she was nine years old, her parents sent her to a Catholic summer camp for two months. One day she fell while playing and hurt her knee. For the rest of the holiday, she had trouble walking, despite the treatment she received, and the pain continued even after the wound had closed entirely. As soon as she came home, her father examined the knee to discover a small black point showing through the skin. He made her sit on a chair, and equipped with a sharp knife and two spoons, which he sterilized in boiling water, he reopened the wound. With a pair of tweezers, he removed a piece of rotten wood that was deeply embedded. He then cleaned up the wound and put a bandage on it. "In spite of the terrible pain and all the fears of a child, I had to sit there without uttering a sound."[4] The terror she experienced during this home operation remained with her for the rest of her life and was very apparent, as her granddaughter Nechama Davidson recalled in an interview with me. Despite all this, Ruth reaches an interesting conclusion: "I feel that I have reason to be grateful to him for having trained me to endure pain from my earliest childhood." Indeed, Europe would go into great turmoil in the years to come, and Lucette surely benefited from her strong personality, her ability to show no fear, and her ability to endure pain, whether physical or psychological.

Her father's family lived in Switzerland, and she had minimal contact with them during her childhood. However, she adored her maternal grandmother and was very close to her. Her grandmother had a hard life raising a family in poverty. Ruth says she was inspired by her advice and noble example. Lucette was twelve when she used to take her blind and aging grandmother for walks each week; the blind old lady would lean on her and tell her of her misfortunes. Ruth describes her grandmother as a woman of great beauty, tall and slender, with delicate classical features, black eyes, and short hair. Her grandmother had Spanish ancestry. In her last year, she lived with them in their house, although her father objected, calling her "la Carmencita," the name of a famous Spanish dancer. Lucette was fifteen years old when her grandmother died.[5]

The Spanish ancestry of her grandmother inspired Ruth later in her life to study her family tree in great depth. In an interview I conducted with Henie Persitz, a close friend of Ruth who was almost one hundred years old when we spoke in 2018, Henie said that Ruth spent days in vain studying archives in southern France trying to find a hidden family connection to crypto-Jews.[6] Crypto-Judaism is the secret adherence to Judaism while publicly professing to be of another faith. The term is mainly applied historically to Spanish Jews who outwardly professed Catholicism.

Ruth wrote in her unpublished autobiography that her grand-mother had certain habits that were distinctly Jewish, like soak-ing meat in saltwater before cooking it. She recalls that whenever her father came home unexpectedly, he would walk straight into the kitchen, and if he found meat in water, he would become furi-ous. Still, her mother continued the practice, though she would take every possible care to conceal the vessel containing the meat in water from her husband's angry eyes. Her mother also refused to eat pork and shellfish, and Ruth confesses she inherited this aversion from her mother, although oysters were a very popular dish in France.[7]

Her grandmother's family name was Magniez, pronounced Magnies, derived from the Latin Magnus; the name is still found among Jews today. Perhaps the best-known example is Yehuda Magnes, the founding president of the Hebrew University of Je-rusalem. According to Henie, Ruth had Yehuda Magnes in mind as a possible family connection.[8]

Ruth sought to replicate the dichotomy of Jews versus inquisi-tors from the history of the Jews of Spain in her parents' home. She depicts her beloved mother striving to maintain the remnants of Jewish heritage in the way she cooked food, to the displeasure of her virulently antireligious father. In his interview with the *Jerusalem Post*, her son Uriel Davidson (he changed his last name from Ben David to Davidson) discussed his mother's attempts to claim a secret Jewish identity. He states that he spent much time with his grandmother as a child and has no recollection of the process of "koshering" meat that his mother described.[9] Ruth's status as a convert—a newcomer to the Jewish world—irked her throughout her life and created numerous problems. Accordingly, it is only natural that she attempted to credit herself with a Jew-ish background, however flimsy. We may interpret Ruth's narra-tive regarding her relations with her parents in a similar context.

Figure 1.1 Little Lucette in Paris. Courtesy of Nechama Davidson.

Having assumed a secret Jewish origin inherited through her maternal family, this side of the family was depicted in glowing terms. At the same time, her father was portrayed as a cold and egotistical Christian with a brutal hostility to religion. I would add that, in general, Ruth describes agnosticism and antireligiosity in dark terms as a force against which she was forced to wage an active struggle. Despite her predominantly negative depiction of her father, she thanks him for giving her various qualities that would usually be considered negative, such as stubbornness, rigidity, and a fanatical devotion to her goals.[10]

CATHOLICISM

Ruth stated that she had deep religious feelings from an early age and had a strong faith. This did not come from her parents, who were nonpracticing or nonbelievers. Despite this, they ensured that she received a Catholic education at the nearby Church of Saint-Sulpice. She was baptized into the church, and at the age of nine, she entered a course of religious instruction, followed two years later by her first communion. This was a moving occasion for her, where all the girls in the district dressed in white and walked proudly to the ceremony through the streets of the quarter in which she lived.

She remembers that she used to stay quietly in her room as a child, and later her mother told her that she was praying. She recalls that she took her religion very seriously and asked questions about the mystery of the Trinity. However, after she moved to middle school, she began to have doubts. The issue in mind was the grim discovery that there is no "Father Christmas" who brings toys to children through the chimney. "I was most distressed at the thought that I had been living in a world of myth, and determined to verify the truth of all I learned."[11]

Another incident that she describes as unimportant but that clearly moved her deeply occurred at the Church of Saint-Sulpice. At the heart of the church stands a statue of St. Peter that is highly revered by the faithful. When I visited the church, I saw notes, flowers, and candles by the statue. Ruth recalls seeing worshippers walking past, each fervently kissing its foot. She adds that she felt guilty for standing frozen while others were displaying such piety, and accordingly she moved forward to follow suit and kiss the foot. The emotions she felt were not as expected: instead

Figure 1.2 The statue of St. Peter. Photograph by the author.

of a profound religious experience, she was disgusted by the hygienic aspect of the experience. After cupping the cold bronze foot in her palm, she ran away, ashamed of kissing a statue in the same way she kissed her dolls.[12]

Ruth often thought of this incident when she studied history and art. She had doubts and hesitations throughout her youth, but she dared not to take any action and merely intensified her studies. We can trust these testimonies, despite their apologetic tone, given that later she indeed changed her religion, and she embarked on an educational journey that led her to pursue a PhD program at the Sorbonne in theological studies.

The Catholic Church puts little emphasis on the teachings of the Hebrew Bible (the Old Testament). The priests in her church did not encourage the reading of that part of the Bible, but since she became interested in religion as a young child, she asked her parents to buy her the Bible when she saw it on a Salvation Army stand on the streets of Paris. She was about twelve years old when she got her first copy, and the biblical tales thrilled her imagination: "I crossed the Red Sea with Moses and the children of Israel."[13]

From a certain age, which she does not specify, she no longer was obliged to attend religious school. As a result, her visits to the church became less frequent, and she lost interest in the Catholic faith.

POLITICAL ORIENTATION

The years 1932 to 1939, during which she studied at the lycée, were a turbulent and fateful period in European history. In 1932 the National Socialists rose to power in Germany amid a global economic crisis; France's political and economic situation was also tense. Her father, a skilled radio engineer, suffered from the economic depression, while her mother had to take a second job as a dressmaker.

The political streets of Paris were divided between opposing movements. Many of Ruth's friends were Socialists, Communists, or supporters of the right-wing Croix-de-Feu, and they joined the associated youth movements. The teachers at school were also divided between these movements. Ruth declares that she was not political, but out of interest she participated in a Communist event together with one friend and even read *Mein Kampf* on the advice of another.

The rise of antisemitism and the persecution of Jews in Germany attracted heightened attention to the Jewish situation as more and more refugees flooded the streets of Paris. At this time, Ruth perceived Jews merely as the Old Testament people, but following the rise of Hitler, she realized that some girls at her school were Jewish. For the Socialist girls, Jewish students became friends in need of political defense; for the Fascist students, they were the object of scorn and humiliation.

Ruth's father paid a Jewish refugee living in Paris to teach his daughter German. From him, she learned the language, which helped her considerably later in life, and had an opportunity to learn about the political situation in Germany.[14]

Her father had a Jewish colleague of Russian origin who was also a Communist. This man fell in love with Lucette when she was sixteen years old, and he asked her father for permission to marry her. Ruth tells us that she felt nothing for him. His personality, coupled with his Communist ideas, did not make him particularly attractive. Her father declined the proposal. Ruth initially assumed that this was because the candidate was Jewish, but later she realized that her father was simply a negative person. She said that her father was no more antisemitic than the average French man.[15] In her father's letter during the war, he used the term "the wandering Jew" to describe his grandson, a very energetic child.

OCTAVE FERRAILLE'S LETTERS

Although Ruth decided to cut her father out of her life entirely after she became independent, she held on to five letters he wrote, and these were later found at her son's apartment in Jerusalem. The letters include one sent by her father to her mother just after they married in 1918; three sent to Lucette during and after World War II, and a fifth sent to his mistress at an unknown date. Although he asked his lover to destroy the letter after reading it, it fell into his daughter's hands and possibly into his betrayed wife's hands.

Octave's first letter, dated September 27, 1918, was a sweet missive to his wife, Jeanne. He said he was a wreck without her and was desperate to see her again due to his great love for her. The first letter to his daughter, dated September 8, 1943 (during the war), was full of emotional manipulations. He began by thanking Lucette for the money she had sent him; he also thanked her for visiting him in Paris earlier. He mentioned an earlier argument with his daughter on March 29, 1939 (about four years earlier). Octave did not mention the cause of their fight in the letter but commented that "even the greatest sponge will not be able to erase that day from my memory." In the letter, he told her that he missed his grandson Claude and complained that his daughter was blocking her child from his "terrible grandfather, who despite it all has a heart like anybody else." He signed his letter "Your daddy, who despite his sadness thinks of you." The letter strongly suggests that Octave loved his daughter and was upset that she had decided to exclude him from her life.

From Octave's letter to his mistress, we learn that her name was Angele and she was much younger than him. She was from Calais, the same town as his wife, Jeanne, and perhaps they were acquainted. The letter is dated only "Paris, the 28th," but the year is unclear. We may recall that Octave had a major argument with his daughter on March 29, 1939—perhaps the day after that letter was written. In the letter, Octave expresses love and affection for his mistress and urges her to move to Paris. He even makes intimate comments about their relationship. He instructs Angele not to send letters to his home address since his wife opens all letters; she should use his work address instead. The letter ends: "Burn the letter when you finish reading it, for we must be careful." The letter was torn but had been taped back together.

On May 12, 1946, Octave sent another letter to his daughter expressing disappointment that she had not attended his remarriage ceremony two weeks earlier. At that point, Jeanne was still alive, so she and Octave must have divorced. "Why your silence? What do you hold me responsible for?" charged the father. "I always have been quite unhappy to see your indifference toward me." At this time, both Lucette and Octave were living in Paris, and their homes were no more than a few stations apart on the Métro. Lucette decided to ignore him. He begged her: "Come visit me and all will be forgotten." He pleaded to see his daughter and grandson, but as we know, she had determined to cut him out of her life.

In March 1939, Lucette and her father had a big fight. Six months later, she lived in southern France, married and pregnant, with her mother by her side. We do not know what happened between the father and the daughter. However, it seems that Octave's letter to his mistress was probably never sent; someone, presumably his wife or his daughter, appears to have caught it and ripped it apart but later taped it back, perhaps so that it could be used as evidence when filing for a divorce. The fight might have been over discovering that the father had a mistress; maybe the mistress was a close relative or mutual acquaintance. In a short time, both mother and daughter left the father to himself, Lucette to get married and leave home. This could be the reason she treated him so poorly. Still, Ruth kept these letters until her death. She wanted to have a memory of her father, even if only a bittersweet one.

CONCLUSIONS

From observing her childhood, there are no clues that could hint about the life she would have as an adult. Lucette appears to have had a normal childhood, receiving a secular and religious education and enjoying the life of a typical girl living in Paris at that time. She developed spiritual feelings from a young age and was a curious and critical thinker. Her parents' marriage was not happy, and Ruth portrays her father as an abusive husband. We also know he cheated on his wife, and his behavior was a source of tension and bad blood between him and Lucette. Ruth declared that she hated and pitied him and blocked him from her life, but his influence on her character and personality was significant. Although she detested him, she was close to him, and he was special to her.

TWO

RESISTANCE

ON OCTOBER 16, 1944, THE French military intelligence agency, the Deuxième Bureau, issued a confidential memo with the order to arrest Lucette Ferraille. The notice indicated that Lucette was on the run and gave two addresses where she might be hiding, one in Toulouse and the other in Paris.

The memo described Lucette as an elegant blue-eyed woman aged twenty-three to twenty-four, with a height of 1.60–1.65 meters (5'2"–5'4"), blond (most likely dyed), and rather stout. It added that she held a bachelor degree in literature and spoke English. She was a school teacher in several locations from November 1939 to October 1944. However, from October 1943 through October 1944, she was employed as a teacher in Arrau in the Pyrenees only by title and did not actually work.

The charges against "Baud's wife," as the document said, were that she had socialized with a certain Captain Martin of the Luftwaffe, the German army, who was last seen in Dijon in eastern France, and that Martin also belonged to the SRA, the German Intelligence Services. The document included the accusation that "the Baud's wife may herself have been part of the GESTAPO" (capitalization from original).

About a week later, the French police found Lucette in Tarbes, and she was held for interrogation between October 23 and October 28, after which they released her. After the liberation of France, women who collaborated with the Nazis or even had affairs with Nazi soldiers had their hair shaved in disgrace, were stripped naked, and were paraded in the streets while people around shouted, spit, or even hit them. After five days of interrogations, not a single hair fell from Lucette's head. But still, where did these accusations come from? What does it mean that Lucette was a teacher only by title: If she was not teaching in the classroom, what else was she doing? Who was Captain Martin, and how does he relate to the Gestapo? The documents found at the Service Historique de la Defense, France's military archives, reveal a story Ruth never told.

DAS REICH

A few months before D-Day, in a conference room at his headquarters in East Prussia, Adolf Hitler and his staff discussed what additional units they should remove from the eastern front to reinforce their forces in France. The Nazis anticipated an Allied invasion, and Hitler decided to relocate the Second SS Panzer Division, known as Das Reich, to France.[1]

Das Reich was one of the most prestigious armored divisions of Nazi Germany. It had scored some spectacular victories in the war, but its most significant challenge was yet to come on the French front. Captain Martin was a high-ranking intelligence officer in Das Reich, while Lucette's destiny became embroiled with the soldiers in the division.

Das Reich was part of the Waffen-SS, a wing of the Nazi military headed by Heinrich Himmler. By late 1943, the Waffen-SS had won the führer's trust and had grown exponentially. The SS formations became the spearhead of Germany's armies on the eastern front and served on every major front except North

Africa. The Waffen-SS as a whole earned a dual reputation for their remarkable aggression and stamina on the battlefield and their murderous atrocities against civilians and prisoners. The Waffen-SS had become the fire brigade of Hitler's empire, rushing to each new crisis. In January 1944, Heinrich Himmler said: "So far, the Waffen-SS has never under any circumstances caused disappointment."[2]

Das Reich's first great victory came during the Nazi invasion of France, where the division defeated the French and British armies at Calais in 1940. In 1941, Hitler redeployed it to invade Yugoslavia, and from there, it marched toward the Soviet Union. The division captured Kyiv, massacring the city's Jewish community, and then headed for Moscow, reaching a point just ten miles from the city's center. As winter arrived and the war became a battle of attrition, the division was reassigned to Krakow, Poland. Even during the retreat of the Nazi army, Das Reich fought with distinction throughout the great summer battles of 1943, especially in the slow fight back to the Dnieper in August. After losing Kyiv by the end of 1943, the remnants of Das Reich were sent to France to combat the Resistance and prepare for the Allied invasion.

By the spring of 1944, Germany had already lost around one million soldiers on the eastern front, which consumed endless men and resources. Divisions that were sent to France had either been decimated in Russia or were untrained and medically unfit. It would be an exaggeration to suggest that Das Reich was merely a shadow of its former glory, but it was far removed from the elite all-volunteer force that had swept into Russia with the Wehrmacht in June 1941. To fill the ranks, nine thousand replacements flooded the division: untrained boys, almost all aged seventeen or eighteen, many of them Hungarian or Romanian, and with a large contingent from Alsace. Three months before one of the great battles of history, the recruits held a weapon for the first time.[3]

Hitler decided that the division headquarters and training center would be in Montauban, just north of Toulouse. There Das Reich could prepare for the battle in a quiet area, well-positioned to intervene along France's north or south coasts when the Allies landed.

The division had three main wings: Panzer tanks, infantry, and secret police (Gestapo). The Gestapo's primary mission was to crush the Resistance, and Das Reich's officers did not shy away from brutality. The barbarity of the Gestapo caused dread among the civilian population and the various Resistance movements in southern France. From March 1944, when the division camped in the Toulouse area, until June, with the invasion at Normandy, Das Reich lived up to its appalling reputation.[4]

When the Allies landed in Normandy on June 6, 1944, the division was ordered to move to the frontline from its positions. Along the way, the French Resistance delayed it by frequent acts of sabotage. The soldiers responded furiously, executing 99 civilians in Tulle in retaliation for the death of some 40 German soldiers. On June 10, the capture of an SS military camp by the Resistance served as an excuse for the Das Reich soldiers to destroy the peaceful village of Oradour-sur-Glane near Limoges. This act entailed the murder of 640 civilian men, women, and children.

The German armies could not uphold the Allies invasion, although they fought ferociously. By January 1945, Das Reich had collapsed on the French border, but the division was revived and sent to Hungary to save the country's vital oil fields. After failing on that front, what was left of the division retreated to Austria and Dresden, Germany. Its last operation was to evacuate German civilians from Prague. Das Reich was the most decorated division in the history of Nazi Germany.[5]

As a secret agent, Lucette penetrated the headquarters of the Das Reich Gestapo section in Montauban after she joined the Alliance resistance underground.

LA RÉSISTANCE

France fell on May 10, 1940, and on June 22, France and Germany signed the Second Armistice at Compiègne. The so-called neutral Vichy government, headed by Marshal Philippe Pétain, superseded the Third Republic. Germany occupied the north and west coasts of France and their hinterlands, while the collaborative Vichy regime controlled its southern parts. The Allied invasion of Normandy, D-Day, came nearly four years later on June 6, 1944, and by September 1944, most of France had been liberated.

As Nazi troops marched into Paris in June 1940, over six million French citizens flooded the south, the most significant single movement in Europe since the Dark Ages. According to American diplomat and historian George Kennan, who witnessed the flight, the scene was one of "panic, defeat and demoralization of a disintegrating society."[6]

In a radio broadcast to his countrymen, the eighty-four-year-old Marshal Pétain blamed the defeat on "too few arms, too few allies" and also on the country's moral failures, which included a lack of discipline and "an unfortunate spirit of pleasure." Many in France were joyful at Pétain's capitulation; they laughed, kissed each other, and drank to Pétain's health. On June 25, 1940, the marshal announced the terms of the armistice. In a speech he gave that day, he demanded that the French people show a new spirit of sacrifice. France was to be divided between occupied and unoccupied territories.[7]

A week earlier, a relatively unknown French two-star general, Charles De Gaulle, sat in front of a microphone at BBC Broadcasting House in London and gave his own speech. Lasting less than six minutes, his words were a passionate rejection of the armistice with Nazi Germany. Very few French people responded to de Gaulle's speech, primarily because it was difficult not to accept Pétain's logic that Nazi Germany had won. Indeed, most saw de Gaulle as irrelevant, while Pétain won massive support.

As scholar Olivier Wievioka has shown, out of a population of some 40 million people, there were no more than 300,000 to 500,000 women and men in the "army of the shadows," the French Resistance.

Moreover, the Resistance itself was not a united movement but included many subgroups that were not always on good terms with each other. Not all the Resistance was military— many of the groups concentrated on publishing a clandestine press that challenged the Vichy regime and Nazism on the ideological level. Furthermore, the Communist Party adopted an ambiguous position. In light of the Nazi-Soviet Non-Aggression Pact of August 1939, the party only engaged in full-blown anti-Nazi resistance after Germany invaded the Soviet Union on June 22, 1941.[8]

Among the millions who fled out of Paris was Marie-Madeleine Fourcade, who refused to reconcile herself to France's defeat and, as early as 1940, decided to defy the Nazis. In 1941, at the age of thirty-one, she became *la patronne* (the boss) of what would emerge as the largest and most important Allied intelligence network in France. It supplied the British and American high commands with vital German military secrets throughout the war, including information about troop movements, submarine sailing schedules, fortifications, and coastal gun emplacements as well as the Reich's new terror weapons, the V-1 flying bomb and the V-2 rocket.

Throughout the conflict, Fourcade, the only woman to head a significant Resistance network in France, commanded three thousand agents, infiltrating every major port and sizable town. As we will see, her group also entered Nazi headquarters. The agents came from all segments of society. Thanks to Fourcade's determined efforts, almost 20 percent were women—the highest proportion in any Resistance organization in France.

Her group's formal name was Alliance, but the Gestapo called it Noah's Ark because its agents used the names of animals and birds as their aliases. Fourcade was the Hedgehog, an animal that, though small, even a lion would hesitate to bite.

Until July 1944, Marie-Madeleine Fourcade managed to elude her foes like the animal she named herself. Many others in her network were less fortunate. For the previous year and a half, the Gestapo had engaged in a full-scale offensive to wipe out the Alliance. Hundreds of agents had been captured in subsequent arrests and killings; entire organization sections had been annihilated. By the summer of 1944, Fourcade had no idea how many of her people were still alive. Dozens, including some of her closest associates, had already been tortured and executed. After each crackdown, the Gestapo were sure they had destroyed the group, but she was able to cobble together a new infrastructure each time.[9]

One of the recruits to the network was a young woman living in southern France, Madeleine Lucette Ferraille.

MARRIAGE AND DIVORCE

In 1937, a German friend suggested that Lucette (age seventeen) spend the summer with his family in Stuttgart, and all involved were happy to send Lucette off on the proposed vacation. Over the course of the correspondence between her father and his friend, it transpired that the friend had become a Nazi. Accordingly, the father decided not to send her to Germany but, instead, for a French Rivera vacation.

In Nice, Lucette met Henri Baud, a young man who two years later became her husband. From Ruth's autobiography, we learn that he was handsome, had no parents, and lived in a boarding school with his brother, under the supervision of an uncle. The summer ended, but Lucette and Henri maintained a long-distance relationship; she returned to Paris while Henri remained in Nice. He proposed to her in 1938, and Lucette received her mother's approval but not that of her father, who disliked and never met his son-in-law. Ruth later remarked that had her father been reasonable, she would certainly have paid attention to his views, but he offered no grounds for his rejection of the match except to claim that she was too young. On September 5, 1939, the couple married in southern France: Henri was twenty-one, and Lucette was nineteen, just finishing high school. Four days before their wedding day, war broke out. The groom had already been drafted to the army, and the wedding took place in the town where he was stationed. Very shortly after that, Henri left for the Maginot Line, a chain of concrete fortifications, obstacles, and weapon installations built by France in the 1930s to deter invasion by Nazi Germany.

Lucette became pregnant but suffered a miscarriage. She decided to remain in the Pyrenees in southern France near the Spanish border, anticipating that Paris would be bombarded, and she invited her mother to join her. She found a job as a teacher, and when her husband came to visit for a few days after three months of the war, she became pregnant again.[10]

In June 1940, France capitulated, and Germany seized two million French prisoners of war, sending them to camps in Germany, among them Henri Baud. The pregnant Lucette rented a small house in Tarbes in the Pyrenees. A few weeks before she was due to give birth, Henri suddenly appeared, having managed to jump off a train carrying prisoners to Germany.

On October 1, 1940, Claude was born. Lucette had to stay in the nursing home for two months after she developed phlebitis in her legs and could not walk. During her long sickness, she lost her job, but after returning home, she found another job, as did her husband, who found a job at the postal office.

When Claude was one year old, Lucette enrolled at the University of Toulouse to become an art and philosophy teacher. Lucette had lost interest in her husband a little more than a year into their marriage. She felt that she had matured and become a mother, while Henri had remained "the same typically thoughtless southern French young man." After returning home from work, his

main ambition was to dress up in fine clothes and go for a walk in
the center of town, where the youth would gather. Ruth later said
that Henri was proud of her, her looks, and their splendid son.
But she had enough of that. She recalls that her parents forced
her almost every Sunday to walk for hours along the boulevards
of Paris. They would sit in cafés and stare at the passing crowd,
and she found the experience boring and pointless: "I could not
spend my life like that and be happy." She wanted to advance her
husband socially and spiritually, but he had no interest in studying and showed no evidence of any spiritual needs. He still loved
her, but there was no intellectual or spiritual bond to hold them
together. She realized that she desired him only for his looks, but
she aspired for more and eventually decided to divorce him. The
couple signed their divorce papers in 1942. Henri was shocked
and bitter, and he left Lucette and their son without ever paying
alimony or seeing his son.[11] Only seventy years later would father and son finally meet again in Nice, France, on the initiative
of Claude (now called Uriel); by this time, his aging father was
already in his nineties.

Choosing to divorce in the middle of the war and the harsh
conditions in the unoccupied part of France was not an easy decision. Even before the war, France had been a male-dominated
society where women were expected to be in a family and take
care of the household.

Under the Vichy regime, however, the emphasis on the family
was accentuated, and the government clearly favored the traditional family model. The regime blamed women for the failure
of France, claiming that they had neglected their duty to the nation by failing to produce enough children. Marshal Pétain even
said that "the state should strike down laws permitting divorce,
against the winds and storms of public protest."[12] As a result,
divorces became more challenging to obtain and were approved
only after three years of marriage; this explains the delay in Lucette and Henri's divorce proceedings.

Figure 2.1 Lucette and Claude. Courtesy of Nechama Davidson.

The regime also encouraged French women to make themselves more attractive morally and physically and condemned
them for their vanity and material concerns. The regime fiercely
opposed the ideas of feminism and women's emancipation. It
condemned ambition, pride, and even intellectualism, and it argued that pronounced femininity would lead to frivolity, flirta-
tiousness, seduction, and, above all, infidelity. The Vichy regime

discouraged equal education for the sexes, and its approach to education, in general, was marked by anti-intellectualism and anti-individualism. Women were viewed as unsuitable for professional careers; the only suitable vocations for them were in education.

At the same time, the government encouraged large families and declared that "a single child is a spoiled child." The Catholic Church applauded the imposition of measures intended to bolster the family and the morals of the French nation, and most French women agreed with this worldview and supported the regime's policies.[13]

Lucette Ferraille, of course, embodied everything the new regime detested. She was separated from her husband. She had a mind of her own and nurtured ambitions that stretched beyond housekeeping. She gave up on having a large family, satisfying herself with one "spoiled" child. She wanted to learn and be educated in philosophy and art, against the general understanding that women should not pursue higher education. She did not fear living in poverty as a result of her separation. She was disgusted by the regime and everything it stood for, and she refused to be silenced and fought for her freedom and dignity.

Given her character and convictions, it is hardly surprising that Lucette found herself in opposition to the regime. The fact that she did not know fear made her a perfect candidate for a journey in espionage and resistance.

The new recruit Madeleine Lucette Ferraille and her patronne, Marie-Madeleine Fourcade, had more in common than the similar-sounding names. Both women were young Parisians who now lived as refugees in similar locations in southern France. Both were divorced or separated from their husbands and had young children. Both were independent women in a patriarchal society who refused to obey society's rules and assumed responsibilities generally regarded for men only.

THE GLOVIEZONER FAMILY

Lucette settled in Trabes during the war (1939), supporting herself by working as a teacher. In 1941 she began to study for a bachelor's degree at the Faculty of Letters at the University of Toulouse. In November 1943, she graduated in geography, modern and medieval history, and ancient literature.[14]

Her first act of resistance to the regime took place in September 1943. A short entry in her file in the military archives confirms an episode she wrote about in her autobiography regarding her actions to rescue a Jewish woman from a concentration camp in Nice.

By the summer of 1940, there were around 340,000 Jews in Metropolitan France, on top of that there were some 70,000 Jewish refugees who had fled to France to escape the Nazi persecutions in Germany and elsewhere.

Based on the Nuremberg Laws, the Vichy regime enacted anti-Jewish laws, depriving the Jews of civil rights and dismissing them from many state-sponsored positions. The regime also established concentration camps for Jews in southern France. Around 75,000 Jews were sent to the death camps, mainly Auschwitz, although some 330,000 Jews were able to escape deportation and survive the Holocaust in France. Generally speaking, Jewish refugees in France were rounded up by the Vichy regime and sent to their death, while most Jews who were French citizens were spared.[15]

In her autobiography, Ruth says that in Tarbes, she was approached by friends who asked her to help a woman who was caught in Nice, some seven hundred kilometers away. The woman had been arrested together with her husband by the Gestapo. The husband had disappeared while the wife was waiting in a concentration camp. The city was closed, and a permit was required to enter or leave. The friend had no idea how Lucette could enter the city, but she had forged identity papers that she could use to leave.

Lucette decided to go to the German headquarters, the Kommandatur, and find a way to get into Nice. She sat in the lobby and an officer approached her. She told him in German that she was a student who wished to travel to Nice to obtain some books she needed for her exams that would begin in a few days. The officer denied her request, but she continued to beg him for a permit and eventually asked him whether there was a way to get into the city without a permit. After nagging him for a while, he finally told her of a way to get in and out of the city unhindered. She thanked him warmly and went home to prepare for her journey.

She began her trip in the evening, traveling by train the whole night and the following day. The trains were very slow, and she had to change often as accidents were frequent owing to sabotage actions by the Resistance. She completed the final part of her journey on foot, entering Nice before sunrise.

Lucette went straight to the address she had, where all the Jews were concentrated, awaiting their uncertain future. She met the person she was looking for and told her of the escape plan. In the autobiography, she referred to the woman by the pseudonym Mrs. Segal, but her real name was Mrs. Gloviezoner (her first name remains unknown). At first, Mrs. Gloviezoner was too afraid to consider the escape plan. Originally a refugee from Poland, she ran from the Nazis, was arrested by the Gestapo, and lost track of her family. Her traumatic experiences had reduced her to a nervous wreck, subject to uncontrollable fits of trembling.

She was afraid to leave the house and dreaded encountering a Gestapo inspection on the train, which was quite common in this period. It took several hours to persuade her to agree to leave for Tarbes the following day. They decided that Lucette would present the documents to the Gestapo, if they were questioned, and say that she was too sick to do anything by herself. This would spare her from direct contact with them, something that was enough to put her in a state of terror. Luckily for them, there was no inspection during their journey back home, and they arrived safely in Trabes. As they reached the place of shelter, a wonderful surprise awaited Mrs. Gloviezoner. Her husband, Abraham, had managed to escape the train taking him to Auschwitz and had arrived safely at the hiding place with only minor injuries. The couple remained in Tarbes with their false identities until the end of the war. They stayed in touch with Lucette and used her house as a safe haven whenever there was a state of alarm.[16]

Abraham Gloviezoner's statement to the police in Tarbes on August 25, 1944, confirmed the story Ruth wrote in her autobiography. In a short testimony, he thanked her for saving his wife's life. He said that on September 29, 1943, "Madame Lucette Baud, born Feraille, went to pick up my wife at Nice, hunted by the Germans carrying on her fake but necessary documents to save my wife. I acknowledge all the devotion this young person was capable of while putting her life on the line."[17]

"THE FAIRY"

The reign of terror of the Gestapo worsened as the war progressed. As the Nazis prepared for the Allied invasion, Chateau Bonrepos-Riquet, a castle built in the seventeenth century, and the eighteenth-century Chateau of Avignonnet were converted by the Nazis to serve as training schools for Waffen-SS officers who would lead the fight against the maquis, the rural guerrilla bands of the French Resistance.

In one of their raids, the Gestapo managed to arrest in 1944 the commander of the local Resistance group, a man called Pouey whose alias was From Osso. In a confidential report dated September 12, 1945, and written by M. Rougier, head of the intelligence bureau, we learn that the Resistance recruited Lucette in January 1944 and charged her to find Pouey in the Nazi prison and help him escape. In his report, Rougier interviewed Francois Haran, the commander of the Deuxième Bureau in Tarbes, the military intelligence agency, who told the story of Lucette's recruitment and actions.

When Mr. Haran recruited Lucette to the Resistance, he emphasized that her mission was dangerous, detailing the risks she would have to accept if she chose to undertake the task. If caught, he told her, the Resistance would not be able to help. Haran said that Lucette responded that "it did not matter to her to be killed to save a French person." She accepted the mission.

Lucette had to penetrate the Nazi headquarters and win their trust. The confidential reports state that Captain Martin was a Gestapo officer, head of the Bonrepos-Riquet school for Waffen-SS officers, and a specialist in the fight against the Resistance. Captain Martin was around thirty-five to thirty-eight years old in 1944, 1.72 meters (5.6") tall, slightly hunched, with light brown hair, a bare forehead, and an elongated, lightly blotchy face. He had a vertical scar from his forehead to his chin due to a car accident. He was originally from Alsace, like many of the Das Reich division recruits stationed in southern France in preparation for the Allied invasion. The last time he was spotted by the Resistance was on August 10, 1944, as his team retreated through Dijon, in eastern France.

The report leaves many details unknown. But it is clear that Lucette was able to get into the castle and win Captain Martin's trust by becoming his mistress. Indeed, Martin trusted her enough to make her a Gestapo officer herself.

Lucette was unable to save Pouey, though the documents do not tell us whether he was killed on French soil or deported. Throughout her time in the Nazi headquarters, she informed her commander, Haran, of all of her initiatives with Captain Martin. The report states: "Mr. Haran declared that he had nothing negative to say about her. Even if her initiative concerning Martin did not save Commander Pouey, she could not be considered to have committed any action against the resistance network of Tarbes."

Mr. Haran concluded in his declaration [that Mrs. Ferraille] "...
acted on her orders and it was proper to absolve her of all charges."

Moreover, Lucette helped the French intelligence identify
ten people who were members of Martin's team. One of them, a
French citizen called Eugene Marty, a deputy to Captain Martin,
was caught and detained by the French police in 1944.

The report concluded that no charges were to be brought
against Lucette Ferraille, who entered the Gestapo on the orders of the Resistance and "never ceased to keep communicating
with the Resistance." The report ends that "the person of interest was thus released."[18] A separate document, signed by Marie-
Madeleine Meric (Foucade changed her last name after she
remarried) on November 16, 1945, states that Lucette was indeed
part of the Alliance network and had completed the missions that
were assigned to her. Accordingly, she performed "a great service
to the network, despite the delicate situation of her district."[19]

There is a document listing twenty-six members of Captain
Martin's team in the archive. The information is basic, including
physical attributes and limited personal information. The list was
comprised mainly of men, but there were also a few women. The
names included two North African Arabs, Russians, and Hun-
garians alongside French citizens. Some were undercover agents
in the Resistance, pretending to be maquis. Lucette was able to
add information about ten of them. The gang used to gather at a
bar on Bayard Street in Toulouse.

Unfortunately, the reports in the archive do not tell us vital
pieces of information: How did Lucette enter the Gestapo gang?
How did she win their trust? What were her roles as a Gestapo
agent? Did she meet the gang at the bar on Bayard Street?

After the war ended, Lucette was investigated on suspicion of
collaborating with the Nazis. In her unpublished autobiography,
Ruth devotes two pages to her arrest and questioning at Villa St.
Joseph in Toulouse at the end of the war. She claimed that she was
the victim of a plot by two Resistance fighters who were affiliated

with the Communist Party. They tried to enlist Lucette to their group during the war, but after she declined, they adopted a vindictive attitude toward her. In her manuscript she stated that she was arrested for forty-eight hours, but the records show that her interrogation actually lasted five days. As noted, her lieutenant cleared her of all charges, and she was released after receiving an apology.

The screams she heard in the corridors of the interrogation rooms of men and women tortured by the interrogators left a strong impression on her. Although she admits not all the people in the villa were guiltless, "those who professed to be administrating justice had adopted the methods of those whom they were supposed to have fought and driven out of our country." Her chief, she said, had played a heroic role in the Resistance. The Gestapo had caught him several times but had always managed to escape. He had been tortured and lost an eye but refused to torture others. "This experience of human beings descending to such levels of conduct had a deep affect on my mind. In my despair I came to doubt men's capacity for genuine progress," Ruth writes in her autobiography.[20] Her undercover membership of a Gestapo unit where brutal violence must have been a common sight may explain her profound revulsion for violence. However, it is worth recognizing that she later acted violently against others, including kidnapping a child.

The facts that Ruth spent five days under interrogation and that she vividly recalls in her autobiography the acts of torture she witnessed against others suggest that she may have been a victim of torture during this time.

SPYING IN MOROCCO

In October 1944, by the end of the war, Lucette decided to move back to Paris. In January 1945, her mother and son also moved to Paris. She got a job, and she was delighted to be in Paris again, looking forward to everyday life. But within a few months, her

Figure 2.2 Lucette's military ID card. Photograph by the author.

mother became seriously ill, eventually dying at fifty-four. Ruth states that at her mother's funeral, two aunts accused her of "driving her mother to the grave" because of the terror she lived in during the war's years. Ruth remembers this episode as an experience that alienated her from her family. In response, she decided not to wear black, the color of mourning. After this incident, the gulf between her and her family grew, and in time, they became completely estranged.[21]

A classified document found in the military archives Service Historique de la Defense dated September 13, 1945, sparked my interest. At first glance, the contents seem innocent enough. The document reports that the Department of Aviation in the French government decided to hire Lucette as a copy editor—an unsurprising area of activity given her qualifications as a literature major from the University of Toulouse. Her admissions file includes a copy-editing test she performed to gauge her suitability for the profession. It is logical that the postwar French government would want to help former Resistance fighters by providing them with positions in the government bureaucracy, including the pension rights this entailed.

However, why was the unremarkable news that Lucette received a low-key job in the government regarded as "classified information"? An answer might be found in the archives.

When I visited Ruth's son's house in Jerusalem in 2018, I saw in the old photo albums a picture from a trip Lucette took in 1946 to Morocco. As far as the family was concerned, this trip was no more than a pleasant vacation in an exotic location after the stressful years of the war. The family was surprised to learn from me that the trip was not as innocent a vacation as the photographs implied.

It emerged that Lucette applied to become a member of the French secret service and counterintelligence; her appointment in the Ministry of Aviation was merely a disguise for her actual function.

Documents in her military files confirm that Lucette pledged on her honor to be loyal, to act in secrecy, and to not break French law. She was also required to swear that she was not a Communist or a past member of any Fascist organization, among many other details.[22]

A classified document in the archive dated September 4, 1946, states that Lucette was arrested in Meknes, Morocco, in June 1946, after she was seen together with Salvatore Collica, an Italian citizen born in September 1924 in Casablanca. The document defines Collica as an "Italian suspect" who was under surveillance by the Moroccan secret service. Accordingly, Lucette was arrested because of her relationship with Collica. The report determines that while Lucette claimed that Collica was simply a "date," "she was actually the mistress of this Italian man." Regarding Collica himself, the report states that he had recently been released from a concentration camp where he had been held since December 1942 "for his Fascist opinions and his anti-French behavior."

On her arrest by the Moroccan police, Lucette submitted her identity papers. Among them was an order mission number 520, delivered in Paris on June 14, 1946, by the Ministry of Armament, requiring her to go to Rabat to contact high-ranking civilian public servants and military personnel from Air Maroc, Morocco's national airline. Unfortunately, the report does not mention the purpose of the trip besides the "aim to resolve the situation."

The report also mentioned that Lucette met Jewish and Muslim acquaintances in the upper town of Meknes. The police found in her possession a French passport, the order of mission mentioned previously, an ID card issued in Tarbes, and a military ID card that says that she was recruited under the pseudonym "the Fairy." She also held an employee card from the Ministry of Aviation, which might explain her mission with Air Maroc, and a visa to Switzerland, which she had already used.

The investigation by the Moroccan services also discovered that Lucette had contacted rug and leather artisans to obtain an exportation license allowing her to export Moroccan rugs to France. From Rabat she traveled by bus to Casablanca, and she then planned to return to Meknes and on to Paris on a military flight.

Since we already know that Lucette had become Captain Martin's mistress during the war to spy on him, and we also know that she was recruited to the French Secret Service by 1945, it seems clear that Lucette's mission in Morocco was to spy on Salvatore Collica, an Italian Fascist and someone who was regarded as a suspect by both the French and Moroccan secret services. She appears to have had another mission regarding Air Maroc, and this may have been the background to her employment by the French Ministry of Aviation.

Another interesting and recurring pattern is her interest in international trade. The documents noted that she planned to open a business of importing rugs and leather—a field of activity that can provide a perfect cover for spies, particularly since it requires frequent travel in and out of a given country.

The assignment in Morocco lasted seven weeks, much longer than originally planned. Meanwhile, her son stayed with people who were paid to take care of him, but after his mother disappeared for a much longer time than expected, without making contact or paying them for the additional period, they assumed she had abandoned her son and began to take steps to remove him from their charge.[23]

The French archives do not yield any other information regarding further secret operations. In her autobiography, Ruth tells us nothing about her mission in Morocco, confining herself to recalling that she soon became tired of her job as a copy editor at the Ministry of Aviation. She was interested in finding more exciting venues for herself that offered intellectual and spiritual meaning, but at the same time, she also sought opportunities in the business world. It is possible that her secret service episode ended quickly on her resignation from the government position, but there is nothing in the records to confirm or disprove this hypothesis. The thrill of adventure and the adrenaline that comes from secret activities would end for a while—until she was recruited to kidnap Yossele Schumacher fifteen years later.

Figure 2.3 Morocco 1946. Courtesy of Nechama Davidson.

CONCLUSION

To sum up, Lucette Ferraille emerges as a character constantly swimming upstream—an independent woman in a conservative society, a rebel, even. She was very loyal to her causes. She was willing to undertake life-threatening missions for France's independence and well-being, fighting for freedom. However, she was not loyal to the people in her immediate environment. She rid herself of men around her, including her husband, and betrayed her lovers. Later we will see that when her lofty ideals clashed with her son's well-being, she put principles above people. It is also clear that she was not shy about using her sexuality as a weapon. All the intelligence documents emphasize her elegance and beauty—tools she used to her advantage. She put herself in dangerous situations, but she knew how to emerge from them with the upper hand, probably by using her looks and intelligence to talk herself out of complicated situations. Another point worth noting from this period is her dislike of Communists, which will play a crucial role in the Yossele affair.

THREE

—꘏—

"YOUR GOD IS MY GOD"

Lucette's Quest for Spirituality

BACK IN PARIS, RUTH WRITES in her unpublished autobiography, she registered for a master's degree in history at the Sorbonne. She enrolled in a theological studies program in 1946 and eventually graduated in June 1954 with a major in the classics.[1]

She felt overwhelmed with work, study, and taking care of her son by herself as a single mother. She said that at that time, the only happiness in her life was her son.[2] After a year of living in Paris, she decided to move to Geneva and get close to her father's family. She found a place to live and enrolled her son at a Catholic boarding school.[3] He stayed with her at the weekends while she wrote her thesis in the city's library during the weekdays. In the evenings, she worked selling insurance policies.

In the summer of 1948, she started an import-export business of chemical products. She purchased products in Switzerland and sold them in France. Later she expanded her business to textiles.

She succeeded in negotiating several deals. Although the business world was very new to her, she preferred it to working as a civil servant for the government. It seems that her business was eventually relatively successful.

An important episode in her life, and one she describes in detail, began when Elizabeth and Philippe Schneider, members of the Seventh-day Adventist Church, a Protestant movement whose members believe that God chooses them for redemption, refused to purchase a policy from her, declaring that her insurance was of no use to them, since the Messiah would be arriving soon.[4] Lucette became a close friend of the couple. Over the twentieth century, the Seventh-day Adventists announced six times that the End of Days was imminent. The members of the church observe certain Jewish customs, including the Sabbath (hence their name). Lucette comments that she indeed met the couple in the city of Calvin, but she was the daughter of a Catholic mother, and her son studied at the time in a Catholic educational institution. She describes the jolting effect of her discussions with the couple. She began to explore their doctrines in some detail: "I read all kinds of books at night, apart from long discussions I sometimes had during the day." She attended Catholic services during the same period, but she said Catholicism did not satisfy her, neither appealing to her logic nor speaking to her heart.[5]

Her friends' declaration that the Messiah was about to arrive, and their attempts to win her over to the Seventh-day Adventist Church, had a profound influence on Lucette. She did not consider them extremists and happily joined in their Sabbath meals. She confessed that the words "the Messiah is soon coming" suddenly made her heart beat quicker.[6] In a comment that underscores some similarities between this movement and Judaism, she recalls that she found the Friday night meals pleasant and interesting. She was able to discuss the Old Testament with them.[7] The draft of her autobiography describes in detail her affectionate response to the couple, but the relationship was omitted from the published Hebrew version of her book.

In 1948, her friends were struck by misfortune. Elisabeth was found to be suffering from cancer, and by the summer the family decided to hospitalize her in Paris; however, there was no improvement in her health. Ruth said that she prayed for her constantly, and one day she suggested that Elisabeth might be given a blood transfusion. The doctors objected, but Lucette insisted there was no risk since her condition was terrible anyway. Against all medical logic, this procedure was a success, Ruth wrote in her manuscript; Elisabeth's condition improved, she recuperated, and she returned to Switzerland.[8] This story is mentioned in the English and French versions of her manuscript. However, the French version is not identical to the English one; the former adds essential details that explain why this episode was so crucial in Ruth's life.

In her French book, Ruth tells that she was devastated by the sickness of her friend. She went back to her hotel room and prayed for her well-being. That night she had a vision in which she saw the sacrifices at the ancient Temple. The dream gave her the idea of offering a sacrifice to God to save Elisabeth's life. She did not tell the readers what she sacrificed. But it was after this night that she had the idea of a blood transfusion. And although the doctors were opposed, "it was a miracle," and Elisabeth regained her former strength. "It was a resurrection, and I had played a part in it! . . . The gates of heaven had opened, God responded to my prayer." For Ruth, this experience was a sign of God's existence. She had never imagined she would be given such proof, and as noted, she had been raised by an agnostic father who challenged the presence of God—but God accepted her sacrifice. "Heaven's response to my prayers was for me the proof that I need to advance my spiritual quest," she concluded.[9] This episode was viewed as a mystical experience, and she concluded that she had mystical powers. She could offer sacrifices, and with God's help, she even changed the course of nature. God was listening to her prayers.

Unfortunately for Ruth, she could not stay in Geneva with her friends. In her unpublished manuscript in English, Ruth relates that she was caught by the police living in Geneva without proper documents. In addition, the customs authorities caught her importing raincoats without a proper export license and without paying taxes; all of her merchandise was confiscated, and she was left penniless. As a result, she had no choice but to leave Switzerland. She remembers this period as a nightmare.[10] This may explain why she disconnected from the company of the Adventists and moved on to other spiritual venues.

Lucette returned to Paris again opened an import-export business with a new partner. At first, she did poorly in business.[11] She sent her son to the care of a family in a village, where she would join him at the weekends. She lived alone in Paris for several months, preparing her thesis in solitude and reading extensively, mostly on religious and esoteric experiences. She read about China, India, and the Middle East.

It seems that Lucette was suffering from depression during this period and could find comfort in religion. She was disappointed by the morality of society and found her peace in religious teachings. She felt that her existence was unbearable, saw no meaning in life, and even contemplated suicide. She was living all alone, reading and rereading, comparing and examining religious texts in an effort to ease her suffering.

Lucette was attracted to the compassion and unconditional love (including love for one's enemies) advocated by Christianity, particularly as manifested in Jesus's Sermon on the Mount (Matthew 5–7). However, she was unable to overlook the hostility of the New Testament toward those who refused to accept Christ. She quotes: "Woe to thee Chorazein, woe to thee Bethsaida . . . thou wilt be thrown into hell" (Luke 10:13).[12] She found little mercy, love, and tolerance in the Gospels, but by contrast, felt these values were embodied in the Hebrew prophets. The values she sought in this period led her to reconsider her own faith. The gulf between the lofty standards of faith in Christ and their human implementation, including the Inquisitions and the Crusades, led her to question the essence of Christianity. While her agnostic father found the antithesis to Christianity in his antireligious fervor, Lucette turned to the morality of the Hebrew prophets: "Perhaps that was why the genuine humanity of the

Pentateuch and the Psalms had such appeal for me. . . . I read the
word of G-d through Moses and the prophets, that calls his children back to him, and grants his forgiveness to patient sinners;
the promise to eternal life and peace to the world."[13]

Another Catholic teaching Lucette found repelling was the
doctrine of predestination, as articulated by St. Augustine of
Hippo (354–430), one of the most important of the Church
Fathers. This doctrine argues that grace is bestowed on some,
while those excluded have no right to complain. In her unpublished manuscript, she writes that the pope assigned St. Augustine to write the Gospels for all Christendom. Accordingly, she
concluded that the Gospels are not of supernatural origin but a
product of the weakness of man's reasoning.[14] She thus effectively
came to believe that St. Augustine fabricated the Gospels. According to her words, she saw proof of this in an original letter
that St. Augustine sent to the pope. In her collection of letters at
her grandson's home, I found a letter from the Bibliothèque na-
tionale de France from August 1963, responding to an inquiry she
sent in June concerning the original St. Augustine manuscripts
available at the library. The librarian explained that Ruth had
confused St. Augustine with St. Gerome, who was mentioned in
the letters as the figure who had revised the texts of the Gospels.
I find it amazing that even in 1963, years after she graduated from
her classes at the Sorbonne (1954), after her conversion, and after
the Yossele affair that will be discussed later, Ruth was still interested in ancient Christian manuscripts. This episode provided
intellectual support for her conviction that the Christian religion
is a fraud fabricated by the Church Fathers.

Ruth emphasizes that all those around her in Paris, as in the
Western world in general, had no interest in religion at that time,
so that she had no one to speak with about her feelings. She could
not explain, even to herself, what drew her so deeply into this
particular path, despite her attempts to push it aside.

To overcome her spiritual doubts, Lucette spoke with a Catholic priest called Father Vincent, with whom she still maintained friendly contacts when the biography was written. She remarked that one of the books he gave her—Edouard Schuré's *Les grands initiés*—impressed her considerably.[15] First published in France in 1889, this book describes the author's lifelong quest for spiritual truth. The book examines the lives and deeds of human beings of exceptional stature: Rama, Krishna, Hermes, Moses, Orpheus, Pythagoras, Plato, and Jesus.

This book was a best seller and an influential volume of its time. Schuré was influenced by Friedrich Nietzsche's warnings against the death of God and the demise of religion in society. He believed that society was moving toward a world deprived of values. Schuré was concerned that the giants of French literature in the nineteenth century had rejected any evidence of the existence of the spiritual world. He accepted science, saw no contradiction between science and religion, and advocated a middle path. He feared the moral decline that would come with the rejection of religion. The book's central argument calls for reconciliation between science and religion—between the seen and the unseen.[16]

Of the various figures in Schuré's book, Lucette was particularly impressed by the character of Pythagoras. Schuré's interest in the Greek philosopher led her to explore the world of philosophy. In her unpublished biography, she devotes many pages to quotes from the writings of Pythagoras, which she felt spoke directly to her.[17]

It should be noted that no authentic writings of Pythagoras have survived, and almost nothing is known for certain about his life. A principle of Greek philosophy Lucette found particularly impressive was the belief that man can master his passions by subjecting them to the might of his free will. Based on philosophical deliberations, she believed that instead of blaming God, humans must blame only themselves for the troubles they suffer.

"You have to accept your pain as the result of your actions, and not to be angry," she concluded. She found this message similar to the Mosaic laws, and this led her to investigate the Hebrew Bible.

Pythagoras also advocated the concept of metempsychosis, according to which all souls are immortal; after death, the soul continues to a new body. Lucette said that she was moved by the idea of reincarnation, whereby in each new life the individual is rewarded or punished for the soul's past behavior. However, she eventually concluded that the teachings of the Hebrew Bible were superior.[18]

She found in Greek philosophy a refuge from a world enslaved to political doctrines that fostered despair and sacrificed individuals for the good of the nation, class, or race. As noted, Lucette's intense interest in religion and philosophy came during a period of personal crisis, including her expulsion from Geneva and her conviction for financial offenses, and at a time when she had been living on her own for several months. It is also essential to bear in mind that she evidently had something of a tendency to depression. The absolute political ideologies such as Communism, Nazism, and nationalism that were playing a central role in Europe at the time utterly repelled her. She also remained unimpressed by Catholicism, expressing doubts about the place of eschatology and the idea of the physical Second Coming of Christ.

In the spring of 1951, she abandoned philosophy and decided to move to what she saw as the source. "It was Judaism which met my sense of universalism, my concept of unity, my need for a convincing theology, and, above all, an increasingly strong inner calling." In the Hebrew Bible, she found the roots, people, and truth she had been seeking. Her conclusion was final.[19]

THE PSYCHOLOGY OF CONVERTS

Religious conversion is an intellectual process of transformation that resolves the individual's questions of identity. William

James's *The Varieties of Religious Experience* is a celebrated milestone in the philosophical and psychological study of religion. In his discussion on the origins of conversion, James begins with the assumption that happiness is the main concern of human life. Some men, whom he describes as "healthy-minded," are born with the inclination to happiness, and everything makes them happy—the flowers, the butterflies, and the green grass. These "once-born" people have a healthy consciousness; James mentions the poet Walt Whitman as an example of such a personality.[20] The second type of personality is the "sick soul." James describes a radical pessimist who has a "pathological melancholy"[21] and has lost his appetite for all life's values. He offers the Russian novelist Leo Tolstoy as an illustration of this type. Tolstoy considered suicide, saw no meaning in life, and eventually chose to disengage from the ordinary pleasures of life.

According to James, the "divided self" is a person who is deeply melancholic yet seeks inner peace. The "sick soul" longs to be happy and reborn as a "healthy mind." This gap between the bad condition of the self and its need for healing is referred by James as "unification": "It may come gradually, or it may occur abruptly; it may come through altered feelings, or through altered power of action; or it may come through new intellectual insights, or through experiences which we shall later have to designate as 'mystical.'"[22] The purpose of this unification is to make men happy. Religion is one of the ways to gain this gift, but it need not necessarily assume a religious form. Tolstoy needed two years to reach unification, James said. He realized that his problems were not with life per se, but with the life of the elite; he was living wrongly and had to change, escape falsehood, and embrace truth. Tolstoy found the existence he was seeking in the simple life of peasants.

This process of overcoming sickness and moving to be "twice-born" is referred to by James as "conversion." It occurs when a divided self who feels inferior and unhappy becomes unified, consciously superior, and happy. To be converted means to gain grace and assurance. James argues that to be converted means that religious ideas that were previously peripheral in the consciousness now assume central place, and religion becomes the center of men's personal energy. Sick souls who suffer from depression, feelings of imperfection, anxiety, and sin, may convert to feel happiness, hope, security, and resolve.

Conversion can be a long process or a rapid event, but it is usually a gradual process that builds up piece by piece to form a new set of moral and spiritual habits. James explained that there are critical points in this type that move the process more rapidly. The individual needs to abandon his own will. Resistance to change breaks, and a person embraces a new identity. James concludes that conversion is a personality change: "The man is born anew."[23] The new man obtains a state of assurance and produces happiness.[24] In contrast to William James who referred to converts as having a "divided self," Charles Taylor has compared conversions in late modernity to "self-authenticating experiences" and acts of "creative renewal" often affecting highly self-reflective intellectuals and often turning them, as in the case of Ruth, into fanatical resisters to liberal modernity.[25]

Since James's pioneering research, the knowledge of religious conversion has advanced. Scholar Chana Ullman has found that conversion can better be understood in the context of the individual's emotional life. It occurs against a background of emotional upheaval and promises relief through a new attachment. Conversion can be understood as a search for psychological salvation.

Ullman, who interviewed some forty converts in the Boston area during the 1980s as part of her doctoral dissertation, argues that for the population of converts tested in her research, the religious quest is best understood in the context of a search sparked by emotional distress. The converts she interviewed were more likely to report an unhappy and stressful childhood. In addition, a sizable majority of the converts in her study described the

two-year period preceding their conversion as fraught with negative emotions, and many reported that their conversion offered
relief from this turmoil. The conversion process was an experience of love and acceptance; after their conversion, converts tend
to espouse their religious beliefs more rigidly than nonconverts.[26]
Also, people with particular personality trait mixture might seek
conversion as a way of dealing with life issues, finding expression
through religion.[27] In support of Ullman's conclusions, Raymond
Paloutzian, James Richardson, and Lewis Rambo have said that
available evidence seems to indicate that people with a particular
personality trait mixture might seek conversion, finding expression through religion, as a way of dealing with life issues.[28]

One of Ullman's most interesting findings is that conversion
stories often include a complex father-child relationship, including instances of an absent, passive, or aggressive father. She found
that such relations occurred in around half of all cases she studied. Ullman claims that the emphasis on this relationship in the
conversion stories suggests that it played a vital role in the religious transformation. Whereas converts tend to hold bad memories of their fathers, they develop an infatuation with a powerful
authority figure who serves as a leader and mentor. Ullman suggests possible ties between the lack of benevolent parental presence and the actual conversion process.[29]

Scholars Granqvist and Kirkparick show that those with insecure or avoidant attachment relationships with parents are
more likely to undergo a religious conversion. Children raised
securely tend to retain a sense of security during adulthood. They
do not seek security and safety by developing a new relationship
with God. But children raised insecurely need a haven in times
of danger, and this need is met by accepting a loving God who is
always there to protect and sustain them. A theoretical implica-
tion is that people with insecure childhood attachments are more
likely to convert to another religion as part of a compensatory
process.[30]

Scholar Mark Bear shows the conversion process entails a process of acculturation, adhesion, syncretism, or transformation. Not all converts end up with a radical break from their past. However, those who chose the path of transformation are taking a sharp new way of life in place of the old. These converts turn toward a new axis or set of ideals that motivate them to transform themselves and their environment. They reject or denounce their past and former beliefs or practices. Transformation entails a turn to piety within one's religion or a change from one religion to another.[31]

This process of transformation endows the convert with new powers. A wish to unite with a perfect, idealized object, a sense of being pawned in a struggle of giants and yet being chosen or called for a special mission, and the perception of personalized miracles—these themes also viewed in Ullman's research among converts. She refers to these feelings as "narcissistic." Finally, about one-fourth of the cases studies in Ullman's research expressed the reason for their conversion in an existential quest, an interest in ideological and existential questions that reach beyond the circumstances of the individual's life.[32]

RUTH'S SPIRITUAL QUEST

These psychological traits can illuminate the biography of Ruth Blau, who reported that she experienced an unhappy childhood with a tyrannical father; profound feelings of unhappiness, and perhaps even depression, following the Second World War; a turbulent life that saw her spend time in jail; an attraction to men "greater than life" as part of her conversion process; and kidnapping a child out of a sense of mission and a need to prove herself fit for the community, as will be discussed in the following chapters.

Ruth's story of conversion meets many of the characteristics of the profile of converts. She fits William James's model of a radical pessimist and melancholic; she saw no meaning in life besides her toddler son, who was physically distant from her. Struggling to find inner peace, she looked into spirituality, a process that started with Seven-day Adventism and progressed to philosophy and the occult. Ultimately, she found in the Hebrew Bible to be a place of refuge for her tormented soul. She believed in free choice and the notion of reward and punishment, and accordingly interpreted her sufferings as the product of her past actions. She may even have feared her coming reincarnations.

At this point, it is interesting to wonder whether she saw any connection between her engagement with the Gestapo just a few years earlier and her choice of Judaism. Her biography offers no insights on this question, but I believe that she left clues that may indicate such a connection. She may have seen her conversion to Judaism as a way to correct her karma and gain happiness.

The profile that Ullman portrays in her research into converts also fits Ruth. Her spiritual quest began with what she was convinced was a personal miracle. Ullman associates the conversion process with emotional turmoil, and Ruth indeed endured severe emotional distress before her conversion; moreover, she connected her emotional life to her upbringing. Ruth tells us that she had an abusive father and a loving mother, a pattern that is common among many converts. Part of her conversion process included her falling from the Christian faith and an intellectual process through which she concluded that the Christian sources had been tampered with by St. Augustine.

After choosing the Hebrew Bible as her spiritual compass, her next step would be to find Jews.

FOUR

—〰—

"YOUR PEOPLE SHALL BE
MY PEOPLE"

Conversion

BY 1950, LUCETTE CONCLUDED THAT she was interested in discovering Judaism and needed to act. As noted, she had been living in solitude for several months and had had plenty of time to engage in profound philosophical thought. She had no Jewish acquaintances in Paris.

Without any practical solution to her dilemma, her mind turned to the newly created State of Israel, which was attracting interest around the world at the time. She recalls that the holy city of Jerusalem became the center of her world, and she was mesmerized by the State of Israel, a "sensation" that was only two years old. In Israel, she would find Jews living in the Holy Land.[1]

The same week she developed these thoughts, she came across two Israelis of her age in the reading room at the National Library in Paris. They became friends, and the friendship became more intense with one of them. She called him Simon in her unpublished manuscript, but from her family, I learned that his real name was Ephraim Harpaz (1920–2011); he would later become a professor of French literature at the Hebrew University of Jerusalem.

Harpaz had taught Ruth some Hebrew to read the Bible in the original with the help of a dictionary, but he was not a religious person. His view of Judaism was national, and he wanted to build his country so that Jews could find refuge from antisemitism. She quoted him as saying, "We are not adherents of [the prophet] Jeremiah and have no time for Jeremiah in Israel."[2]

Soon after, Harpaz left France. Before leaving, he asked her to marry him, but she was torn. On the one hand, she longed for a Jewish family, and her son would surely benefit from a father figure. On the other, Harpaz was not religious. She enjoyed talking with him since he was intelligent and cultured, but she was worried about his secular lifestyle. Harpaz invited her to visit Israel and consider the possibility of marriage. In 1951, she renewed her business activities with great success, and in the spring, she traveled to Israel. At that time, Israel was in a period of austerity, so she brought suitcases packed with gifts and said that everyone treated her like a long-lost friend. She recalls how emotional she was at seeing the Holy Land from the sky for the first time, and her religious sentiments caused her to shed a tear of joy.

Ruth says that Harpaz's family welcomed her, especially since they knew she was interested in converting. According to her narrative, his parents were observant Jews and refused to eat in their son's home since he did not keep a kosher kitchen; they hoped his converted wife might bring him back to tradition.

Harpaz took his potential wife on a tour across the country. She visited kibbutzim where she ate delicious grapefruit; they traveled to Tiberius on the shores of Lake Kinneret, to Haifa and Mount Carmel, and Nazareth and its churches—but he did not take her to see Jerusalem or its Orthodox Jewish community.

Ruth was filled with regret when the visit came to its end after one month. She felt her time in the country "had passed like a dream." She decided to continue her conversion plan and promised to revisit Israel.[3]

In the manuscript, Ruth includes some comments concerning Zionism. However, we must be careful in examining these, since they were written when she was already anti-Zionist and may not reflect her true feelings at the time of the visit. She felt respect for all the people she met who were working hard to develop their national home, but she was not attracted to their ideal: "It was Judaism, not Zionism, that I wanted to embrace; the Holy Land, not the fatherland, to which I was attached. I wanted to come and live among Jews, in order to worship Him—not to sing Hatikvah, even though I was not unmoved when this Israeli anthem was sung."[4]

From this quote, we can see that at this point she had positive feelings toward the State of Israel and the Zionist anthem made her feel emotional. But she felt something was wrong. Only at a later stage would she be able to articulate that, for her, Judaism was primarily a religion, not a nationality.

A professor from the Hebrew University who knew Paris well gave her the name and address of a rabbi who could convert her. She went to meet in person the leader of the liberal synagogue on rue Copernic, a man she calls Rabbi Elbaz but whose real name was Rabbi André Zaoui (1916–2009), a Reform rabbi based in Paris. Zaoui was one of the pillars of French Jewry in the postwar period, an active intellectual who authored several books. He also translated Maimonides's letters into French.[5]

Ruth said she was happy to meet the rabbi who showed understanding and sympathy for her ideas and plans. On page 79 of Ruth's unpublished autobiography, several sentences were deleted by pen strokes. Deciphering these lines reveals an important detail: when Lucette met with Zaoui and explained that she was interested in converting, she stated that her motivation was her desire to marry an Israeli man. In fact, she had reached this decision at an earlier stage, though she postponed its implementation. Thus, while she showed an interest in Judaism, her decision to convert seems to have come after she met a man she considered suitable. In Orthodox Judaism, such motivation is unacceptable—a "true convert" is by definition someone who chooses Judaism for pure motives and not based on any mundane self-interest, such as marriage.[6]

Zaoui accepted her to his conversion program. She studied the Torah diligently, with particular attention to those commandments that Reform Jews kept in part, like the prohibition on pork and some form of Sabbath rest. She attended services over the weekends, driving her car to the synagogue. The rabbi and his wife invited her for a Passover meal in April 1951 for the first time in her life. She also attended a confirmation service for girls. Afterward, the rabbi asked her what she thought of it, and she responded it reminded her of church services. He replied that something has to be done for girls, and his remark led her to think that Jesus must also have been a Reform rabbi in his time.[7]

I interviewed Zaoui's widow, Bianca, and she commented that there were a considerable number of converts to Judaism during this period, as a reaction to the Holocaust.[8] I tried to obtain Ruth's conversion file from the synagogue, but the community stated that its conversion archives were destroyed after the building was flooded.[9]

Her family and close friends were puzzled by her choices, but they were even more concerned by her decision to drag in her son with her. According to the Talmud, Jews are not allowed to force the child to convert. According to her testimony, she gave her ten-year-old son the option to wait with his conversion, but he strongly demanded to have it, which meant he would need to be circumcised. She hired a surgeon to conduct the operation, unaware that a ceremonial ritual was also required.[10] She went to immerse herself in the Mikveh (ritual bath), together with her son. She completed her transformation by changing her name to Ruth Ben David—a name suggested by Zaoui. The biblical Ruth is traditionally considered the first convert and accordingly, this is a trendy name among female converts.[11] According to the Bible, Ruth was the grandmother of King David—a further factor behind her choice of this name.

Everything was going well for her: she had converted to Judaism and her business was flourishing. She imported textiles and sold them in France and its colonies. She expanded her studies in Jewish texts and spirituality.

However, the more she progressed, the more she felt that Reform Judaism was not the right path for her. Although she declared with hindsight that she opposed the approach of Reform Judaism from a principled standpoint, she was extremely positive in her comments about Rabbi Zaoui, who converted her and brought her into the world of Judaism. Reform Judaism was her entrance gate, and at the time when she went to pray in the Reform synagogue in Paris, she was unfamiliar with the different branches in Judaism and had never even heard of Neturei Karta.

Her relationship with Harpaz ended; there are several different versions of the story. In the unpublished English version of her manuscript, she tells that a few weeks after she started her studies in conversion, she wrote to Harpaz to tell him she could not be his wife because she wanted to live her life and raise her family in a religious setting: "He did not understand me nor empathize with my feelings."[12] But then she detailed that in August 1951, she came back to Israel and met Harpaz again, as they had remained good friends.[13] In the French manuscript, she wrote that she decided not to marry Harpaz after she finished her conversion.[14] Henie Persitz, Ruth's close friend at that time, remembers things differently. In an interview, she told me that Harpaz's religious parents rejected her because she was a convert, and this possible match was a great disappointment for his mother. Accordingly, he broke off the relationship.

Henie was born in Poland, and her family escaped persecution and immigrated to Mandatory Palestine before the Holocaust. She served in the Israeli army and later won a fellowship to study in Paris, living in the dormitories. Harpaz connected Henie and Ruth, and Ruth later invited Henie to move in with her and help her raise her son. At that time, Ruth's business was growing fast, and she used to come home late; thus, she sent her son to boarding schools. In our interview, Henie criticized how Ruth raised her son, and she also disapproved of Ruth's decision to block her son from his biological father.[15]

Ruth recalls that she loved Henie like a sister, and they discussed all kinds of subjects. From her, she learned a lot about Jewish history and customs. Indeed, Henie confirms that they became very close while taking care of Claude. Eventually, the two would separate because of Ruth's life choices and her sharp turn toward ultra-Orthodoxy. However, Henie, who was one hundred years old when I interviewed her in the summer of 2018, said good things about Ruth, whom she loved dearly.

In May 1952, Ruth left the Reform synagogue and entered the Mizrachi movement—the bastion of Orthodox Zionism. She became involved in the circles around the Consistoire, the umbrella organization of French Jewry. There, she met Jean Poliatschek (1914–1993), a modern Orthodox rabbi from Alsace, in an encounter that would eventually bring her much heartache.

She heard him give a lecture, and after the talk, she gave him a ride to his apartment. They talked about philosophy and continued corresponding. A few weeks later, he returned to Paris to a rabbinical conference, and they met again. According to Ruth's testimony, it was at this point that she told him that she was a convert. He reacted negatively, and she was upset: "I am not a leper, after all!" As we have noted, Ruth was an attractive woman, and many men were captivated by her charms. Like others, Rabbi Poliatschek fell in love with her and wanted to marry her.

Ruth recalls that the rumors of their engagement spread like wildfire. The news went out that she was not only a convert, but a Reform convert and then—"all hell let loose."[16] In a campaign to protest the marriage, all joined forces: people from the Consistoire, the Mizrachi, the disappointed girls who wanted to marry the rabbi, and their mothers. The community was divided between her opponents and her supporters.

Ruth faced accusations that her conversion had been insincere and that she had converted solely to marry Poliatschek. After this claim was proved to be inaccurate, it was alleged that she had converted to marry Harpaz, which, as we know, was partly correct. Another criticism focused on her Reform conversion. Decades of animosity between the two movements have shown beyond all doubt that Orthodox Jews do not accept Reform conversions.[17]

Ruth insisted that her motivations for entering the gates of Judaism were pure and free of any self-interest. She struggled for several months to defend her reputation, fighting for her right to marry a Jew and even a rabbi. Ruth identified two possible solutions to the challenges she faced. First, she would have to undergo a second conversion of an Orthodox character. Second, the couple would need to marry outside of France.[18] These two decisions proved to be fateful to the future course of her life. Over a decade later, she would have to confront a similar situation within the world of Haredi (ultra-Orthodox) Judaism when she sought to marry Rabbi Amram Blau, despite the united opposition of the Haredi community.

During this troubled period, she felt that no one was on her side and that even those rabbis who spoke in her favor were insincere. The sole exception was Rabbi Avraham Elijah Maizes (1901–1961), a strict Haredi rabbi who had managed to flee the oppressive regime in the Soviet Union and moved to France. She recalls that Maizes took an interest in her plight and led her to understand that her ordeal arose from heaven's will.[19] The rabbi convinced her that her problems resulted from predestination; her acceptance of this belief marked a retreat from her earlier adherence to the principle of free will. She now accepted that she was doomed to suffer in the complicated situation in which she had become embroiled—a situation that was exacerbated by further developments on the financial front.

One result of her emotional distress was that she neglected her business. She worked with a business partner, a Jewish man called Leon Swergold who lived in Brussels. In December 1952, Ruth was arrested by the French customs authorities on suspicion of tax evasion of 39 million francs (equivalent to around $1.5 million at 2015 rates). In Ruth's personal archives, I found a letter from the tax authorities stating that the amount of 39,665,369 francs was for importing textile from Italy during October 1951–February 1952. She was convicted of fraud and spent two months in jail. In the City of Paris archives, there is a record of her imprisonment at the Petite Roquette prison. In her autobiography, Ruth claims that her business partner deceived her and was responsible for the massive tax evasion. Her son, Uriel, claimed that Swergold fled to Israel and later to the United States after the French authorities requested his extradition.[20] This claim is problematic since Israel and France only signed an extradition agreement in 1958.[21] I found evidence at the court in New York of a commercial suit filed against Swergold and his brother Maurice, the directors of a company called Corta Corporation. In 1952, Swergold was fined approximately $20,000 for failing to pay his debts.[22] These findings suggest that while Ruth was penalized severely, spending time in prison, her business partner received a relatively lenient fine from the court. As will be recalled, this was the second time that Ruth had been apprehended for tax evasion. In the first incident, she was fined, and only after the second offense was she sentenced to prison. Her fiancé Poliatschek said in an interview for an Israeli newspaper that Ruth had lost all of her money. "I was sure that after all that these two Jewish partners have done to her behind her back, she would renounce the Jewish faith, turn into an anti-Semite, and return to Catholicism, but this experience only strengthened her ties to Judaism," said Poliatschek.[23]

Ruth described the two months in prison as humiliating and shameful. She said she knew that the business was not doing well, but her business partner had begged her not to incriminate him. As a Holocaust survivor, he was a stateless Jew awaiting his Belgian citizenship any day; he feared that exposure would deprive him of the chance to acquire a nationality. She trusted her partner would solve the problem, and it seems that his Jewish background was a weak spot which he exploited against her.[24]

"No one who has never entered the grim world of prison can ever imagine what it is like." Ruth devotes a long section to this two-month episode in her unpublished manuscript.[25] It seems that this was the first time in her life that she could not extricate herself from her troubles and was forced to pay the price for her actions. I find this episode particularly interesting since she would kidnap a boy a decade later—a serious criminal act that could have resulted in a lengthy prison sentence. When she kidnapped Yossele Schumacher, she knew what it meant to be imprisoned and willingly risked protracted incarceration.

Petite Roquette is a citadel that was built in the eighteenth century and used as a prison until 1974. Although her prison time was during the winter, Ruth remembers that the rooms were not heated. Each cell hosted six inmates, and the wardens were nuns. Upon arriving at her cell, she witnessed a scene too revolting to describe. She just covered her head with the blanket and sobbed.

The incarceration papers mention that her religion was Jewish. She had issues with the food that was provided, which was not kosher, and she did not participate in the daily Catholic prayers. As such, the nuns developed a dislike toward her and called her "the Jewess."

After a few weeks in prison, Ruth began to struggle; the cold winter and her strict diet caused her health to deteriorate, and eventually, she was hospitalized in the prison infirmary. Ruth described the nun at the clinic, Sister Monique, as a sadist who gave her painful injections as punishment, causing her to faint from the pain. In the second month of her imprisonment, a rabbi helped her move into solitary confinement at her request. Ruth says that the second month was better for her being alone. She got used to the prison situation; had a chance to rest, which helped with her back pain; and read many books.[26]

Coming out from prison, she continued her Orthodox conversion, which Rabbi Samuel Jacob Rubenstein conducted in 1953. After her conversion, Claude changed his name to Uriel.

Rabbi Poliatschek resigned his position in France, and in May 1953, Ruth moved to Israel to prepare for their marriage. She also applied to the rabbinical court to register her as a convert, presumably so that she could get married in Israel. On May 25, 1953, the court approved her request.[27]

The couple had already announced their marriage, but the groom had doubts. Ruth said that she decided to break the engagement after she felt that Poliatschek could not commit himself to the relationship. Henie's opinion was that Poliatschek was afraid of Ruth since she was such an assertive person. Henie recalls that Ruth wrote her a letter saying that Poliatschek was "a bastard," but in her manuscript, Ruth said she forgives him. However, she portrays him as mentally unstable and suffering from delusions and nightmares.[28] Poliatschek was a refugee during the Second World War, hiding from the Nazis in southern France, and this may have been the source of his demons.

Henie and Claude, now Uriel, traveled to Israel, and Uriel was admitted to a boarding school at Kvuzat Yavneh, a religious collective settlement, where he would prepare for his bar mitzvah (as he was close to age thirteen). After celebrating his important day with him, Ruth returned to France while Uriel remained in Israel.[29]

Returning to France after the failure of her engagement, Ruth found Rabbi Leon Ashkenazi (1922–1996), also known as "Manitou," as her new spiritual mentor, and she spent every Sabbath and festival at his beit midrash. Ashkenazi was one of the leading figures involved in rebuilding French Jewry after the Holocaust and adhered to an educational approach based on a combination of Orthodox Jewish principles and a modern lifestyle. Following the Six-Day War of 1967, Ashkenazi became identified with

Merkaz Harav and Rabbi Zvi Yehuda Kook—the core of Israeli
Orthodox Zionism. Rabbi Ashkenazi became the principal of
the Orsay School in 1951, while Professor André Neher served as
president.[30]

Converting to Judaism with an Orthodox conversion was an
important milestone in Ruth's life. She had radically turned a
page in her life: "my entering Judaism meant the absolute an-
nulment of my past, a life entirely new."[31] The words she uses to
describe her new condition are reminiscent of William James's
definition of a man "twice-born." Now, she had the strongest
gravitation toward Judaism. She felt she belonged. But this was
not enough. She needed more, and she drew her attention to the
ultra-Orthodox enclave of Meah Shearim in Jerusalem.[32]

NEW DOUBTS

Ruth spent every weekend and Jewish holidays at the Orsay
School for close to two years. The place gave her the peace of
mind she needed so much while she continued her studies in
Jewish sources. She did not visit her son in Israel once during
these two years.

In 1954 she returned to Israel to celebrate Passover with her
son on the kibbutz; she also took him on long trips around the
country. She explained that she wanted to tour the land to decide
whether she would like to immigrate to Israel or stay in France.
She began to feel that the branches of modern Orthodoxy she had
become part of—the Consistoire-based Judaism to which most
French Jews adhered and the Mizrachi movement of which Kvuzat Yavneh formed a part—were not satisfying enough. During
this visit to Israel, she declared that Zionism and the Mizrachi
had lost their appeal for her. She could not share the excitement
about building a new country and the pride in its achievements
that so many Jews shared around the world.

She went to see a military parade in the city of Ramle but did not find the sight pleasing. She could understand why many Jewish hearts were overfilled with joy seeing a state of their own, with the soldiers, sailors and airmen, officers and generals, and ambassadors that go to make a state. "After the horrors of Hitler, the Jewish people embraced the sight of marching armies of their own with tanks on the ground, airplanes in the sky, and ships on the seas, and this sometimes came to be regarded almost as the ultimate goal."

But she, by virtue of her past, could not find excitement or spiritual elevation in uniforms and military parades: "I have left all my past, all my natural bonds, all the human attachment to family and friends. I have forsaken my land and my people, and crushed the gates of Judaism, for elevated reasons, for the longing of my soul to be included in the eternity and the holiness of the Jewish people; to participate in their sorrow and to share their hopes for eternal glory."[33]

This quote provides several insights into Ruth's character. She understood why so many Jews were attracted to Zionism as a response to genuine distress, and she accepted that Jewish sovereignty could be the height of their aspirations for those born Jewish. But for herself, as a convert, manifestations of nationalism held no particular interest: her motivation in joining the Jewish people had been spiritual and not nationalistic. As a native of France, French nationhood could have satisfied her; and it is difficult not to agree that the military parades on Bastille Day in Paris exceed their Israeli counterparts.

It is interesting here to turn to Ruth's son Uriel, who paints a different picture: "He (Uriel) believes that the establishment of the State of Israel made a great impression on her. She visited Israel for the first time in 1949 and came away fired with Zionist fervor. She became a member of French WIZO, and paid dues from 1950 to 1953."[34]

Uriel's testimony appears to be credible. As discussed above, Ruth indeed visited Israel in 1951 (Uriel appears to have made a mistake regarding the year) because she was planning to marry a secular Israeli. Her remarks, as quoted here, support the conclusion that she could understand the appeal of Zionism. The Orthodox circles she was part of at this time, such as Kvutzat Yavne, the kibbutz identified with the Hapoel Hamizrachi movement where her son lived, and her friendship with Rabbi Leon Ashkenazi and circles close to the Consistoire, all confirm her affiliation during this period with modern Orthodoxy and Orthodox Zionism. Ruth supported the Zionist enterprise in the 1950s, regularly made donations to its institutions, and was moved by hearing the Israeli anthem. However, she was disturbed by the fact that Zionism was essentially a secular movement detached from the observance of the commandments. At this stage, she admits, she did not yet understand what she found lacking in this religious experience, but she sensed that Zionism as a national movement could not meet her spiritual needs. As we have seen, her narrative highlighted her suspicions regarding nationalism in general, particularly Jewish nationalism.

She admits she had doubts and could not decide whether to settle in Israel.

CHOOSING ULTRA-ORTHODOXY

Ruth decided to return to France, and her son returned with her. She enrolled him at Rabbi Ashkenazi's yeshiva, but the institution later closed due to financial difficulties. Uriel moved in with his mother; however, she said he was lonely, so she wrote to Rabbi Maizes, who recommended a new yeshiva for the boy, Yeshivat Chachmei Tzarfat, a stricter Haredi yeshiva in Aix-les-Bains.

Ruth arrived at the yeshiva on Friday afternoon, with a fully loaded car, wearing a short-sleeved dress. She was unaware of the Haredi lifestyle or dress code, and this was a world that was entirely new to her. The first comment she heard was: "Here one dresses differently. You are in a yeshiva here." She had to change into a long-sleeved garment. The incident baffled her, but she found the Sabbath experience charming and worth the trouble of changing her clothes. "I felt during the Sabbaths I spent in Aix-les-Bains that spiritually, after many years, after many peregrinations and misfortunes, I have reached port."[35]

She spent her annual summer vacation in the yeshiva at Aix, located close to the French Alps. She went bathing in spas nearby during the days while studying the Torah and contemplating the new religious lifestyle she encountered. She was on a spiritual search for true religion, and as she was seeking purity, she realized she found what she was looking for: "I found, in this environment, brotherhood, equality and peace of mind, complete observance of the Mitzvot and endeavor to help others to understand and draw ever nearer to true Jewishness."[36]

This quote was written when Ruth was already fully committed to the ultra-Orthodoxy way of life, and indeed she appears to have internalized the Haredi worldview. However, from this quote, we can identify Ruth's mindset at that time. For a long time, she had been embroiled in a psychological crisis that forced her to make drastic changes in her lifestyle while seeking spirituality as a cure for her pain. This search brought her to the gates of ultra-Orthodoxy. There are different shades even within this movement, and Ruth eventually found her home in Neturei Karta, the most extreme and uncompromising section of ultra-Orthodoxy.

Becoming ultra-Orthodox requires a change in many aspects of life, and Henie told me in our interview that Ruth's discovery of the yeshiva was a transformative moment for her; it was here that she made the switch. The transition to the modest dress code was hard for Ruth, requiring her to wear long-sleeved dresses and to cover her hair. Ruth, who was known for her beauty, found it hard to cover herself according to the modesty guidelines of the

community. In her manuscript, she recalls arguing against covering her hair since she was not married and only married women
needed to cover their hair. However, this was to no avail: the rabbis demanded it and conditioned her continued presence there
on a modest appearance.[37] She accepted these demands because
she believed she had finally found the place that would bring her
peace of mind. This was another stage in her conversion process,
and she was, at last, nearing its final stages.

The man who introduced ultra-Orthodoxy to Ruth was Rabbi
Avraham Eliyahu Maizes. He served as an archetype of absolute Judaism and absolute truth for her. This explains the vital
role Maizes played in shaping the religious practices Ruth later
adopted. As Ullman has shown, the conversion process often
entails an attachment to a charismatic figure. Maizes provided
Ruth with a role model and a source of imitation.[38]

Uriel found it challenging to settle in his new surround-
ings. He even suggested that he not go to the yeshiva so that,
accordingly, Ruth would not need to cover her hair, but she
insisted. After the summer ended, Ruth returned to Paris. At
Aix, she met Rebbe Moshe Yitzchak (Reb Itzikl) Gevirzman
of Pshevorsk (1881–1976), a Hasidic leader from Poland who
survived the Holocaust and later settled in Paris. In February
1957, Gevirzman established a permanent base for his Hasidic
court in Antwerp, Belgium. Upon returning, she connected
with this Hasidic court in Paris, spending Sabbaths with them,
and Ruth recalls she traveled to Belgium often to be close to
her new rabbi.[39] The atmosphere in the rebbe's house calmed
her and eased her troubles. During the same period, the French
customs authorities demanded a payment of seven million
francs, money she did not have, toward her debt, and she almost had to go to prison again, but she avoided it by paying
some of her debt.

By spending time with the Hasidic Rebbe and observing him,
she learned a lot about Hasidic customs, and in hindsight, she

says this was the Jewish life she had always been searching for. Staying with the rebbe required her to do a lot of dishwashing and helping set up and clean the tables until late in the night, but the whole atmosphere at his home made her feel that she had truly become Jewish.

Yet here, too, Ruth failed to find the respite she sought. After rumors spread that she was a convert, she was forced to leave the Hasidic court. Nevertheless, she continued to be attracted to the Haredi lifestyle. She concluded that she should live in the Haredi enclave in Jerusalem, close to Rabbi Maizes.[40]

TRAVELING TO THE HOLY LAND

In November 1959, Uriel decided to move back to Israel, and he lived in Jerusalem under the supervision of Rabbi Maizes. He wrote to his mother that he hoped to get married (he was already nineteen years old), and he believed she would also find a suitable match in Israel. Ruth indeed decided to immigrate to Israel. She realized that traveling through the Arab world would be cheaper, so she embarked on a thrilling adventure.

She left France on March 14, 1960. First, she traveled to Aix, where she spent Purim; continued to Trieste; and took the Orient Express train to Istanbul. In Istanbul, she spent the weekend with the local Jewish community before flying to Beirut.

From Beirut, she flew to Kalandia, East Jerusalem's airport. At that time, East Jerusalem and the West Bank were under Jordanian control, and Jews were not allowed to visit their holy sites. She found a hotel room to stay in and headed to the Western Wall (also known as the Wailing Wall). She hired a young tour guide to show her the holy city. After a long tour, she finally reached the wall: "My heart was beating rapidly." She wanted to pray, to pour out her heart at the wall, but the tour guide would not leave her alone. The following day, she gave it another try, but again there were people by the wall, and she could not pray.

On the third day, she went alone to the wall, and on the way, she saw a boy, whom she described in her unpublished manuscript as a "child that Heaven has sent to guide me." The boy showed her the way to the site, and by the wall, she had an emotional break-down: "I prayed and cried." The child climbed the wall and broke off five little stones from the giant rocks of the wall for her that she would cherish forever.

The following day, she took a taxi to Hebron, to visit the Tomb of the Patriarchs and the Rachel Tomb in Bethlehem. The Muslim tradition of generations was that only Muslims were allowed inside the Tomb of the Patriarchs, while Jews were permitted to stand only by the site's entrance. Ruth, visiting as a tourist, was allowed in. She walked barefoot inside the mosque, as Muslim custom requires. While the tour guide was giving explanations, she silently prayed next to a crowd of Muslim wor-shippers. Since her behavior inside the site was unlike that of a regular tourist, it caught the guards' attention, and a female guard escorted her out. In her manuscript, Ruth devoted more than twenty pages to describe these trips to holy sites, an indica-tion of how important they were for her.[41] This was indeed an almost unique experience, since only in 1967, after the Six-Day War, were these locations again accessible to the vast majority of Jews for visits and worship. Paradoxically, however, Rabbi Yoel Teitelbaum, the Satmar Rebbe who later became her spiritual leader, prohibited his followers from visiting the Western Wall after the war so that they would not take advantage of the Israeli victory.[42]

After a short vacation time, Ruth headed toward the Mandel-baum Gate, the checkpoint between Jordan and Israel, and her dream trip was over. Crossing the checkpoint marked the begin-ning of the most difficult time of her life, as she described it. Her son came to pick her up on a motorcycle and took her straight to meet Rabbi Maizes in the ultra-Orthodox enclave in Jerusalem. She told the rabbi and his wife about her adventures at the holy sites and showed him the stones from the Western Wall. The rabbi was so moved that she begged him to keep a stone for himself.[43]

Uriel and his mother took a vacation together after being apart for several years, and she reported that the state had progressed considerably. They visited Eilat and Beersheva in the Negev, Jerusalem, Tel Aviv, and Haifa. "Everywhere fields and plantations had taken the place of sand and rock. Towns like Eilat and Beersheva have developed, other towns and villages were born." The Zionist narrative was that the State of Israel had "made the desert bloom," but Ruth's approach differed. She commented that billions of dollars had poured into this small land with a small population. Accordingly, these achievements were no miracle: "There is hardly anything which money cannot buy."[44]

The secular nature of Israel hurt her. She had already internalized the radical ultra-Orthodox narrative that Zionism is a danger to true Judaism. The true guardians of faith are not soldiers but the Torah scholars. Her Judaism was not inherited but acquired, and for her, Judaism was embodied in the image of Rabbi Maizes and Meah Shearim, the ultra-Orthodox enclave: "I came to Judaism because of the impression that Judaism made on me. . . . What moved me was Jewish teaching—the teaching of the Torah . . . Six years ago, when I was last in Israel, I was, at times, carried away by general enthusiasm. . . . During the last six-year, in which I became closer to the real Jewish religious concepts, I have moved still further away from my non-Jewish past and, together with that, from Zionism."[45]

Ruth increasingly identified with the paradigm of the Haredi world, according to which Zionism is a secular-nationalist movement that lacks any religious sentiment and, indeed, is sometimes hostile to such belief. She came to see the desire of Reform Judaism or Orthodox Zionism, through which she had entered the world of Judaism, to strike a balance between the modern world and the Jewish religion as a distasteful compromise that she was no longer willing to support. Moreover, ultra-Orthodoxy was not

anti-Zionist during this period, and the Agudat Yisrael movement, which represented the mainstream Haredi community,
actively cooperated with the Zionist enterprise.[46] In ideological terms, Ruth was thus attracted to the most extreme Haredi
circles, led by Neturei Karta, that opposed and fought against
Zionism.

Here, we can discern a process of increasing extremism fueled
by a desire for spiritual perfection. The Reform synagogue or
the Consistoire contained modernity and saw no contradiction
between a modern way of life and Judaism. For Ruth, by contrast,
her disconnection from Catholicism also implied the abandon-
ment of modernity and its values, including nationalism.

CONVERTS IN EUROPE AFTER THE WAR

With the aftermath of the Shoah and the destruction of European Jewry, a new phenomenon emerged in Europe. As the
dimensions of the Nazi destruction became apparent, a wave
of European Christians seeking to convert to Judaism reached
out to the Jewish communities. To date, there has been little
research into this wave of seekers. Still, a young generation of
German scholars is now beginning to pay more attention to this
fascinating historical phenomenon. The research is solely in the
German context, but a similar interest in conversion to Judaism
also developed in Paris after the war. From my conversations
with Jewish community members, I believe that similar motivations stood behind German and French Christians who wanted
to join Judaism.

To understand the dimension of this movement, I will begin
with figures quoted by several scholars. By June 1946, 2,500 applications for conversion had been filed with the Berlin Jewish
community, which numbered some 7,000 members.[47] In 1950,
Nathan Peter Levinson, then rabbi of the Jewish community
in Berlin, received about 6,000 applications for conversion to

Judaism. With such a demand, the Jewish community decided to establish a special commission to check all applicants. Among the applicants were people who hoped to gain advantages from their conversion to Judaism—for instance, to receive a CARE-Paket (a gift of emergency supplies from the American allies) or to gain financially from compensation payments. Many former Nazis also wanted to become Jews, whether out of genuine regret and a desire for repentance or to disappear unnoticed by taking cover in the Jewish community. Many people wanted to belong to Judaism for religious reasons. Many Germans, horrified by the crimes committed against Jews, requested to convert out of solidarity with the Jewish people.[48]

The scholar Barbara Steiner has concluded that there were three broad groups of German converts to Judaism after 1945; the boundaries between them were, of course, somewhat fluid. The first group of converts consisted of the non-Jewish female partners of Jewish men and the children of Jewish fathers. The number of religiously mixed marriages in the Jewish community remained high even after 1945. The majority of converts to Judaism probably belonged to this category. The community saw the integration of these gentile women as a moral obligation, and priority was given to this type of conversion by the few rabbis serving the community.

The main factor for most Germans who wished to convert was their guilt regarding Germany's past. Solidarity with Jews created a counteridentity for converts. For them, this was a conscious act and a commitment to join the community of victims. Conversion marked the end of a transformation process, in which a Christian German, raised and socialized under Nazism, became Jewish. Most converts were women. Non-Jewish German women made every effort in the first postwar decades to compensate for the injustices done to Jews. These women specifically sought to marry Holocaust survivors; for them, marrying a Jew was an act of repentance. These women made a significant contribution to starting Jewish families and rebuilding Jewish communities in Germany.

The second type of converts decided to join the Jewish ranks because of theological motivations. The experience of the Holocaust had elevated the Jewish faith in their eyes. The fact that Jews had survived mass extermination was taken as a sign of Judaism's superiority as a religion. The persecution of the Jews stood as evidence for the truth of their faith. Over time, however, this argument fell out of fashion, being replaced by a general theological critique of Christianity. They wished to convert because, for them, Christianity was false.

A third group used conversion to Judaism to deal with personal and existential crises. Judaism served as a type of alternative identity that enabled them to opt out and offer an "alternative" to the milieu of their parents.[49]

Steiner argues that in the 1960s and 1970s, most converts immigrated to Israel, a place where they could wash their guilt away. In Israel, converts had found a new home, a place they could be proud of.

The converts' earnest desire to belong to the Jewish community encountered the reality in Jewish communities. Historically speaking, converts have tended to occupy a somewhat special status and not be regarded as entirely equal to those born into the faith. As much as the appeal of Judaism grew among Germans, the acceptance of converts has been a hotly debated topic. Rabbis have yet to reach any kind of consensus about the extent to which converts should be considered entirely legitimate members of the Jewish people.

Converts sometimes attempt to look for Jewish ancestors, thereby justifying their conversion because they already had Jewish blood. Presenting themselves as Germans of hidden or previously unknown Jewish origin satisfies their desire for a Jewish (that is to say, "untainted") ancestry. This desire was sometimes created in the first place by their experience of being rejected by the Jewish-born.[50]

RUTH BEN DAVID—THE CONVERT

Steiner's analysis fits nicely into the biography of Ruth. Her conversion started with a marriage proposal she received from an Israeli Jew she met in France, and later she continued her conversion after she got engaged to a rabbi. Although she never mentioned this explicitly, guilt may have played a role in her motivations, as she repeatedly noted that the condition of Jews during the war touched her heart. Her associations with the Gestapo might have been in the backdrop of her mind when she decided to convert. As we see in this chapter, she indeed mentioned that she was repelled by French identity and found in Judaism a counteridentity. Ruth used intellectual arguments to counter Christianity; meanwhile, her dislike for her father, whom she stigmatized as a cold agnostic of Catholic origin, motivated her to oppose him with her fascination with religion in general and Judaism in particular.

The fact that Jews by birth tend to view converts as second-class members of society was a problem for Ruth, who would have to fight for her right to marry Jews by birth and particularly rabbis. She would always be known in Israel as "the convert." In her biography, she mentioned how the children in the ultra-Orthodox enclave of Meah Shearim would giggle behind her back about her unique status as a convert, something very unusual in that community; their laughter and stares broke her heart.

In 1953, Ruth immigrated to Israel out of her desire to live among Jews. Like most other converts studied in Steiner's research, she was supportive of the Jewish state. Later, in 1960, she would make Israel her permanent home, but she would change her loyalties to ultra-Orthodox anti-Zionism, a move that was indeed rare but reflected her desire to be the most Jewish she could be while viewing the Jewish state as a sinful entity.

Ruth's conversion led her to become a new person. This was a long process that took years, and it included an intellectual, spiritual, communal, and psychological transformation. The process was catalyzed by marriage opportunities and motivated by a desire for perfection, but it also exposed a certain level of insecurity. Her transition to the extreme resulted from her inability to make the compromises needed by anyone who seeks to combine the spiritual world with the modern world. As time passed, she found these compromises distasteful. Another point to note is that she did not find insular religious communities, such as the Seventh-day Adventists or ultra-Orthodox Judaism, to be extreme; on the contrary, she was captivated by their isolationist character.[51] In the Haredi lifestyle, Ruth found a balm for the psychological difficulties and personal disappointments she had experienced during that period.

Her decision to join ultra-Orthodoxy marked a turning point. Ruth would join the defensive struggles of this community against the modern world and the secular way of life, which included fierce battles against the secular State of Israel. Ruth would become embedded in one of the most ferocious battles for the soul of the State of Israel, the kidnapping of Yossele Schumacher, an affair that would make a lasting impact on the young Jewish state, the ultra-Orthodox community, and on Ruth's life.

WHERE IS YOSSELE?

IN THE EARLY 1960S, THE State of Israel was thrown into turmoil. A family dispute in which a grandfather refused to return his grandson, Yossele Schumacher, to the custody of his parents developed into an affair that threatened the social stability of the state. Neturei Karta, an anti-Zionist ultra-Orthodox movement that had resisted the Zionist movement and the State of Israel since its founding twelve years earlier (1948), decided to show that they were serious in their anthem: "We do not believe in the government of heretics—and we will not follow their laws." The little boy was kidnapped from his parents, and the court order to return the boy was disregarded. In their actions, which were supported by a broader circle of ultra-Orthodox rabbis, Neturei Karta attempted not only to highlight its resistance to Israeli law and court orders but also to convey the message that the State of Israel, which had just celebrated twelve years of independence, cannot confront a small group of religious zealots who claim to be loyal to God alone and to execute his commandments. The kidnapping of Yossele Schumacher marked the peak of a series of confrontations initiated by Neturei Karta, but the state's forceful response had a profound impact on the organization. After resolving this affair in 1962, Neturei Karta lost much of its strength and public support, and the movement never again risked criminal confrontations with the state.

This political achievement can be credited to David Ben-Gurion, Israel's first prime minister. Ben-Gurion was an enormously influential figure in the Zionist movement and played a seminal role in shaping the emerging Jewish society in Israel before and after independence. During his years in government, he led Israel through international recognition, military victories, and impressive financial and demographic growth. Ben-Gurion had a clear political vision that prioritized the supremacy of the state and the stability of its institutions. In the Yossele Schumacher affair, Ben-Gurion was guided by his conviction that no group, even if religious principles govern it, enjoys privileges that place it above the law. The Yossele Schumacher affair constitutes a formative event in the early history of the State of Israel, and Ruth Ben David was one of the central figures in this episode.

THE YOSSELE AFFAIR

Nazi Germany invaded Poland in September 1939, marking the beginning of World War II. Among the many refugees who escaped the Nazis was Alter Schumacher, a young Jewish man from Lublin, Poland, who would become Yossele's father years later. Alter fled east as far as he could go, by foot, on farmers' wagons, and on trains, until he reached Kazakhstan. There, with tens of thousands of other refugees, he worked in hard labor in the coal mines for eighteen months, grateful to be alive. However, he was sad to have left his family behind, with no clue about their existence.

When the Soviet Union liberated Warsaw in January 1945, there was a celebration at Karaganda, Kazakhstan. At the event, Alter met his future wife, Ida Starks. Ida was the daughter of Nahman and Miriam Starks, who would later become Yossele's grandparents. The family originally came from Uman, Ukraine, the historical center of the Breslov Hasidic movement. Nahman maintained his Hasidic identity during the Soviet period, but he had to practice his Judaism in secret as the Soviet Union banned the practice of religion. During the war, the Starks also escaped to Kazakhstan.

The Starks had five children. The oldest, Ovadia, reached London after the war, and became a member of the Chabad Hasidic movement. The second, daughter Rivka, remained in Russia. The third, son Israel, was murdered during a romantic feud over a woman. The youngest children were Ida and Shalom.

While Miriam Starks was pregnant with Shalom, Nahman was arrested and sentenced to five and a half years' imprisonment in a labor camp in Siberia for following his Jewish faith in public. During his time in prison, Nahman lost an eye and three toes.

Ida and Alter married and later had two children: Zina and Yossele. After the marriage, Ida became a Polish citizen.

In 1956 the Soviet Union and Poland signed a treaty allowing Polish Jews who had migrated to the USSR during the war to return to Poland, from where they could immigrate to the State of Israel. In early 1957, Nahman, Miriam, and Shalom Starks arrived in Israel and found home and shelter among Breslov Hasidim in the Meah Shearim neighborhood of Jerusalem. In April 1957, the Schumacher family arrived in Israel and set up residence in the northern town of Nahariya.[1]

Meah Shearim is an insular community in the heart of Jerusalem. With its Haredi and overwhelmingly Hasidic population, its streets retain many of the characteristics of the prewar shtetls of eastern Europe. Life revolves around strict adherence to Jewish law, prayer, and the study of Jewish religious texts. Traditions in dress include black frock coats and black hats for men (although styles vary according to the particular religious subgroup to which they belong), and long-sleeved, modest clothing for women. The lifestyle of Haredi Jews resists the innovations of the modern world and strives to maintain a largely premodern way of life.[2]

Immigration was a complicated process for the Schumacher family, and the parents struggled. By the end of 1957, Ida had found a job opportunity in Jerusalem. She thought that it would be too difficult for Alter to take care of the young kids by himself, as Yossele was five years old at that time, so she moved them both to the guardianship of her parents. After five months, her parents enrolled Zena into a Chabad boarding school for girls, under the care of Shalom, Ida's brother, who was affiliated with the Chabad Hasidim and studied in the movement's institutions in Lod, near Tel Aviv.

After a few months, Ida and Alter found an opportunity to purchase an apartment in a housing project in Holon, near Tel Aviv, provided they could prove that they were working in the city. This was a challenging time for them: they could afford to buy the apartment, but they had to move to Tel Aviv. Yossele stayed with his grandparents while his parents moved away, and the family would only meet together on weekends in Jerusalem.[3]

Yossele grew up in this community for about two years, but finally, in the summer of 1959, the Schumachers received the keys to their new home. They enrolled their kids at a state-religious (modern Orthodox) school. Zina returned home with no problems, but when Ida called her father to get Yossele back, the old man requested that his grandson remains with him for the upcoming summer break. Alter wanted his son back, but Ida was willing to accept her father's request as she knew that her father was very attached to his grandson. When the school year started on September 1, the grandfather requested an extension for Yossele to spend the upcoming High Holidays with him. Ida arrived at her parents' home during the Succot holiday to spend the Sabbath and take the boy back with her on Sunday. In the morning, Nahman sent Yossele to morning prayers. Since it was a cold day, the grandmother suggested that the boy remain with them one more day so that he would not catch a cold; Shalom would bring him to his parents the following day. Ida, who had to rush to work, agreed to the suggestion, a mistake that would cost her dearly. "How could I have guessed my mother was lying? She is my mother; she knows how a mother feels for her children. Oh, dear, if only I had the slightest suspicion!" Miriam escorted her daughter Ida to the bus stop, and Yossele stayed home with his grandfather. She said goodbye without knowing she would not see him again for a long time.[4]

When the High Holidays were over, grandfather Nahman still refused to return the child to his parents, and his opposition became clear: a modern Orthodox education would ruin the boy's soul, and he would not allow his grandson to dwell among heretics and apostates!

Alter became impatient: "I will call the police!" Nahman responded, "You will see him only in your dreams!" In one of their bitter arguments, the grandfather said, "Even if you take me to court, I will not comply."

Ida went to the Chief Rabbinate to arbitrate, but Nahman did not accept its authority, so she had to cancel her appeal, and she took her grievance to the police, who advised her to take her father to court. On January 15, 1960, the court ordered the grandparents to explain why they would not return the boy to his parents and ruled that in the meantime, neither side would be allowed to take the boy out of Israel. In their deposition, the grandparents made several points that would become central in the dispute. They argued that the parents had asked them to take care of their children and had only infrequently visited them; indeed, they claimed that Alter Schumacher barely came to visit his son. The grandparents had never planned to smuggle Yossele to his uncle in London, but they opposed the parents' plan to return to Russia. In addition, the boy himself had expressed several times his desire to remain under the supervision of the grandparents.[5]

The court ordered the grandparents to return the boy to his parents in no more than five days, but the grandfather refused. In

February 1960, the court called the police to find the boy, but the grandfather said he had no knowledge of Yossele's whereabouts and could not comply with the court's order. After five months, in July 1960, the court ordered the arrest of Nahman Starks until the boy was returned to his parents.

Police Lieutenant Zvi Rudin composed a report submitted to the court in July 1960 detailing the police's activities. The police took action in six distinct tracks to find the boy. They initiated a meeting between the grandfather and the parents; they negotiated with important rabbis to influence the grandfather to return the boy; they placed informants in ultra-Orthodox circles; they surveilled, made arrests, and conducted detective work around the grandfather and anyone in his close circles; they investigated and collected information; and they followed up on tips as to where the boy might be.

The lieutenant said that the grandfather was an extreme Orthodox Jew with no interest in the modern outside world and no respect for secular courts. "He has a mystical belief that he stayed alive throughout his ordeals (in Russia) only due to his grandson. He will merit the afterlife only by saving his grandson from apostasy, and he will do that by removing the boy from his parents, because he believes they intend to immigrate to Russia where he will surely lose his religion."

The report mentioned that the grandfather sent a person on his behalf to Rabbi Tzvi Pesach Frank, the chief rabbi of Jerusalem, on January 29, 1960, and the rabbi ruled: "Since the father wants to take his son back to Russia, the ruling of the Torah forces R. Nahman Starks to hide his grandson so that he would not leave the Land of Israel to a place where apostasy is forced on Jews . . . and anyone who can help him must do so with all of his might." The police report continued that the grandfather regarded this ruling as binding and saw his struggle as a holy war.

The report described a mediation attempt between the parents and grandfather on March 3, 1960. The two sides agreed that the boy would stay with the grandfather for nine more months and that he would attend a state-religious school. The grandfather demanded to be the boy's guardian, and this demand led to the collapse of the negotiations. In the meantime, the police expanded their searches.

The lieutenant emphasized that the response of the ultra-Orthodox community to the searches worsened over time. At first, they responded with cynicism but without showing resistance to the police. For example, some would call their children "Yossele" when the police came to their communities or hide boys in closets to confuse the police. Later, the report added, the responses included curses, insults, and spitting on the police. Eventually, the police encountered incitement and even assaults on its officers. For example, during the Purim holiday in March 1960, some three hundred young men, many of them drunk, stood outside the grandfather's apartment, dancing and cheering him. The grandfather stood on the balcony and declared that the police in Israel was worse than the USSR and Nazi Germany, accusing it of abducting children to make them apostates. The following day, the grandfather assaulted a police officer next to the synagogue while two hundred worshipers closed in on two police officers, shouting at them "Nazis," "murderers," and "Bolsheviks." A special force had to break into the synagogue to rescue the two officers.

The report added that Rabbi Maizes entered the scene the next day. He met Nahman Starks on his way to the synagogue and praised him for his struggle against the police. He told Starks that the police was worse than "the Gestapo and the Inquisition." He referred to the police raid to rescue the officers the previous day as "a pogrom." Later that day, Rabbi Maizes appeared at the police headquarters and demanded that the police not send any more officers to synagogues and yeshivas.

The police report concluded on a pessimistic note. There was no information as to the boy's whereabouts, and the police did not anticipate that its officers and informants would be able to crack the secret. The report added that many Orthodox and secular Jews supported the grandfather due to his willingness to sacrifice himself and fight for his ideals. Some of this support was due to the unconfirmed assumption that the parents were planning to return to Russia. The police assessment was that the resistance would only grow stronger as long as the grandfather remained firm in his opposition. The police also believed that the boy did not wish to return to his parents and was cooperating with his abductors.[6]

The report exposed the weakness of the police in handling the situation while the grandfather was taken to prison. The two systems, the Israeli courts on the one hand and the ultra-Orthodox community, on the other hand, clashed in a war of principles. The police were helpless because the Orthodox community supported the kidnapping and hid the abductors and the boy.

The Schumachers and their lawyer established a public committee that included influential figures to create counterpressure and keep the affair in the news. As public opinion turned in favor of the parents, the ultra-Orthodox newspapers came up with a counterattack that included three main arguments: There had been no abduction; the parents planned to move back to Russia; and this was a personal family feud in which the public should not interfere.

The claim that the father was an ardent Communist who planned to return to the Soviet Union was utterly groundless. From any objective perspective, the story raises serious problems. If Alter Schumacher was so firm in his Communist beliefs, why had he left the Soviet Union in the first place? If he was fiercely antireligious, why did he marry the daughter of a Breslov Hasid and enroll his children at religious and even Haredi educational institutions? If he was planning to return to the Soviet Union, why did he purchase a house in Israel? The parents chose a state-religious (i.e., Orthodox-Zionist) school for their son—an

improbable educational choice for a Communist longing to return to the Soviet Union. In an interview with Yossi Schumacher
in April 2020, I asked him about this subject. He replied that he
had been deeply disturbed by this aspect and after researching
it in depth had concluded that the allegations were false. Among
the immigrants to Israel from Poland, some became disillusioned
by the difficult immigration process, and a few hundred of them
signed a letter to Comrade Voroshilov, a high-ranking member
of Stalin's office, asking to return to the USSR.[7] However, his
parents were not among the signatories.[8]

Member of Knesset Shlomo Lorentz from Agudat Yisrael tried
to mediate the dispute and to secure an agreement for the child
to return to his parents, provided that they agreed to ensure
that he continued to receive an Orthodox education. However,
the kidnappers rejected the proposal.[9] Rabbi Yitzhak Yedidia
Frankel also attempted to mediate. The parents agreed that the
grandfather be released from prison for two weeks to allow him
to find the boy, and they also agreed that Rabbi Frankel would
serve as the boy's legal guardian and attend the Ponevezh Yeshiva in Bnei Brak. The rabbi urged the police not to persecute
the abductors. After ninety days of delays, the rabbi reported that
his mission had been unsuccessful.[10]

The tension between the secular and Orthodox communities
grew. Attorney Cohen-Sidon, who represented the family, mentions in his book a letter he received in 1962 that illustrates the
level of anxiety in Israel at that time. The letter was written by a
young female soldier, who provided her name and identifying
details. In her letter, she noted that the Yossele affair worried her
and many others who felt helpless regarding the religious zealots.
Her parents were moderate Orthodox Jews, and she knew this
community well. In her letter, she said that the threat of prison
would not deter the kidnappers and would only serve to make
them feel like martyrs, just as the grandfather's imprisonment
had not deterred him. She wrote: "Yossele will return only if his

abductors would face an unconditional choice. . . . I suggest kidnapping a boy from a Haredi family and holding him until Yossele
returns. This is the only way to make them understand that the
peace-seeking public that does not interfere with other people's
business would not stand helpless in front of their crime."[11]

The lawyer quoted this letter at a press conference to warn
against the deterioration in relations and culture war between
the two groups, which created a sensation. Meanwhile, in Tel
Aviv, some secular youth took the law into their hands and
stoned the Belz Yeshiva complex, shouting: "Bring back Yossele!"
Similar slogans were shouted by youth by yeshivas in Tel Aviv
and Bnei Brak.[12] The situation appeared to be spiraling out of
control. Both the Orthodox and the secular sides were becoming
impatient, and the threat of violence and perhaps even civil war
was looming.

THE KIDNAPPERS' TRAIL

In an interview Yossele gave to Cohen-Sidon, he described his
kidnapping trail. He remembered watching his mother going to
the bus stop, while he stayed at home. After a few days, his grandfather and uncle told him that his parents wanted to return to
Russia and turn him into a Communist. "Do you want to move to
Russia?" "No way!" They suggested he would go to study at a yeshiva, but Yossele wanted to stay with his grandparents. "Grandpa
told me: 'If you study, you will become a great Torah scholar.'"[13]

He stayed in the yeshiva for a while, and from time to time, his
uncle Shalom came to visit him. After a period, Yossele returned
to Jerusalem and stayed with a grandparents' neighbor. After a
few days, the uncle came again and took him to Moshav Komemiyut, an agricultural settlement of ultra-Orthodox Jews associated
with the Agudat Yisrael movement.

The police received a tip that Yossele was being held in the
moshav and began to make arrests. After investigation, the Kot

family was summoned for questioning. At first, they denied any involvement in the affair, but eventually they admitted that Yossele had stayed with them for a while. Zalman Kot confessed that Shalom Starks had brought the boy to his home, but had taken him away after three weeks. With this testimony, the police asked for the extradition of Shalom Starks, who had already fled to London, joining his brother Ovadia in the Chabad Hasidic community.[14]

The person who orchestrated the hiding of Yossele in Israel was Aryeh Schechter, who served as the personal aide of Rabbi Yaakov Yisrael Kanievsky (1899–1985, commonly known as "the Steipler"). Kanievsky was one of the leaders of the Haredi public in Bnei Brak and was well-known for his criticism of the Agudat Yisrael movement.[15] The police had already conducted some four hundred raids in ultra-Orthodox centers and they were closing in, making arrests in Moshav Komemiyut. When Schechter realized that he could not hide Yossele anymore, he contacted Rabbi Maizes.

Rabbi Abraham Eliyahu Maizes (1901–1961) grew up in Slutsk in Belarus, faced both physical and spiritual hardship, and suffered appalling persecution at the hands of the Communist authorities and their Jewish supporters in the Yevsektzia, the Jewish section of the Soviet Communist Party. The rabbi was willing to give up his life to maintain traditional Jewish life, and he indeed paid a heavy price. He was harassed, tortured, interrogated, and eventually sentenced to seven years of exile in Siberia. After returning from exile, he managed to leave the Soviet Union and reach France, teaching at a yeshiva in Bailly, near Paris, that had absorbed many refugees and Holocaust survivors. In 1953 he immigrated to Israel, joining and later heading the Torah VeYirah Yeshiva affiliated with the anti-Zionist Neturei Karta movement. Ruth claims that Maizes agreed to serve as head of the yeshiva since he considered Zionism to be no less evil than Communism and was determined to continue his war against atheism. The fiery rabbi inspired her: "Maizes was of very high intelligence and with deep penetrating eyes."[16]

As the leaders of Agudat Yisrael felt they could not safely keep Yossele under their supervision, they decided to transfer him to the hands of Neturei Karta.

RUTH BEN DAVID ENTERS INTO THE AFFAIR

After arriving in Israel, Ruth rented an apartment in the Bayit VaGan neighborhood of Jerusalem, which was a bastion of the Orthodox Zionist community. She found a job as a translator. One day, Rabbi Maizes, whom she knew from Paris, asked her to come to him urgently.

As she walked into his study, she saw Aryeh Schechter, who was in charge of hiding Yossele, leaving the room. The rabbi was in a serious mood, and there was silence for a few minutes. As the minutes passed, Ruth realized this was a moment of great importance. The rabbi began to talk quietly, as Ruth recalls the conversation:

"Listen," he said. "There is a great Mitzvah before you, and as I see it, only you can carry this through. It is Yossele Schumacher. Take this child and get him out of the country quickly. I am afraid we cannot do it much longer here. The salvation of a Jewish soul is at stake here—a world on its own. This is your job, go and do it, and G-d will be with you."

Maizes repeated the incorrect assertion that the boy's father, Alter Schumacher, was a Communist who wanted to return to Russia, and reassured her that the child agreed with his abduction. "You must get the child out of Israel!" ordered the rabbi. "But how? I cannot put him in my luggage or pretend that he is my son Uriel, who is twelve years older," Ruth responded. The rabbi looked at her and said: "You are the one destined for this, and as such God will help you on your way." Ruth accepted the mission and promised to come back the following day with a plan.[17]

As noted, Maizes had considerable power over Ruth, who enormously admired the charismatic rabbi. Neturei Karta justified the kidnapping based on the traditional maxim that "the preservation of a human soul overrides the Sabbath"—by extension, to save the boy's spiritual soul, it was permissible to kidnap him and ensure he received an Orthodox education.[18] Ruth herself was equally appalled at the father's apparent intention to return a pure Jewish soul to the Soviet Union and detach him from Judaism.

Ruth went back to her home and could not sleep all night. By the morning, she had an idea. She rushed to the rabbi and told him: "I have found a solution and I can accept the Rabbi's proposal. I shall take the child, and I shall carry out this mission." The rabbi responded: "Boruch Hashem—G-d be praised."[19]

Ruth's plan was to begin by calling Uriel and discussing the details with him. She needed to fly to Europe alone and come back with fake papers for two persons, herself and a girl; if all went well, she would be able to get the child out of Israel and return to Europe. The rabbi responded that he did not need to know all the details; he gave her the address of Aryeh Schechter in Bnei Brak, who concealed Yossele in his home.

She called her son and arranged to meet him in the afternoon. When they met, he supported her decision and gave her his blessing. The false narrative that the parents were planning to return to Russia won the abductors strong support, at least at the beginning of the affair. Even the secular *Davar* newspaper, the mouthpiece of the ruling Mapai Party, published an op-ed supporting the grandparents,[20] and the support for the kidnapping was especially strong among Orthodox circles, with senior figures from Agudat Yisrael collaborating with the abduction. Uriel became an accomplice in the abduction, helping his mother in essential ways.

The following day Ruth traveled to Bnei Brak to meet Schechter, and after discussing the plan with him, he let her meet Yossele. Ruth described the child as beautiful and bright and claimed that he participated knowingly in the fight for his faith. This description is correct to a degree. The child had been manipulated to believe he would turn into a Communist if he returned to his parents, and over two and a half years, he indeed collaborated with his kidnappers. Ruth quoted Yossele saying: "They [my parents] don't want me to be a proper Jew." Unfortunately, she could not recognize that the abductors had manipulated his young soul and maneuvered him to collaborate with them. She also fell into this false narrative, blurring her ability to see right from wrong: "I drew my courage from the aim of my mission, from the sincerity and authority of Rav Maizes, from the fact that I was rescuing a Jewish child from atheism, Communism, and the misguided ways into which his parents were bent on leading him."[21]

Ruth said that Rabbi Maizes had for a long time been considering the possibility of smuggling Yossele out of Israel disguised as a girl, and with this in mind, the kidnappers had let his hair grow. In the early morning, Uriel and Ruth bleached his hair blond and took his picture on the balcony dressed up as a girl. Uriel developed the film and printed the photos. To better disguise Yossele, they used one of the worst pictures.

In her Belgian passport, in the section for recording children, she changed her son's name, Claude, to "Claudine." She also had to forge her visa stamps for Jordan and Lebanon to make it appear that she entered Israel with two people.

Her next step was to board a ship that took her to Genoa, Italy, and from there, she went to Aix-les-Bains, France. In her manuscript, she relates that the following day she traveled to nearby Geneva, Switzerland, looking for an art photographer to improve the picture. From there, she traveled to Antwerp to study the appearance of Belgium passports, including details of children. Ruth's granddaughter, Nechama Davidson, recalled her father Uriel telling his children that he was the one who forged the documents. He saw in a movie how to fake documents, and he applied the technique to his mother's passport. Thus, Ruth traveled to Aix-les-Bains and Antwerp to set up a plan for hiding the boy in European Haredi institutions.

The following day she traveled to Milan and applied for a travel visa at the Israeli consulate for herself and her daughter Claudine. She purchased a ticket to Israel on a Zim ship line, and the consulate issued her a visa. She went back to Paris, where she heard that Knesset member Shlomo Lorentz of Agudat Yisrael was trying to influence Rabbi Maizes to abort the plan and return the boy. Accordingly, she felt it was urgent to return to Israel and act quickly.

She celebrated the Shavuot holiday in Paris and then returned to Italy to board the ship *Jerusalem* from Naples. When she held up her passport at the passport control, the officer asked her where was "the little one." She pointed her finger toward the hall and said, "Over there." The officer let her pass. She could not believe how easy this was; her only explanation was that heaven came to her help. She embarked on the ship without any further issues.[22]

She met a French-speaking family on the ship with seven children immigrating to Israel from Morocco, among them a ten-year-old girl named Claudine. Ruth made friends with the family, especially with Claudine, and later she invited her to join her for dinner with her two tickets. The following day Ruth asked Claudine's mother to let her daughter stay with her because the two sisters shared a bed in their cabin. Claudine did not leave Ruth for three days.

Jerusalem berthed in Haifa on the afternoon of June 12, 1960. Because of the large number of passengers, the disembarkation took three hours. When the police officer asked where her daughter was, Ruth responded: "We have been waiting for three hours. I could not keep the child beside me all time. I left her upstairs on the deck." The officer asked her to bring the girl back, and suddenly Claudine appeared in the line to say goodbye after her family had already passed through the disembarkation check. Ruth used little Claudine to pass the customs checks.[23]

Ruth was back in Israel five weeks after she left. Now she could take Yossele out of the country.

Over these five weeks, the tension in Israel had grown as the police continued their raids. The Knesset held a debate on the affair, including sharp exchanges between the speakers. Knesset member Shlomo Lorentz had visited Rabbi Maizes several times, trying to change his mind.

On the day after she arrived, June 13, Ruth visited Rabbi Maizes. As soon as he saw her face, he knew she had been successful in her mission. He ordered her to go immediately to meet Yossele at Schechter's custody so that he would get used to her. They spent three days together. In the meantime, she booked plane tickets to Italy.

On June 21, 1960, Yossele, dressed up as "Claudine," together with Ruth, took a taxi to the airport. Aryeh Schechter and his wife accompanied them, and Uriel met them at the airport. They all said their goodbyes. Ruth instructed "Claudine" not to look at people in the eyes. She passed through the security checks with her "daughter" without any difficulties. They boarded a plane and took off: "I knew that Yossele was flying to freedom."[24]

Uriel drove his motorcycle straight to Maizes, to find the rabbi and a group of followers praying fervently. He said nothing, but his face told it all. In the air, Yossele/Claudine was so thrilled at the experience that Ruth was afraid he would blow their cover.

Landing in Rome, Ruth purchased a train ticket to Lucerne, Switzerland. She had a few hours to wait, so she took a hotel room and dyed Yossele's hair back to black. In Lucerne, Ruth went straight to meet Rabbi Moshe Soloveitchik (1914–1995), a friend of Rabbi Kanievsky and the Satmar Rebbe Yoel Teitelbaum. Teitelbaum had spent nine months in Switzerland in 1944 after leaving Hungary, thereby avoiding the annihilation that befell the Hungarian Jewry. Soloveitchik had hosted Teitelbaum at his yeshiva in Switzerland, and the two men had continued to cooperate on various matters over subsequent years.[25]

Ruth presented Soloveitchik with a letter from Maizes, and he agreed to admit "Claudine" to the yeshiva. Yossele resumed his identity as a boy under the pseudonym Menachem Levi. There was an issue with Yossele's education because the yeshiva admitted much older children, so eventually, they decided that older students would teach him Jewish studies. He would have a private teacher to teach him secular subjects, and Ruth was to pay for all of that.[26] In my interview with Yossele, he recalled that he was very happy during his time in Switzerland and they treated him well.

After a few days, Ruth left the boy at the yeshiva and traveled to Antwerp to meet her rabbi. She needed to raise funds for this operation, as the costs were mounting, and he sent her to London with a letter of recommendation. Although she does not admit this in her manuscript, in London, she met with Yerachmiel Domb, a successful businessman and supporter of Neturei Karta, who offered her logistical support and raised funds for her. Isser Harel, the head of the Mossad, claimed that the committee that was ostensibly formed to raise funds for the legal defense of Nahman and Shalom Starks actually collected money to pay for the concealment of Yossele Schumacher.[27]

Ruth faced a serious problem with the identity papers of Yossele/Menachem Levy/Claudine. Soloveitchik demanded that she supply him with an identity paper, but she had no solution. Thus, she traveled to Vienna. Some Hungarian Jews, some of them ultra-Orthodox, escaped to Vienna in 1956 after the Hungarian revolution, received refugee status in Austria, and they tried to help Ruth; however, by this time it was 1961, and the authorities were no longer offering visas to refugees.

Ruth decided to return to Israel. Surprisingly, on August 21, 1961, Ruth applied for Israeli citizenship (later, in May 1963, she renounced this citizenship).[28] Uriel rented a room for her near his yeshiva. On the same night she arrived at the yeshiva, the police conducted a raid, and her son was questioned. This episode made her realize that the story was far from over, and she wondered whether the raid's timing was a coincidence. The following day she traveled to Jerusalem to meet Maizes, noticing his deteriorating health. She could not keep Yossele in Lucerne for long, so while in Israel, she consulted with Rabbi Kanievsky, who had assigned his personal assistant to hide Yossele during the early stages of the affair.

According to Ruth, Kanievsky advised Ruth to alter Yossele's looks by performing plastic surgery on his face and removing a scar he had on his head. In her manuscript, Ruth said that she opposed this idea;[29] however, Yossele himself later claimed several times that Ruth had, in fact, suggested plastic surgery but that he had opposed the idea and threatened to expose his identity, leaving them with no option but to drop the idea.[30]

Kanievsky was considered one of the greatest ultra-Orthodox authorities of his generation and provided Ruth with a letter of support which she found extremely useful. Despite this, and despite the culture of deep respect and admiration toward senior rabbis, Ruth describes him in her manuscript in unflattering terms, calling him as anything but an ordinary man.[31] She showed such profound disrespect because he ultimately attempted to reach a compromise to end the kidnapping saga.

Ruth stayed in Israel for four weeks before returning to Vienna. However, she could not obtain the refugee documents, so she returned to France. She contracted jaundice and was sick for several weeks. She traveled to Lucerne, but Rabbi Soloweitchik had traveled to Israel to meet with Kanievsky. This led Ruth to fear that they were negotiating a deal behind her back. She had to wait for him patiently to return.

Rabbi Maizes died on June 16, 1961, aged fifty-nine. When Soloweitchik came back from Israel, he asked that Yossele leave. Yossele had been in Switzerland for over a year and was happy at the yeshiva. Even as an adult, he returned to Lucerne to visit the yeshiva and meet those who had concealed him. In my interview, he declared that he had forgiven Rabbi Soloweitchik. Yossele also stated that two youths in Lucerne identified him as the missing boy and called him by his real name and that this was why he had to move out.[32]

Ruth dressed up Yossele again as Claudine and crossed the Swiss-French border at a checkpoint she knew well, assuming they would not face serious checks during heavy rain. She took him to a new yeshiva in Fublaines in rural northern France, headed by Rabbi Gershon Liebman, a Holocaust survivor and a friend and colleague of Rabbi Kanievsky. Liebman recruited most of his students at the yeshiva from Morocco. Yossele indeed recalls that all of the students and some of the teachers were from North Africa, and there was only one child who spoke Yiddish like him. The language spoken at the yeshiva was Hebrew. At the yeshiva, he learned to curse in Arabic and regularly got into fights with other boys. He remembers that the food cooked in the institution was Moroccan style and was too spicy for him. He also recalled that one of his teachers, Haim Turgeman, used to hit the boys with a ruler as an educational method. Yossele was also beaten, but this did not bother him. What concerned him more was that all the other boys got letters from their parents, but he never received any. He said he was very jealous of them, and he missed his parents.[33]

An interesting memory Yossele had from France was that Ruth arrived and took him into a room alone one day. She showed him a letter written in Yiddish and asked him to copy it five times, but each letter had a different address. There was one address in Israel and one addressed to the court in London. According to Yossele's recollection, the letter stated that his uncle Shalom had taken him to Moshav Komemiyut at his own request and that he never saw him again. In the end, the letter presented Yossele's request to free his uncle. As noted earlier, the British court had ordered that Shalom Starks remain in prison pending his extradition to Israel. There was also another letter, shorter and also written in Yiddish. Ruth asked him to read it aloud, and she recorded him. He remembers the following words: "This is Yossele Schumacher. I ask the court in London to release my uncle Shalom Starks. He only brought me to Komemiyut, and nothing more." When Yossele asked who wrote these letters, Ruth responded: "A man called Domb. He is in London."[34]

After putting him in his new temporary home with new temporary friends, Ruth traveled to Morocco to find a place for Yossele among followers of Chabad in Casablanca. As noted, the child's uncle Shalom Starks, a follower of Chabad, had been involved in the early stages of the kidnapping. Given the highly centralized nature of a Hasidic court, it is impossible that the movement's leader Rabbi Menachem-Mendel Schneersohn (the "Lubavitcher Rebbe") was unaware of this involvement. After Yossele was transferred into the care of Neturei Karta, Schneersohn decided not to continue to cooperate with the operation. Accordingly, Ruth met with a cool response when she visited the Chabad followers in Morocco; they refused to join her plan and told her they would cooperate only if their Rebbe told them to do so directly. In her unpublished book, Ruth is sharply critical of the Lubavitcher Rebbe for his refusal to help while instructing his followers to ignore her pleas for help. However, I should note that despite desperate requests from Agudat Yisrael, the Lubavitcher Rebbe does not seem to have helped in the efforts to locate the child. His position was not to assist the kidnappers, but at the same time, not to hand over the boy to the authorities.[35] This approach embodies the Halachic principle of *din moser* (the Law of the Informer): according to Jewish religious law, a Jew must not inform on a fellow Jew to the authorities and any disputes must be resolved within the Jewish community.[36] Thus, in general, the Haredi world did not support the kidnapping and attempted to find a compromise that would allow the affair to be resolved in a dignified manner while ensuring that all those involved would be pardoned. However, the Haredi circles did not cooperate with the investigation or provide vital details needed to locate the child, despite this information being known to several figures involved in the affair, including the Lubavitcher Rebbe and Rabbi Kanievsky.[37]

In his interview with Cohen-Sidon, Yossele recalled that an older child at the yeshiva had shown him an article with his picture and asked him if he was Yossele Schumacher. Yossele reported the incident to the principal, and he knew that his time at the yeshiva was limited. Shortly after that, Ruth duly arrived and said that the yeshiva was too dangerous and that the French police were looking for him. "Where will we go?" asked Yossele, and Ruth responded: "We will take you to Morocco. Over there, you could study and progress quietly."

Yossele vetoed the idea:

> I knew that if I said no—they would not force me. This is how it was on everything. Whatever I did not want to do—I did not do. Moreover, if they had forced me, I would have told a police officer at the border that I was Yossele, and they would catch Ruth and me and I would not have gone to Morocco. So she said: "Fine, I will travel to London tomorrow morning and I will consult with Domb."
>
> And I responded: "I want to go to America."[38]

Before this reported incident, Ruth again traveled to Israel. The timing was strange, as her son was not in Israel at that time: he was traveling in Turkey, Lebanon, and other countries in the region and had a girlfriend in Lebanon. She came to meet Aharon Katzenelbogen, who was Amram Blau's partner in the leadership of Neturei Karta and who had assumed the management of the Yossele affair after Maizes's death. Katzenelbogen persuaded her to leave the country. Based on this request, Ruth decided to leave Israel, but this time, she traveled to the United States to meet Yoel Teitelbaum, the Satmar Rebbe.[39]

In her autobiography, Ruth is cautious not to implicate Teitelbaum in the kidnapping. Accordingly, she does not describe any meetings with him on this subject. Though she criticizes American Haredi leaders, including Rabbi Aharon Kotler of the Lakewood Yeshiva and the Lubavitcher Rebbe, for failing to help her, she has nothing but praise for Teitelbaum. The Satmar Rebbe informed the press that he was not involved in the kidnapping: "I was unaware of Yossele's whereabouts from the day he disappeared in Israel and until he was found on Saturday evening in New York."[40] An interesting testimony regarding a meeting that is not mentioned in Ruth's book but that nevertheless took place is provided by Isser Harel. Mossad agents who had penetrated the Haredi community in Antwerp heard a rumor that helped them focus their investigations on Ruth. A woman in the community told a Mossad agent that when she visited the Satmar Rebbe in New York, she had been forced to wait for three hours after he entered into an unscheduled meeting. She was amazed to see Ruth leaving the Rebbe's office after such a protracted consultation.[41]

Uriel wrote his own version of events in his autobiography in French, which he shelved, and his daughter Nechama found it on her father's computer. In his unpublished autobiography, Uriel adds further details about that meeting. He wrote that, over the years, his mother told him with astonishment that when she introduced herself and the Yossele case, the rebbe literally fainted, and they had to call a physician. The rebbe said to her that he did not want to have anything to do with this affair, directly or indirectly, since, in his words, in America you can get the electric chair for kidnapping a child.[42] Katzenelbogen put Ruth in touch with the Gertner family, who subsequently hid Yossele in New York. The Gertners were not part of the Satmar community but of an affiliated court known as the Malochim (angels).[43]

After Ruth had arrived in New York, the situation in Israel intensified further. In August 1961, Shalom Starks was arrested in London because of the request to extradite him to Israel. His defense line enraged Israeli public opinion: he argued the court in Jerusalem had no jurisdiction since Jerusalem should not be viewed as part of the State of Israel, in accordance with UN resolutions from 1947 defining the city as a separate international entity. The London court rejected this line of defense, but Starks was only extradited in November 1962; in the meantime, he was held in a British prison. In Israel, the police arrested Rabbi Benjamin Mendelson, the spiritual leader of Moshav Komemiyut and an important rabbinical figure, and brought him to trial.

These developments raised the level of Ruth's anxiety. Mendelson was in touch with Schechter, and Ruth feared Mendelson would crack under investigation. Ruth pondered: "Will he (Mendelson) be able to hold out? Will he not one day give up under pressure and mention the name of Aryeh Schechter, the last link leading to me?"[44]

According to Ruth's manuscript, Rabbi Liebman from the yeshiva in Fublaines arrived in New York with the troubling news that Yossele's identity had been exposed and, thus, she must transfer him to a new location.

In London, in the spring of 1962, Domb contacted Stanisław Albrecht "Stash" Radziwill, a former Polish-Lithuanian royal whose family was related to the Kennedys. Radziwill met with Robert Kennedy, the US attorney general, to discuss the Yossele affair and Kennedy promised to check the possibility of legalizing Yossele's presence in the United States. A hope for legally solving the case was at last within sight.[45]

Fearing that Mossad agents were monitoring the Paris airports, Ruth decided to travel first to Brussels, from where they flew to America the following day. Since she was afraid of checks by American immigration, she decided to fly to Canada, where the checks were less rigorous.

In the air, after a few hours of flight, the captain announced that one of the plane engines had failed and they would have to make an emergency landing in New York. Yossele remembers: "That was the first time I saw Ruth scared. I knew why. Because in America, if you take a child that is not yours, it is called 'kidnapping,' and this is forbidden. Ruth told me of that once. She told me of a pilot in America whose child was taken by others. Later, when they caught them, they were put on the electric chair and died."[46]

When they landed, Ruth remembers, she ordered Yossele not to look at the immigration officers' faces, but he intentionally did so: "I deliberately stood next to the officers and let them look, but they discovered nothing, and Ruth kept telling me, 'Turn around, turn around!'"[47] They were able to pass immigration, and Yossele switched his identity again, assuming the new name Jacob Frankel. Ruth took him to the Gertner's house in Brooklyn, New York.

In her narrative, Ruth stated that Yossele had enjoyed his time at the Gertner's in Brooklyn, and he liked their children, with whom he played. However, Yossele had a different recollection: "It was really bad. It was like a prison. Everyone was afraid the police would discover me, and if they let me go outside once— they warned me a hundred times that I could get them in trouble. I was fed up, and many times I often thought about the electric chair and the pilot's child, and I thought to myself that I didn't care if the police discovered me."[48]

Yossele was misbehaving and the Gertners were unable to discipline him. The boy himself felt that he was unwelcome in their home. He once overheard them saying that although they were being paid well for their services, they still did not want him in their home. He saw Haredi newspapers in the house with articles about his case, and he read that it was time to return him to his parents, which made him think about the matter.

Because of Yossele's behavioral problems, Ruth was looking for other alternatives. She tried to meet Rabbi Aharon Kotler, one of the most prominent ultra-Orthodox leaders in the United States, head of the Lakewood Yeshiva in New Jersey, but he refused to meet her. The Lubavitcher Rebbe, for his part, stated to the press at precisely the same time declaring that he had nothing to do with this affair. Yossele recalled that once when Ruth came to visit and talked over the phone, he went into another room, picked up the phone, and heard that Ruth was willing to go to *din Torah* (a religious court hearing) with the Lubavitcher Rebbe, but the Gertners refused. Thus, the rabbi's statement might have been related to these negotiations.[49]

During Passover week in 1962, Ruth recalls that Aryeh Schechter made a surprise visit to New York to meet with Ruth. She suspected he had come to "betray" her. According to her manuscript, he told her, "Things are going badly, the Zionists are persecuting the religious. It is a real war, and the situation has become untenable." Schechter said that Rabbi Mendelson, who was arrested at the time, had asked him several times to return the boy. He continued: "Ruth, we must return Yossele. The Gerer Rebbe and Rav Kanievsky both agree that Yossele must be handed back and that we must put an end to this affair, which is endangering the whole community." Schechter presented Ruth with the compromise suggested by Rabbi Yedidia Frankel, emphasizing that it was acceptable to Kanievsky. Ruth refused to cooperate and said that "the affair had become a symbolic fight and I could not give up the cause." Schechter, in return, showed her a letter from Rabbi Kanievsky, asking her to return the boy. She concluded: "Now, I thought, Yossele must be hidden from the Zionists and their police, from Aguda betrayers, and from Aryeh Shechter too."[50]

Yerachmiel Domb also arrived in New York to celebrate Passover with Rabbi Teitelbaum. As the summer was approaching, Domb agreed to provide resources to remove Yossele to the country; the Gertners would rent a farm for a while until construction of a new yeshiva would be completed and Yossele could be admitted to the institution. Yossele recalled that indeed the Gertner family tried to take him to the rented farm at night so that no one would see him, but their car broke down on the way, and with great fear, they had to wait for it to be repaired. In the meantime, they decided to return home, and the summer plans were canceled: "I felt like heaven wanted me to stay in Zangwill Gertner's house."[51]

An episode that Ruth failed to mention but that Yossele mentioned in detail occurred following the failed attempt to remove him to the country. He remembers that one day Ruth came and held his hands. She looked him in the eyes and then asked him: "Do you want us to return you to Eretz Yisrael?" The child understood that they were planning to return him to his grandparents or his parents, so they must have made peace with them and he did not need to hide anymore. Then Ruth told him how dangerous it was to hide him in America: many good rabbis would go to jail if he were to be found. She again reminded him of the story of the pilot's child.

Then she said: "I have a passport that says I am a gentile. We can go to Jordan without problems. We will go to the Old City and stay there with good Arabs, until we can find a way to cross to the new city, in the State of Israel." Neturei Karta indeed had connections with the Palestinian leadership, which might have been the source of this idea. Yossele was excited, but then Ruth raised another issue:

> Before we leave, we need to make a plastic operation on your face!
> I screamed: "No! No!"

Yossele flatly refused the idea of undergoing an operation on his face, and his reaction put an end to the idea. With no other options, Ruth told him that they would not take him to Jordan or make plastic surgery. He saw that she was upset, but he did not care. After that, they left him in peace: "They would give me food, wash me, give me clothes, and that is it. We were all waiting for something to happen."[52]

SIX

THE HUNT (1962)

AS THE YOSSELE AFFAIR INTENSIFIED, the State of Israel could no longer see it as merely a family dispute over school choices; it was a challenge to the state's rule of law and social stability. Liberal states must be inclusive toward religious minorities who may not respect liberal ideas, but where should they draw the line? What should be the limits of tolerance toward religious minorities that deliberately and consciously break the law and kidnap a boy? If a religious community claims that religious education is something it is willing to martyr itself for, how should liberal democracies respond to that challenge? How should they react to criminal activity that is justified in the name of God?

These questions became the working challenges of Prime Minister David Ben-Gurion when he called the director of the Mossad at his home on a night in March 1962.

Isser Harel (1912–2003) is one of Israel's most decorated soldiers. Under his leadership, Israel developed a highly respected secret service. When Israel became independent in 1948, Harel was chosen to lead the Shin Bet, Israel's internal intelligence agency. In 1952 he also became head of Mossad, the foreign intelligence agency.

Harel's most notable achievement was an operation in May 1960 intended to identify, capture, and transport Adolf Eichmann, head of the Jewish Section of the SS, from hiding in Buenos Aires, Argentina, to justice in Israel. The Israeli court found Eichmann guilty and executed him in May 1962, just as the Yossele affair was emerging as a new focus of concern for the Mossad. In retrospect, Harel would comment that solving the Yossele conspiracy was the most challenging case he had ever undertaken. The Yossele affair was also one of the last cases he resolved as the head of the Mossad: in March 1963, Harel would resign from the position of director of the Israeli secret service.

Harel decided to take on the mission and described the problem in the following words: "It has been two years and a half since this crisis erupted, and not only has it not been resolved, but from day to day, it becomes more complicated. . . . It is imperative to find the boy and return him to his parents and reveal, without partiality, the root of this malignant disease that has spread over the national body."[1]

As a dispute over domestic matters, the Yossele affair fell outside the jurisdiction of the Mossad, which is an intelligence agency. Nevertheless, Harel justified Ben-Gurion's decision to involve the agency in the matter, explaining that the state must protect law and order and the freedoms that are established in a democracy. The state's inability to offer security is a major threat to its stability. If the state failed to meet its obligations to its citizens, and in this case, to return a kidnapped boy to his parents, citizens might feel exempt from fulfilling their duties to the state. Thus, the assignment of the Mossad was not just to save a boy from abduction but to rescue the sovereignty and dignity of the state. If ultra-Orthodox anti-Zionist circles were encouraged by their success, they might try to replicate their actions and draw in more moderate circles.[2]

OPERATION "GUR"

Early in the investigation, Harel realized that the boy was not in the hands of Agudat Yisrael. He sent his agents to look for information within the more extreme ultra-Orthodox circles, but they faced a wall of silence.

He soon realized that the boy was no longer in Israel since there was no clue about his whereabouts. As they moved their operations overseas, the first problem was language. Mossad agents are well versed with most of the languages of the world, but the one language they hardly knew was Yiddish, the only language used by the ultra-Orthodox.

Harel used to have two daily meetings at which the senior leaders of the Mossad met and discussed the information they had obtained that day. After the first analysis, he concluded that Yossele might be with either the radical ultra-orthodox anti-Zionist movement or in the hands of Chabad Hasidic followers. He reached the former conclusion because of the involvement of Rabbi Maizes of Neturei Karta in the early stages of the affair. At the same time, the Chabad connection was possible given the involvement of Shalom and Ovadia Starks. Another clue for Harel was the silence of the Lubavitcher Rebbe, who never condemned the kidnapping of Yossele, unlike the Council of Torah Sages of Agudat Yisrael, who publicly opposed the abduction.[3]

One of the tips the Mossad received was that Yossele might have been taken to an Arab country, likely Morocco, where Chabad has a presence. Two agents were sent to Morocco and investigated the yeshivas and airports for two weeks, but without any results.

In Europe, the Mossad first looked at the yeshiva in Lucerne and other Haredi centers in Switzerland. They also planted an agent at the yeshiva at Aix les-Bains—a former student but a strong supporter of Israel. Mossad agents carefully investigated tens of orphanages, yeshivas, and charitable organizations in Europe. Harel recalled that searching for a boy who looked like thousands of others in the various ultra-Orthodox enclaves was exhausting and discouraging to many agents.[4]

A month and a half after the operation began, Harel moved his headquarters to Paris and took complete control of the investigation. His deputy stayed in Israel to take care of all other Mossad businesses. Harel had a small operational apartment, and over time the Mossad was able to study the world of the Haredi zealots very closely. Their attention turned first to England, and specifically the activities of Yerachmiel Domb (1915–2013).

Domb was a wealthy businessman who also was involved in "dubious business," according to Harel. Domb hated the State of Israel, and he was the man behind the Committee for the Defense of Shalom Starks. London was also a center of the Chabad Hasidic movement. For these reasons, the city was Harel's first priority in the investigation.[5]

Based on unconfirmed information, Harel sent agents to Ireland, Scotland, and Manchester looking for Yossele, but they returned no results. However, his agents were able to rule out the involvement of the Chabad movement in the abduction. Harel was convinced that Shalom Starks had no idea where the boy was being held, and that the Lubavitcher Rebbe had no control over the situation, although he could have helped the Mossad much more than he chose to. After eliminating Chabad as a suspect, Harel concluded that Yossele was being held in one of three locations: with the Satmar Rebbe in New York, Domb in London, or the Neturei Karta enclave in Jerusalem.

After two months of fruitless investigations, many agents were exhausted and despairing. Harel knew he could not give up, primarily, because of the damage this would cause to the prestige of the secret services but also because admitting failure could spark a civil war in Israel. The kidnappers became aware of the agents' massive efforts and came under intense pressure. They now needed to move the child from one place to another, which inevitably increased the circle of people involved and implicit in the attempts to hide Yossele, thus weakening the wall of silence.[6]

Moshe Shaked, a Mossad agent, penetrated the Haredi community in Antwerp. He heard an anecdotal rumor that helped them focus their investigations on Ruth. A woman in the community told him that when she visited the Satmar Rebbe in New York, she had been forced to wait for three hours after he entered into an unscheduled meeting. She was amazed to see Ruth and two companions leaving the Rebbe's office after such a protracted consultation.[7] Shaked told this anecdote to Harel while visiting Brussels in May 1962, and he immediately knew that this was a significant lead. Harel said: "The mysterious convert! The woman of many faces, the brave, travelling all over the world on the Satmar Rebbe's mission. . . . And a meeting for three hours with the great Rebbe." Why should he, the admired rabbi of hundreds of thousands of followers worldwide, spend hours of his precious time with a woman—and, moreover, a convert? Harel suspected that the meeting was devoted to resolving a complicated issue that had to be determined by the rebbe himself. What issue could be troubling the rebbe's zealot followers, Harel reasoned, if not the fate of the abducted boy, Yossele Schumacher?[8]

Harel realized that this was the piece of information he had been waiting for all along. It was clear that Ruth was responsible for moving and hiding the boy.

Harel had no information about this mysterious convert, so he called Shaked again to go to Antwerp to find more information. A piece of anecdotal news Shaked picked up while talking with a secretary of one of his friends proved helpful. The secretary's sister had been offered a match with the convert's son, but the family was unhappy because the candidate was a convert himself. Shaked took the initiative and offered the secretary his connections to research the prospective husband if she would give him more information. The secretary learned that the prospect match was studying at a yeshiva in Beer Yaakov. He passed this information to Harel, who made immediate inquiries.

Uriel often traveled to Beirut, using his French nationality, because he had a Jewish girlfriend. He devised a plan to smuggle the Jews of Lebanon and Syria out of their countries and presented it to the head of the Jewish Agency, who arranged a meeting between Uriel and Harel. Thus, Harel knew Uriel from a completely different context. When Harel connected the dots regarding Ruth, he sent agents to Uriel to tell him that his plan to rescue the Jews of Beirut was moving forward, so he should please send a letter to his mother telling her that he would be disappearing for a while. He did as he was requested and sent a letter to Aix-les-Bains.[9]

Harel sent a team to Aix-les-Bains to watch the postal office. The following day they saw a woman whom they suspected might be her as she fitted Ruth's physical description. After picking up her mail, she sat down at the postal office and opened a letter. An agent sneaked a peek and saw the words "Dear Ruth." After identifying her, they followed her into an apartment building where a teacher at the yeshiva was living. After a short interval, she came back with a suitcase, and to the amazement of the agents, she began to hitchhike. Ruth took rides to Paris while changing cars several times. Eventually, the agents lost her.

Hitchhiking was typical of Ruth. Yossele said in our interview that they had hitchhiked several times when moving from one location to the other. Nechama Davidson, Ruth's granddaughter, also told me that Ruth had hitchhiked with her son during a vacation in Spain, so this behavior was not out of character.

Mossad agents were able to steal her mail from the box and saw two letters: one was from Domb in London, which strengthened their suspicion that Ruth was involved in the kidnapping affair. The second was from a real estate agent from Orleans, France. The letter included a newspaper clip of a home sale advertisement. Harel realized that this was a critical piece of information since it would allow his agents to contact the convert.[10]

While the Mossad lost track of Ruth in France, another team of agents were monitoring Domb's house in London. They suddenly saw Ruth and Domb sitting together in his car for a long hour. Harel concluded now that Ruth was undoubtedly the key figure in the affair.

Harel had to decide between two options: One was to continue the surveillance of Ruth, hoping that she would eventually lead them to the boy; the second was to kidnap her and bring her in for interrogation, as he had done with Eichmann. Both options were dangerous, but he realized he could not continue surveillance for much longer since they repeatedly lost track of Ruth. Accordingly, he decided on the second option.[11]

Harel chose for the job two Mossad agents who were living in Europe. One was Austrian who spoke perfect German, and the second was German who also spoke fluent French. He instructed them to make a bid for the house Ruth had placed on the market.

The house had been put up for sale because of Ruth's debts to French customs. A letter found in Ruth's archives dated May 25, 1962, from the Ministry of Finance and Economic Affairs notified her that she still owed a large sum to the state, and if she did not pay her debt, she would be sent back to jail.[12] She put her house on the market, and Mossad agents called the real estate agency that was taking care of the sale and pretended to be two Austrian business people looking for a vacation house for their families. After intense negotiation, they agreed on a price, and they said they wanted to close the deal only with the owner, Madeline Lucette Ferraille. The agent told them he did not have a good connection with the owner since she was always traveling. The ostensible buyers left him a hotel's phone number in Paris and asked him to notify the owner.

In the meantime, Harel instructed his team to rent a house in one of the wealthy suburbs of Paris, while the buyers were waiting in their hotel room for a sign from Ruth. The following day, Ruth called the agents from Switzerland and arranged to meet them the day after. She met with the "buyers" and reached an agreement regarding the details of the sale. They spent two hours together, breaking the ice, and inviting her to go to lunch with them. At that point, she told them she could not join them because she was Jewish and would not eat nonkosher food. In her manuscript, Ruth said that she mentioned her Jewishness to test if the potential buyers were ex-Nazis.[13]

They decided to meet again at the hotel the following day with their lawyer to close the deal. She gave them no contact details but promised to call again. In the morning, she indeed called, and they told her the lawyer could not come to the hotel due to heavy traffic in Paris due to a train workers' strike. They suggested they should visit him at his home instead. They agreed to pick her up, and in good spirits, they drove to the meeting while engaging in pleasant small talk. The door opened at the "lawyer's" house, they walked in, and the door closed. The date was June 21, 1962; the time, 3:00 p.m.[14]

INTERROGATIONS

Ruth admits that she had made a grave mistake by not being careful: "Did I willingly enter that car of the Israeli Gestapo? Why didn't I suspect that I might be abducted?" She could not believe that the Mossad would kidnap her, a French citizen, on French territory, thus violating French sovereignty, particularly since France was regarded as a staunch friend of Israel.

As the door closed, she was asked to sit down. With exaggerated description, she said: "I thought I had fallen into the hands of sadists, of professional killers." A man walked into the room, telling her that she was not brought in to sell a house but to reveal where Yossele Schumacher was. She denied any connection to the affair.[15]

Harel knew that Domb was at the center of the abduction, so he also sought to kidnap Domb's close associate and bring him into interrogations. Mossad agents identified Gadol Halpern, a *mohel* (circumciser), and were able to trick him into coming to Paris to perform a circumcision. On June 21, 1962, he was also kidnapped.

When Ruth was kidnapped, there were many letters inside her bag and a phone book. Among them was a suspicious letter signed by "Lea's father" written in a very conspiratorial style, and it was clear to the agents that it was written in some kind of a code. Eventually, they broke the code, and identified Lea's father as Rabbi Aharon Katzenelbogen of Neturei Karta.

Ruth denied any connections to the Yossele affair. Her strategy was to win time. She believed that as long as she did not break, the interrogators would find nothing; at some point, her friends in Paris would call the police to report a missing person or at least notify Domb, and he would make his moves or even just send the order to have the child moved to a new hiding place.

After two days of futile interrogations, Harel decided to question her himself. "I got the impression she is wise, she knows how to listen and understands what we say to her." He offered her a deal in which if she would give up the boy, she could begin a new life in Israel. If she refused, he warned, she and the circles around her would pay a heavy price: "It was clear for me, as I guessed in advance, that the convert is a tough nut to crack. I had no doubt she was involved in the Yossele affair from start to end, but she was very zealous, tough, intelligent, and sneaky. I assumed that she understood we would not torture her, and accordingly, she decided to exhaust us instead of us exhausting her."[16]

Over the Sabbath, there were no interrogations, and they prepared candles and a prayer book, in addition to kosher food purchased in Paris for her. The first few days of interrogations were concluded in complete failure. Harel called for French-speaking interrogators to join the team from Israel.

The kidnapping of Mohel Gadol Halpern also proved to be a resounding failure. After a night of extensive investigations, it was clear the man knew nothing and that he was not as close to the zealot circles in London as they had thought. He took a lie detector test that confirmed he was not involved in the affair.[17]

The interrogations resumed when the Sabbath was over, and Ruth continued to deny any connections. In the meanwhile, the agents were able to narrow down six addresses from the materials found in her bag, one of which was in New York; they suspected that the child was hiding in one of them.

Harel's next move was to bring in Uriel for questioning in Israel. At first, Uriel denied all connections to the kidnapping. Then, the interrogator showed him "Lea's father's" letter. Uriel, in response, requested guarantees that he and his mother would not face charges. After such promises were made, he told the interrogator his role in the affair—how they smuggled the boy and changed Ruth's passport—and he also told them that Yossele's first stop was in Lucerne, Switzerland. Uriel was transferred immediately to be investigated by the head of the Shin Beth (the internal intelligence agency); over a good lunch, he repeated his testimony and added more details. This new information was sent immediately to Harel in Paris on June 26, 1962.[18]

During that day, Ruth refused to cooperate with the investigations, and her confidence grew. With the new information, Harel decided to join the interrogation. He sat in front of her, and they both knew this was the moment of truth. Harel recalled that he was convinced that she was in a kind of "trance" of righteousness at this time; he could not rule out that the Yossele affair was also intended to further her own career and her prestige among the zealots. He acknowledged that she was intelligent and sensible, "but above all, in front of a character like that, you have to show moral superiority." He had to show her that he was better than her.

Harel told her that he wanted to make a deal with her, and he read Uriel's confession. When she heard it, she almost collapsed. Harel said that Uriel was at the center of events in Israel and that he came to conclude that the Yossele affair must be resolved immediately and without delay. Uriel made a deal that he and his mother would not be persecuted as long as she told them where Yossele was being held; if she failed to do so, she would have to pay the full price of kidnapping, smuggling, and concealing the boy, and so would her son.[19]

Ruth was very upset. She struggled with herself: "I was surrounded, caged, with barbed wire cutting into my flesh." She asked, "How can I know who you are and that you can speak in the name of the government?" Harel knew it was a onetime opportunity, so he pulled out his real diplomatic passport, with his real name, and handed it to Ruth. The people in the room were astonished. Ruth was held illegally in a foreign country, and Harel had just identified himself by his real name and title.[20]

Ruth looked carefully at the passport, and after a while, she said in a voice choked with tears: "Yossele is at 126 Penn Street, Brooklyn, New York, with the Zangwill Gertner family. His name is Yankele." Harel shook her hand and promised that she and her son would be free once the boy was in his hands. It was Tuesday, June 26, 1962.[21]

"I was betrayed. A few informants, not all from their camp, were responsible for the victory. The informants were cheap and weak," Ruth charged in her manuscript. "I was surrounded by enemies from all sides, and the Shin Bet knew quite a lot—nearly all the details of my engagement in the Yossele affair."[22]

Ruth was disappointed at what she saw as the betrayal of the Haredi world in the Yossele affair. She adopted the rhetoric of Neturei Karta and Satmar, arguing that protest has an intrinsic value. Thus, even if the kidnapping was ultimately a failure, it was still a demonstration of bold opposition to the Israeli and Haredi establishment. This distinct value can be gauged in its own right.

Ruth mentioned her concern that her son had given his testimony under torture.[23] The truth is that Uriel gave his testimony willingly due to his desire to end the affair. Although he had ties to circles close to Neturei Karta, including through Rabbis Maizes and Katzenelbogen, Uriel was a Zionist and served in the military. When Ruth's interrogator informed her that Uriel had given testimony against her, she proclaimed, "No, no, no, he is no longer my son."[24] Uriel confirms that she indeed rejected him for a while but adds that he was able to appease her and repair their relationship.[25]

In her manuscript, she said that one reason she was willing to confess was her desire to save the Gertners from serious punishment: "In the United States for kidnapping a child—anything from fifteen years to the electric chair," interestingly she echoed what Yossele has said in his interview.[26]

Harel sent an immediate telegram to the Israeli consulate in New York to check whether the address was correct. He knew he could not conduct a secret operation on American soil, so he sent an arrest request to the FBI. To his astonishment, the response was slow and uncertain: How would they know that the information is correct; how would they ensure there was no violation of the family's rights? Harel understood that the situation was fragile. Many Americans were in on the secret, and someone might leak it to the family, who would quickly transfer him to a different location. Three days had passed, but nothing was done.

On Saturday, June 30, Harel called the Israeli ambassador to the United States, identifying himself by his actual name. It was widely known that the phones were tapped, so they never spoke about delicate issues over the phone. In the call, Harel strongly criticized Robert Kennedy, the US attorney general at the time, for failing to attend to the affair. The purpose was to speak not to the ambassador but straight to Kennedy. Indeed, that night, the FBI broke into Gertner's home and found the child.[27]

What led Kennedy to change his mind? Was it Harel's fervent speech about doing the right thing, or was a deal made between the FBI and the Mossad regarding a Soviet-Jewish spy? On July 1, 1962, Israel deported Robert Soblen to the United States, a week after arriving in Israel with a false identity. Soblen, a Soviet spy, was caught and sentenced to life in prison for espionage in the

Figure 6.1 Yossele at the age of four years old with his sister Zina. Courtesy of Yossi Schumacher.

United States. While on bail, he escaped to Israel with a fake Canadian passport and requested asylum based on Israel's Law of Return. He was arrested in his hotel room shortly after his arrival. The Israeli government declared that the Law of Return was not an open invitation for Jewish criminals to immigrate to Israel. Soblen was denied citizenship, and his appeals were rejected. Although Israel and the United States did not have an extradition agreement at the time, Soblen faced expulsion from Israel and deportation to the United States on charges of illegal entry. Soblen was deported from Israel on a flight to the United States on July 1, a day after Yossele was taken in the hands of the FBI on June 30.[28] Was this timeline coincidental?

YOSSELE IN HIS OWN WORDS

It happened on Saturday night. The whole day had been peaceful,
like every regular Sabbath. Zangwill Gertner went to shul (synagogue) and I stayed alone. I remember that the Torah portion of
that week was Korach. On Saturday night, we sat down for dinner.
Two people walked in. They came to me straight and started talking in Yiddish. From their first words, I knew they had caught me
this time. "Did you ever hear the name Schumacher?" they asked.

"Schumacher?" I responded. "No."

For a long time, I had been prepared for this moment. They
taught me day and night that if anyone asked me whether I
was Yossele Schumacher, I must immediately deny it, without
thinking.

"Aren't you Yossele?" the two men asked.

"No. I have a different name."

"What?"

"Yankel Frankel."

One of them gave me a pen and a pencil: "Sign your name!"

I signed: Yankel Frankel.

The other man asked me: "Did you ever hear of Nahman
Starks?"

I responded: "I don't know him."

"Do you have a grandfather in Eretz Yisrael?"

"No."

"Where are your dad and mom?"

I knew how to respond. They had taught me. "In Argentina."

"Where do they live? What does your dad do for work?"

"I don't know." It was not a lie. I do not know where mom and
dad live or what does my dad for a living.

They kept asking: "If you want to write to them—what is their
address?"

I did not know. For real.

"When were you born?"

"I do not know."

I had a thought running in my head all the time: Maybe I should
just tell them the truth, tell them I am Yossele, and it will be over?
But I thought, this is not going to look good in the newspapers.

Besides that, outside was Gertner and his wife, and I did not want to expose them so that they will take them to the electric chair. Therefore, I continued saying that I did not know Yossele Schumacher.

Suddenly, I had another thought: what if they believed me and went away, and then I would be smuggled out again, to who knows where, and no one would ever find me and all my life I would run away from one place to the other? I was afraid to tell them, but I hoped they would discover me. Finally, they said, "Come with us!"

Yossele stayed in a safe house for the night. The following day, the FBI continued questioning him. Meanwhile, his mother and sister Zina took a flight from Israel to New York. In the evening, the authorities scheduled them to meet finally.

"Come, someone is waiting for you," said the woman who guarded me. Two men took me down, and we went to a different room. It was evening. They opened the door. I saw two women standing there. I knew them immediately: Mommy and Zina. My mother and my sister!

I did not run to them; I said nothing. I stood, and I made myself act like I did not know them. This is exactly how Ruth Ben David told me all the time: "If they find you, tell it is not you!" So I said to myself: Do not look at them. Do not say "Mommy." Do not say you are Yossele.

Mommy called out: "Yossele! My son!" and she ran toward me. I stood straight.

She hugged me. I did not hug her back, and I said nothing.

Mommy started crying. So did Zina. She stood in the corner and cried.

I sat on a chair and held myself. Mom said: "Yossel! Yossele!" but I responded, "I am not Yossele! I am Yankel Frankel!"

Mom took my hat off and put her hand on my head, where I have a scar under the hair. "Do you remember?" she told me, "how you got this wound? You were a little child in Russia. Do you remember?"

Yes, I remember.

She showed me pictures of me and her. She told me about Dad, how they were looking for me all the time, and how they love me and want me back.

I wanted to ask her: "So you did not return to Russia? You don't want to make me into a gentile? Everything they told me about you was a lie?"

I did not ask, but Mom said: "Come back to us. You will study the Torah. We will love you."

In the end, maybe after an hour, I could not hold myself anymore. I started crying. I turned around to my mommy; I opened my arms and said: "Mommy, my mommy."[29]

YOSSELE COMES BACK HOME

After Yossele returned home to live everyday life, he suffered from anxiety and met daily with a psychologist for over two and a half years.[30] His first year in a state-religious school was not a good experience, so the following year, he joined a state (secular-Zionist) school where he was happy and found peace and normalcy.

Nahman Starks, Yossele's grandfather, lived for three more years, but they never met again. Yossele attended Starks's funeral and later made peace with his grandmother. When Yossele came to visit her in Meah Shearim, he prayed in the same synagogue where he was abducted, and he recalls that all the worshipers knew him and that the affair hung over him like a cloud.[31]

Two years after Yossele's release, a yeshiva student came to Holon, where he was living, and asked if he would be willing to meet Ruth. Yossele agreed only if she admitted that she made a grave mistake and committed a crime toward his parents. That meeting never took place. He said, "I never really loved her."

In August 1977, Yossele got engaged, and he invited the former Mossad leader Isser Harel to the wedding, where they met for the first time since the affair. Over the years, they kept in touch annually until Harel died in 2003.

Figure 6.2 Uriel Davidson (*left*) and Yossi Schumacher, July 15, 2021. Courtesy of Nechama Davidson.

Over time, Yossele learned to forgive many of the people involved with his abduction. As an adult, Yossele visited the places of his concealment in Switzerland and New York and met with his kidnappers. In an interview in April 2020, Yossi said that he forgives everyone, except for two people: his uncle Shalom and Ruth. Soloveitchik in Lucerne and Gertner in New York, he said, treated him well and never repeated their crime. However, he learned that his uncle Shalom consulted with a rabbi before kidnapping him; the rabbi advised him not to commit the act, but he ignored the advice and abducted him anyway. He said he would never forgive Ruth because she never publicly apologized.

On July 15, 2021, the ultra-Orthodox weekly *Hamishpacha* arranged a reconciliation summit between Uriel; his wife, Gittel; their two children, Nechama and Itzhak; and Yossi Schumacher.

The meeting was recorded for a featured story in the newspaper, and all sides reflected on past memories and shook hands. The Davidson family apologized to Yossele, and he accepted their remorse.[32]

Isser Harel offered some interesting insights into Ruth's character and actions in his book. He quoted her Hebrew manuscript where she spoke about her reasons for joining the Jewish faith and the moral values she found in the Bible: "You shall not hate your brother in your heart. . . . You shall not take vengeance or bear a grudge against the sons of your people, but you shall love your neighbor as yourself" (Leviticus 19:17–18). He responded to that with the following:

> The life story of the convert Ruth Ben David is in stark opposition to these high values . . .
> Throughout her journey as a Jew, her notable character traits were deep hatred and unbridled hostility: She deeply hates the Jewish state and Zionism. In her hate, she has gone so far as to wish the end of the "Zionist state."

Ruth spoke of how the biblical commandment to honor your father and mother spoke to her heart in her manuscript. For that, Harel had the following to say: "In her actions in the Yossele affair, she completely disregarded the eternal commandment to 'honor your father and mother.' With a gross violation of the principle of honoring your father and mother, she planted— together with all her partners in kidnapping the boy and concealing him—hatred in the heart of Yossele the child, only eight years old, and falsely accused his father and mother of betraying God and leaving their religion."[33]

Harel's strongest comments were on the traits of true converts. Over the generations, the Jewish people welcomed true converts

who came to the aid of Jews. In her manuscript, Ruth said that
the role of converts is to strengthen the Jewish people in times
of weakness and give new spiritual powers to a people weary of
persecutions and trials. However, Harel continued,

> What good can come for the Jewish people from people like you?
> You bring divisions in the nation. You are alienating the most
> fundamental values of humanity, the right of a child to be with his
> parents and the right of parents to raise their child.
>
> It is very doubtful that her joining the Jewish people made
> any contributions to "strengthen the Jewish people in times of
> weakness" or "give new spiritual powers to a people weary of
> persecutions."
>
> On the contrary, the Jewish people can gladly give up the "help"
> and the "protection" of the convert Ruth Ben David.[34]

THE MOYSHALE AFFAIR

In the Hebrew version of her book, Ruth describes her efforts to
find a Hasidic boy who, she alleged, had been kidnapped from his
parents by Christian missionaries. I shall discuss the testimony
and the details of this case in this section and attempt to deter-
mine whether it may contain an implicit expression of remorse
regarding the Yossele affair. First, though, it is worth quoting
Isser Harel, who made the following remark when discussing
the arguments he used for breaking Ruth during her interrogation: "At this point, I decided to provoke her personal anxiety. . . .
What would you say and how would you feel if some extreme
Catholic group decided that, since you abandoned the Church
and adopted the infidel Jewish faith, you have betrayed God and
are unfit to raise your son—and so they kidnap and imprison
your son in monasteries—supposedly acting on divine orders?
What would you do then? Would you relinquish your son?"[35]

Harel's book was published three years after Ruth's, and his
comments may constitute a reaction to the details she provides

regarding the investigation of the missing Hasidic boy. In 1972, Ruth investigated the kidnapping of Moshe Simon, the son of a Hasidic couple, Avraham and Gittel Simon. The couple were Hungarian Holocaust survivors who lived in Petach Tikva in Israel. According to Ruth, Moshe (Moyshale was his nickname) was kidnapped by missionaries in 1957, and her sources suggested that the boy—who had since become an adult—had been concealed in France. She relates that she found a man in France by the name of Edmond Hadad whose biographical details matched those of Moshe Simon. Ruth might have used a pseudonym for him, as Ruth's grandchildren remember his name as Victor Tabbak. However, a medical examination revealed that he was not circumcised and accordingly could not be the wanted boy.[36] Ruth's grandson, Itzhak Davidson, told me in an interview that he recalls his grandmother's intensive engagement with the "Moyshale affair" where she spent a lot of effort finding this man. Ruth stayed in touch with Tabbak and even helped pay for his teeth treatments. I could not find any corroborating testimony for this affair, and the Hebrew press does not mention any such kidnapping after 1957.[37]

In her manuscript, Ruth makes the following comment on the affair: "The death of a child is a terrible and unforgettable experience, but time heals the pain. Humans can accept the fact of death. But the disappearance of a child will never allow the poor parents to be at peace. . . . For as long as they live, they will be unable to forget." As for the kidnapped child, "his childhood was so disturbed, so unhappy."[38]

There is a powerful dissonance here. Ruth's sympathy for the parents of the Hasidic child, whom she claims was kidnapped by missionaries, and her willingness to travel to Jordan, Lebanon, and France to find him, are diametrically opposed to her own actions in kidnapping another child and concealing him around the world. Can she have been entirely unaware of this dissonance? Is it plausible that her sympathy for the parents and child in the Hasidic case is completely inverted when it comes to an Orthodox Zionist child? After all, a child and a mother are universal concepts, and as a convert from Catholicism, Ruth was well aware that all people, not only Hasidim, have emotions.

I believe that Ruth may have used the story as an oblique way to apologize and express empathy for the parents of a child kidnapped by a radical clericalist group and acknowledge the damage this caused to the child himself. Her grandson Itzhak Davidson told me he also feels the same.

THE YOSSELE AFFAIR—THE AFTERMATH

In his book, Harel mentions that the Mossad offered to purchase her home in France to compensate Ruth for her distress due to the affair. Harel also suggested that Ruth should use her skills in more constructive avenues: "I praised her for her capabilities as a secret agent and for her courage while emphasizing that she could use these qualities in a better way and for a more noble cause than in the service of religious zealots."[39] This comment might be interpreted as an invitation to Ruth to provide services for the Mossad. Ruth confirms that Harel indeed made these two suggestions; although her tone is dismissive, she did not reject them: "I answered only that for the moment I need to rest and think."[40] In her archived autobiography, she mentions that she held a further meeting in Paris with Mossad representatives after her release.[41] Is it possible that this connection with the Mossad continued beyond this point? During the 1980s, Ruth was involved in new adventures and some observers had argued that these were in collaboration with the Mossad.

Isser Harel kept his promise and allowed Ruth to resettle in Israel; no charges were brought against her. After the affair ended, she took a vacation in Morocco, traveled to London, and eventually returned to Jerusalem.

In her personal archive, several interesting documents show her activities in the three years after the affair. Two letters show that Ruth and Domb opened an import-export business together called Tovyon Limited, which traded in crystal and china dinnerware. The company appears to have been active for at least two years.[42] On October 31, 1963, Ruth gave up her Israeli citizenship.[43] During the two years after the affair, Ruth also wrote her manuscript. In her personal archive, there is intensive correspondence with her copyeditor. I could not discern his name from the correspondence, but he was a Satmar Hassid from New York who worked on the manuscript without pay, regarding his work as a religious imperative; he worked on her manuscript in the evenings and in his free time, but since the copyeditor complained about the amount of work required, at some point, he did ask for some compensation. Ruth wrote her manuscript originally in English, but the manuscript was never published in the full English version. In 1993, the draft became available, and a few academic libraries in the United States hold a copy.[44] The work was likely shelved under pressure from Haredi circles who feared that some of the material in the book could prove damaging to their community. Amram Blau prevented his wife from publishing the book because it was written in English, which he did not understand. In 1964, the Beit Din Tzedek of HaEdah HaCharedit ordered Ruth not to give interviews to the secular press: "It is an embellishment of His honorable Torah not to meet with secular journalists for conversations or to convey news and opinions, . . . and not to send letters or articles to the above-mentioned newspapers whatsoever."[45] The plan was to publish the book in three languages: French, English, and Hebrew. According to a letter in Ruth's collection, Yerachmiel Domb supported the manuscript and sent a detailed letter to Amram Blau, even stating that for two years he had invested a lot of time and effort into this project. He said that he believed that the book's publication would be of great value to Neturei Karta.[46] Amram Blau refused all the pleas. Faced with such uncompromising prohibitions, Ruth had no choice but to shelve the publication, however reluctantly.

In 1979, however, after the death of her husband and after she was less subject to the influence of his followers, Ruth published a short version in Hebrew and French relating to her former life as a Christian and focusing mainly on the story of Yossele Schumacher and her later life as the wife of Amram Blau.[47] While traveling in Arab countries, Ruth discovered, to her surprise, that the manuscript had been translated into Arabic without her knowledge or approval and published in Lebanon. According to Ruth's daughter-in-law, Gittel Davidson, when Ruth crossed the border to Syria, a border patrol officer recognized her because he read the book, a mandatory reading assignment to border patrol officers. Ruth purchased several copies of her Arabic manuscript in Beirut. Apparently, the Arabic translation had helped her open some doors in the Arab world, and Gittel still has two copies in her apartment.[48]

In September 1962, about two months after the Yossele affair ended, Ruth sent a letter to the president of the French republic, asking for personal assistance. In her collections, there is only the response to the original letter, and I can only speculate on the content of her original letter. She probably requested an official condemnation of her kidnapping, a French citizen on French soil; she may have hoped to provoke a diplomatic crisis between France and Israel. A short response from December 12, 1962, said that after inquiring with the Israeli embassy, they concluded that since this was a private judicial matter involving an Israeli citizen, and since an Israeli prosecutor had not indicted her, there was no need for France to intervene with the Israeli authorities.[49] In September 1964, the French authorities considered prosecuting Ruth for the kidnapping of Yossele,[50] but it appears that nothing came of their investigation. In her manuscript, Ruth mentioned that Yossele's mother, Ida, sued her in a civil court for $34,000,[51] but since Ruth enjoyed the terms of her plea agreement, the parents received only a small settlement.[52]

BEN-GURION, THE STATE OF ISRAEL,
AND THE YOSSELE AFFAIR

This family dispute transformed into a conflict between the secular and Orthodox communities. It became a turning point in defining what is permitted and forbidden in the relations between the two sides. On the one hand, the affair tested the willingness of the ultra-Orthodox community in Israel to confront the authorities on ideological matters; on the other, it tested the tolerance of the state toward ultra-Orthodox circles that do not acknowledge the legitimacy of the state and the rule of law. After the resolution of the case, with the boy's return to his parents, there was never any similar case of ideological crime conducted by the ultra-Orthodox community, including Neturei Karta.

To understand Ben-Gurion's attitude to this episode, and his decision to use the state's intelligence capability to resolve a domestic dispute, it is necessary to examine the principles of *Mamlakhtiyut* (statism) that he tried to impose on the new state and the role of Judaism and the Orthodox communities in his vision for Israel.

According to Ben-Gurion, the government must be the sole source of power in the state. This conviction led him to dismantle the different political underground organizations from the prestate period and establish a nonpolitical national army.[53] This attitude may also explain why he decided to bomb and sink the Altalena ship that delivered ammunition to the Lehi underground, even at the price of killing the Jewish sailors on board and risking civil war.[54] Ben-Gurion extended the principles of Mamlakhtiyut to the minority populations in the state, demanding that they adhere to decisions made by the majority, show national responsibility, and respect democratic rule. According to scholar Nir Kedar, Ben-Gurion acknowledged the right of the minority to demonstrate and to present alternative opinions but insisted that a minority had no right to endanger the security or social stability of the state; the minority cannot impose policies on the majority. His position may be summarized as one of mutual tolerance, whereby the state must respect minorities, while minorities must adhere to the state's laws.[55]

Ben-Gurion led a secular life and saw Judaism as a national culture based on the humanistic values embodied in the morals of the Hebrew prophets.[56] He saw the relationship between the secular and the Orthodox Jewish communities as a given situation requiring both sides to live with each other in peace, based on tolerance and mutual respect. According to Ben-Gurion, disputes should be resolved not through ideological wrestling, but by negotiations based on logic and respect. An example of this attitude can be found in Ben-Gurion's visit to Rabbi Yeshayah Karelitz (the "Hazon Ish") the spiritual leader of ultra-Orthodoxy in the 1950s, with whom he attempted to develop a dialogue on matters of state and religion.[57]

Ben-Gurion's desire to avoid ideological disputes on matters of religion and state led him to prevent the enactment of a written constitution. At the same time, Ben-Gurion unequivocally clarified to his Orthodox partners that the state is sovereign, its laws binding to all citizens, and its offered religious services granted under the authority of the state, not that of religious law.[58]

An understanding of Ben-Gurion's attitude enables us to appreciate why he took such a serious view of the Yossele affair. The support of ultra-Orthodox leaders for the kidnapping of the boy, at least in the early stages of the affair, violated the values of Mamlakhtiyut he established in the young state.

After the Mossad found Yossele and returned him to his parents, the question arose about how to punish those involved in the affair. On the one hand, it was clear that many people had broken the law and that there was a strong case for severe punishment. On the other, strict penalization could lead to public protests that would keep the affair alive. I will attempt to examine in the following paragraphs how and why the official response was transformed from one of strong punishment to no punishment.

At a government meeting in February 1962, before the boy was found, Ben-Gurion said on the affair that "in my opinion, there has not been such a scandal since Israel was resurrected." He blamed the rabbis for remaining silent and failing to condemn the kidnapping.[59] Thus Ben-Gurion adopted an assertive position: he saw the case as a disgrace and a threat to the rule of law. He was furious with the religious leaders for remaining silent and failing to speak out clearly against the kidnapping.

Two months later, in April 1962, the Knesset debated the affair. Zerach Warhaftig, the minister of religious affairs and a member of the National Religious Party, suggested that this was a classic example of a case where it is not wise to insist on the rule of law without compromise. In his opinion, the state should not punish the kidnappers, and it would be better to return the boy to his home without bringing the kidnappers to justice. The National Religious Party held that a general pardon should be granted to all those involved in the affair in return for the boy's safe release.

Itzhak Meir Levin, the leader of Agudat Yisrael, also spoke in the Knesset debate and declared that the affair was first and foremost a terrible family tragedy. This tragedy had been used "for wild incitement, for blaming all the organized religious communities, the rabbis and the religious leaders, that they all joined hands in kidnapping the boy." The generalizations of blaming every Orthodox Jew in the kidnapping, he said, was like the words of the antisemites, "and this is a blood libel." He urged the secular public: "Do not pull the rope too much, because if it would snap, you will be sorry for that later." Levin also agreed with Warhaftig that a general pardon should be offered to all the participants in the affair so that the boy would be returned to his parents.[60]

At a government meeting on the subject after the boy was found, Isser Harel explained the details of the affair, based on the interrogations of Ruth Ben David and her son Uriel. Harel noted that some leaders of Agudat Yisrael had been aware of, and even involved in the kidnapping at first, but later the movement sought to end the affair peacefully. These statements reinforced Ben-Gurion's opinion that the affair did not constitute a rebellion by the entire Orthodox community. He refused to see Rabbi Yoel Teitelbaum, the Satmar Rebbe, leader of the ultra-Orthodox anti-Zionist movement living in New York, or Rabbi Mendelson, the spiritual leader of Moshav Komemiyut, as representatives of all Orthodox Jews. According to his words, these two represent a cancer that had grown on the national body; Ben-Gurion even identified the origin of their zealotry as based on Roman Catholicism. Ben-Gurion defended their freedom of speech and the right of people to be blunt, burst, and sometimes speak inappropriately. He said that he respects people with beliefs and, accordingly, admired Neturei Karta for having a strong ideology. However, they must understand the limits of the law and take responsibility for their actions. He thanked the Mossad for "finding the pus, and if we know we have pus—we can remove it."[61] From these statements we can see that after the uncovering of the plot, Ben-Gurion treated Neturei Karta as a nonrepresentative group; surprisingly, he spoke about the group with respect and defended its members' right to protest within the limits of the law.

At a further government meeting held a week later, Ben-Gurion discussed the proposal to grant a general pardon to all those involved in the affair and emphasized that while he understood the logic behind the proposal, he could not support it at that stage. Ben-Gurion noted that the State of Israel was still young and had absorbed Jews from all over the world; accordingly, it was important to teach them to respect the rule of law: "Let's not subvert the great effort to teach that in the State of Israel there is law and order, and anyone who breaks the law will face trial." He added that if the abductors had returned the child by themselves, there would have been a case to examine leniency. Ben-Gurion emphasized his opposition to any type of vindictiveness or persecution; accordingly, he proposed that law enforcement authorities complete their investigations and prosecute suspects while rejecting the idea that the government should declare a pardon before trials had been conducted.[62]

The government eventually decided that all those involved in the kidnapping of Yossele Schumacher would be granted a general pardon. This can be explained as an attempt to reach national reconciliation and remove the subject from the national agenda once it had been resolved peacefully. This was an expression of Ben-Gurion's Mamlakhtiyut: on the one hand, it was important to show that the rule of law stands above all; on the other, there was a willingness to make compromises and seek peace. Even the ultra-Orthodox leadership understood that the arrangements they were able to achieve with the State of Israel, which enabled them to regain their strength following the Holocaust, would be endangered by confrontation. Neturei Karta appears to have reached a similar conclusion. Although it continued to criticize the State of Israel and to hold countless demonstrations, the movement was careful never again to be dragged into the sphere of ideological crime.

Although the state's attitude is puzzling, to say the least, it is important to see the outcome of this policy. Setting aside questions of principle, hindsight shows that the approach adopted in the Yossele affair—an initial strict response combined with postfactum forgiveness—has proven to be right from the perspective of the state, since the ultra-Orthodox community has almost never repeated similar criminal behavior. This case also taught the ultra-Orthodox leadership that Israeli democracy is its best safeguard for their rights as a minority. They should support it, be engaged in its institutions, and not test its patience excessively. Thus, Ben-Gurion was able to bend the ultra-Orthodox community to his ideas of Mamlakhtiyut and solve the crisis.

SEVEN

"I AM ALSO ACQUIRING RUTH AS MY WIFE"

The Marriage of Ruth Ben David and Rabbi Amram Blau

ON SEPTEMBER 2, 1965, RUTH Ben David and Rabbi Amram Blau got married in what was supposed to be a secret wedding with a small circle of guests; however, the news leaked out and the press reported on the occasion extensively. The day after the wedding, the widely circulated daily *Yediot Ahronot* published the news as its lead item, and even the international press reported it. This marriage affair had all the ingredients of a melodrama: love, sex, manipulations, and power. At the end of the day, the marriage led to the downfall of Amram Blau as a leader and the weakening of Neturei Karta as a movement. After the news of their engagement went public by the end of 1963, almost the entire leadership of Meah Shearim firmly opposed the match. With hindsight, Ruth would say that confronting her opposition and committing Amram to his word after facing this wall of hostility has been the most brutal battle she had ever fought. The events that came before the marriage were scandalous; to some extent, they were unprecedented.

In Ruth's archive, there are about eighty pages of draft letters Ruth wrote to all the figures involved in this affair, and from these letters and her book, I reconstruct most of the details of the events, the leading players, and the path to resolution.[1] The letters also open a window into Ruth's wounded soul and her deep disappointment at the community's behavior she had adored and viewed as flawless. Ruth joined the most radical circles of ultra-Orthodox Judaism because she saw in them an ideal type of spiritual purity. Their suspicion toward her because she was a convert and their blunt opposition to her marriage revealed an ugly side that she found hard to accept. These incidents brought her to a physical and mental breakdown, and afterward, their marriage also suffered.

The opposition to the marriage came from the top leadership of HaEdah HaCharedit, the communal organization of all the radical ultra-Orthodox supporters in Jerusalem. The key to understanding this saga lies in the power struggles within the ultra-Orthodox community. Amram Blau was one of the most senior figures in his community, and the goal of the opposition to his marriage was to undermine his authority and credibility.

HAEDAH HACHAREDIT AND NETUREI KARTA

The English translation of HaEdah HaCharedit is "the Haredi community," and people often confuse this organization with the entire ultra-Orthodox community. HaEdah HaCharedit is an ideological and political association that serves as an umbrella organization for several ultra-Orthodox and anti-Zionist groups. These groups see themselves as continuing the legacy of the Old Yishuv, a long-standing community of observant Sephardi and Ashkenazi Jews who adhered to the traditional understanding that the settlement of the Land of Israel was a religious and spiritual duty of value to the entire Jewish people. Neturei Karta is a protest movement against the State of Israel that served as a political wing of HaEdah HaCharedit. Established in 1937 and headed by Amram Blau, Neturei Karta is one movement under the umbrella of HaEdah HaCharedit, including a few Hasidic courts. Today, HaEdah HaCharedit has around fifteen thousand followers, accounting for approximately 3 percent of Israel's Haredim.[2]

Scholar Menachem Keren-Kratz, who has studied the history of HaEdah HaCharedit, noted that ever since the establishment of the State of Israel in 1948, there had been ongoing tension between Neturei Karta and HaEdah HaCharedit's leadership. After the declaration of the state, Neturei Karta encouraged a civil rebellion against the state, including a boycott of its institutions and disobedience to its laws; HaEdah HaCharedit did not join the rebellion because it was bankrupt and suffered from weak leadership. In the early 1950s, the organization was practically bankrupt and de facto collapsed, but the bleeding stopped only when Rabbi Yoel Teitelbaum accepted the title of president of the organization: although he was living in New York, he agreed to visit Jerusalem occasionally. Teitelbaum infused much-needed funds to the organization, which was able to rebuild itself.

The Jerusalem leadership of HaEdah HaCharedit included Rabbi Pinchas Epstein, the head of the rabbinical supreme court, with two judges: Yisrael Yitzhak Reisman and David Jungreis. The supreme court justices were prominent members of the Old Yishuv who disapproved of Neturei Karta's vocal politics.

In 1956, Neturei Karta's Sabbath demonstrations became more violent after an activist died during a demonstration; the man probably suffered a stroke, but Neturei Karta blamed the death on police brutality. In order to cool down the streets, the leaders of HaEdah HaCharedit met with Minister of Police Moshe Chaim Shapira, but Neturei Karta objected to the meeting and loudly protested against it. The tension between the groups worsened further after Rabbi Pinchas Epstein participated in the celebration of laying a cornerstone for Kiryat Sanz, a community of the Sanz-Klausenburg Hasidism, who are not anti-Zionist like Neturei Karta. In 1957, Neturei Karta followers shamed Rabbi Epstein after he attended the funeral of the Belzer Rebbe, who had allowed his followers to vote in the Israeli elections.[3]

In the early 1960s, Neturei Karta organized massive demonstrations against the State of Israel on several issues. At the same
time, the Kashrut business of HaEdah HaCharedit expanded
greatly; kosher food supervision continues to be a major source of
income for the body. The friction between the two organizations
grew significantly because the riots on the streets threatened the
success of the business. Moreover, the Municipality of Jerusalem offered a large sum of money to renovate the Etz HaChaim
Yeshiva, an institution that belongs to HaEdah HaCharedit. The
organization agreed to take the money, but Neturei Karta argued
that it was unacceptable to receive funds from a Zionist entity,
and its followers painted graffiti slogans against HaEdah HaCharedit on the walls of the yeshiva.[4]

According to Keren-Kratz, HaEdah HaCharedit chose, as a
matter of principle, not to confront the State of Israel, which provides basic infrastructures such as water, electricity, mail, sewage,
transportation, and so forth. They also sought to maintain a reasonable relationship with mainstream Haredi groups, including
Agudat Yisrael, who were the main customers of their Kashrut
services. Neturei Karta, headed by Amram Blau, confronted the
leadership of HaEdah HaCharedit and accused them of extreme
leniency and compromise.

The marriage of Ruth Ben David and Amram Blau allowed
the leadership of HaEdah HaCharedit to settle old scores with
Amram Blau and to remove him from power.

NEWCOMERS AMONG THE ULTRA-ORTHODOX

Scholar Shlomi Doron, who studied the process of *chazara bitshuva*, moving into the fold of ultra-Orthodoxy in Israel by intensifying the religious identity of secular Jews, shows that the
status of newcomers is considerably lower than those who were
born ultra-Orthodox. Bearing the family name of a devout Torah
scholar and ensuring good matches for oneself or one's children

are an essential part of life in the Haredi community. Newcomers to this community find themselves in a complicated situation since chozrim bitshuva are viewed as inferior, particularly if they are Mizrahim: those descended from the Jews who lived in the Arab and Muslim countries.

Doron argues that the ethnic background of newcomers is an essential factor in the matchmaking process and that it is difficult to find "good" matches for newcomers to this community, mainly if they are Mizrahim or divorced.

In many cases, these newcomers are radicalizing their religious behavior just because they are unsure of what the rules require them to do and because they feel like they are being tested. Hence, they need to show intense piety.[5]

Doron notes that the status of "returning" to the fold or "intensifying" one's faith is supposed to be temporary and to dissipate at some point. In reality, however, this status remains permanently, making it very difficult for the newcomers to blend into the new society.

There is no research on how converts are welcomed into the ultra-Orthodox world. However, Ruth Ben David was divorced and a convert, which might be viewed as an even lower status than newcomers to ultra-Orthodoxy who are Jews by birth. Under the codes of this community, she should not have married a great rabbi. This hierarchy explains why Ruth's match to Amram Blau caused such turmoil.

"WHOSE GIRL IS THAT?"—THE ENGAGEMENT

After the Yossele affair, Ruth took a vacation in Morocco, and then she traveled to London for a while, stayed in Aix-les-Bains for ten months, paid a quick visit to New York, and finally returned to Meah Shearim in Jerusalem.

She was accepted as a hero, but still, there were great suspicions toward her. She was different: no other woman in the enclave spoke many languages or was a university graduate. It did not matter that these alien experiences had come before she converted. Moreover, she was probably the only convert they had ever met. Their community was a closed society that did not allow their children to marry outsiders.

With hindsight, Ruth understood that the community was not ready to accept her at that point and did not see her as an insider. Assuming a leadership role as the wife of one of its senior leaders was a jump they could not accept, and they fiercely opposed her.

In her book she recalls that she met Amram Blau for the first time in 1963 at the Bnot Yerushalayim girls' school. The meeting was with Moshe Arental, the school principal, and Amram Blau, who were requesting her to translate documents to French. Hinda Blau, the wife of Amram Blau, who gave him ten children, died of cancer in September 1963. The meeting took place after Hinda's death, although we do not know for sure when this meeting was held. In her manuscript, she mentioned that she had always adored Amram Blau, though she had never met him in person. She was in close contact with Aharon Katzenelbogen (1894–1979), the joint leader of Neturei Karta, who helped her with the Yossele affair. The meeting was the first time she saw Amram face-to-face. She described the man in front of her as handsome, his blue eyes showing intelligence and kindness. His eyes, she said, reminded her of her mother's. "The personality of this great spiritual person hypnotized me."[6]

Ruth said in one of her letters that after she saw him, she knew she wanted to marry him: "I met Rabbi Blau even before the match, but I had hope in my heart he would be my husband." Over the years she had several opportunities to get married, but she refused: "Men are like wolves." According to her descriptions, she could easily marry a young or a rich man, but did not want that: "I was looking to find a strong man with great faith, as I was . . . I waited in patience to find a stable man who would be a servant to God."[7] Thus, we can see that piety, might (power), and stability were the qualities she was looking for in a potential groom.

A few weeks after the first meeting, two men showed up at her apartment in Jerusalem. The identity of the first man is clear: Rabbi Dov Sokolovsky, the principal of a small yeshiva in Jerusalem and a member of Neturei Karta. The identity of the second person is less clear, but I conclude he was Avraham Yaakov Epstein, the son of Pinchas Epstein, head of the rabbinical supreme court, and the son-in-law of Aharon Katzenelbogen.[8]

Sokolovsky offered Ruth a match with Amram Blau, and she immediately accepted. They said they would go and ask Amram and come back, and in half an hour, they duly returned. Amram had agreed to the match on two conditions: Ruth would have to change her tights from beige to black, the color worn by all the women in Blau's circle in Meah Shearim, and she must change her head cover from a colorful one to a black one. She agreed immediately, but Epstein then said that there was a further condition, though he did not specify what this was.

She waited a full day to hear about the additional condition, but nothing happened. She went to Dov Sokolovsky, and he told her there was an issue with the fact that she was young while Blau was old; at that point, Ruth was forty-three years old while Amram was sixty-three. Sokolovsky opened the Bible to the book of Ruth and said that there should be no issue with the age gap, since, according to the tradition, there was a forty-year difference between the biblical Ruth and Boaz. She felt that something was still being withheld from her, so she went to Aharon Katzenelbogen, who told her that "the matter (marriage) is out of the question before a year passes"—Amram would not remarry until a year had passed since the death of his first wife, as is the tradition among some Orthodox circles.

From the correspondence, it appears that Amram deliberately waited a few days to contact Ruth, since he did not wish to seem as enthusiastic about the match as she was. However, this is untrue. He agreed to the match immediately, and indeed, it is likely that he initiated it, sending the matchmakers to her, as Ruth's book implies.

A few days after the conditional agreement, Amram and Ruth were secretly engaged, while Sokolovsky and Epstein served as witnesses. The couple decided that the wedding would be in the month of Tevet, which is around December, in 1964, about a year from the engagement. Amram chose not to share the news with anyone, including his partner and his children.

According to the tradition in these circles, the couple is not supposed to meet before the marriage. Ruth duly traveled to France, returning in November 1963, just before the festival of Hanukkah. During the holiday, she expected to hear from her fiancé, but nothing happened. After Hanukkah was over, Sokolovsky told her that Amram wanted to meet her—an unusual request since, as just noted, meetings between engaged couples were not usually permitted.

All four met at Aharon Katzenelbogen's apartment. During the meeting, Amram told Ruth that there were several complications due to people who opposed their marriage. The opponents, whose identities were unclear to Ruth at this point but would be revealed later, had managed to persuade the supreme court of HaEdah HaCharedit to issue an injunction banning the engagement.

From Ruth's book, as well from the writings of journalists and other scholars who studied this subject, it emerges that Rabbi David Jungreis, one of the judges on the court of HaEdah HaCharedit, had wished to marry Ruth himself and was furious after he was rejected.[9] However, Ruth's correspondence does not support this version. In her letters, she mentions Jungreis twice. The first time is in a letter she wrote after she had already married Amram. She bitterly complains that Jungreis believed the slanders on her reputation published in the secular press without any examination, defaming her reputation. In this letter, she does not mention any wedding proposal from him.[10] In a second letter to Amram, she said that a third person (whose identity is unclear) suggested Jungreis as a match for her, perhaps as an alternate proposal to Amram; however, she was sure that Jungreis would not have accepted such a match.[11] Thus, the idea of matching the two may have emerged by way of consolation after the affair became more complicated, but this does not mean that Jungreis actually sent a matchmaker to make her an offer.

To solve the situation, Yoel Teitelbaum, the Satmar Rebbe, offered Ruth the sum of 25,000 Israeli pounds as compensation for breaking the engagement: "It breaks my heart that the Rebbe sends emissaries to a broken woman on the Sabbath to convince her to break the terms," she responded. The person who presented this offer to her was Aaron Katzenelbogen, and rumors in Meah Shearim suggested that she had accepted the money. However, Ruth's response was firm: "If my haters continue to spread the lie that I agreed to accept the money, I will write an open letter to the Rebbe telling how it all was, so that everyone on the street would know that I am a woman who is willing to give her life to the service of God."[12]

She also learned, to her astonishment, that several of Amram's children had joined the appeal against the marriage, thus opposing their father's wishes. As will be recalled, Amram had decided to hide this information from them and his partner in the leadership of Neturei Karta, but the news leaked out and infuriated his children. They may have been upset about how quickly their father had got engaged following their mother's death. Moreover, Ruth was so different from their mother in every respect. They were also fed with false information, as I discuss further.

In a letter to her fiancé, Ruth presented her feelings and responded to the accusations made by his sons and others. She opened her letter with a statement of amazement that the people who are conspiring against them are called *Zadikim*, righteous men; God does not send righteous people to the world to create blasphemy: "I have no words to describe how bad I feel. I am like a person who lives with knives in their heart."

People in Meah Shearim were gossiping that Ruth was not sufficiently modest. She responded to these accusations by attacking Amram's granddaughters, who, according to her, did not dress according to the modesty guidelines. She told Amram that her son, Uriel, had followed his children and noticed that Zippora, his grandson's wife, wore tight clothes and did not have black stockings. Another granddaughter was wearing a modern suit, so that on sitting the skirt rises. These descriptions came to conclude: "Here we see the contrast between the Neturei Karta's rhetoric and their actions . . . the *Zadik* [righteous man] that preaches morality to Jews needs to show that his own family should have no blemish because everybody is watching them." In effect, Ruth declared that she had discovered Amram's hypocrisy, as someone who preached to others about modesty but allowed his grandchildren to dress as they wished.[13] However, the purpose of her lecture was not to engage in a debate about modesty. Ruth aimed to criticize Amram's lack of control over his children, which eventually led them to send letters to the court and the Satmar Rebbe opposing their father's planned marriage: "You let them do what they want and maybe this is why they lost respect for you. When the Zadik is not governing his children, his children think they know better than him and they will govern him."[14]

Ruth decided to go to New York to speak with the Satmar Rebbe, but in retrospect, she realized she came unprepared because she did not know who was standing behind the plot against their marriage. "I was not aware of the antipathy governing Meah Shearim."[15] We do not know much about this trip.

On May 24, 1964, after Ruth returned from New York, the couple signed the traditional *Wort* matchmaking and engagement agreement. The agreement required Ruth Ben David to adapt her dress to the modesty codes of the Haredi community, including black stockings, and to cover her head with a black scarf. The agreement did not set a date for the wedding.[16]

After the official engagement, Amram received an official letter from the court of HaEdah HaCharedit forbidding him to marry Ruth. The ruling was made without Amram or Ruth being called to testify. In the Blau archive, the court's order is found, which states the following grounds for its ruling:

1. Amram was sterile and accordingly the marriage entailed an element of "deception," since the bride would not be able to have children.
2. There was an enormous age gap of over twenty years between the couple.
3. The rabbi was a leading Torah sage, whereas the bride was a convert—this constitutes a desecration of God's name since a convert was popularly regarded as someone who is not sufficiently decent or modest. This would result in rumors and make a mockery of Neturei Karta.[17] According to the press, the zealots published broadsheets depicting Ruth as an educated and well-traveled woman, and hence someone unsuitable to serve as the bride of a leading rabbi.[18]

I detail Amram's response to the court in the following paragraphs. After the ruling, Ruth decided to return to New York. She visited the Satmar Rebbe's court, and he and his wife tried to persuade her to cancel the marriage. In a letter to the Rebbe on her way back to Jerusalem, probably from February 1964, she described their conversations. The Satmar Rebbe told her that he believed that the match would not be suitable for her due to Amram's sins; his wife, Alta Faige, added that Amram was "a bum, and he is so poor."

Ruth was deeply offended by these comments. Regarding Amram's poverty, she responded that she planned to go to work and provide for the house after the wedding, adding that she did not value wealth as American Jews do. However, her strongest words were reserved for the rebbe. She started by saying that she does not believe that justice can be served in this world; thus, her true judges are not the justices of the supreme court of HaEdah HaCharedit but God alone. She also accused Teitelbaum of perverting the truth in order to bring peace and tranquility among all the groups of Jerusalem. From her letter, we can see that the Rebbe wanted to cool down the flames that the engagement caused among his followers, and tried to persuade her to accept the offer and break off the engagement. Her response was blunt: "Two years ago, I heard the Rebbe preach on Rosh Hashanah that the Messiah has not come not because of the sins of Israel but because of his own sins. Rebbe, you can win or lose the afterlife in a second. Your ears need to listen to what your lips are saying!"[19]

Ruth also complained that she had received an unfair trial and that the verdict was based on only one side. She criticized Teitelbaum for allowing the court to decide without hearing all sides, and she mentioned her legal affairs in France, where she said she also was mistreated. "When I came to Jerusalem I saw that also Jewish judges act the same way" (like gentile judges). She insisted that she was entitled to get married and that this was also what Amram wished. However, the court issued prohibitions and curses: "Not enough that they have not summoned me to tell the truth; after they heard that I wanted to come to court, they said they would not let me in. This is unacceptable worldwide to lean on news and rumors and not let the defendant state his words and instead defame and shame him."[20]

It is time to introduce two new players into our story. The first is "Rabbi Nachum," a pseudonym Ruth used in her book for Rabbi Yosef Sheinberger, the general secretary of HaEdah HaCharedit; the second, referred to as "Yitzhak Guttmann," is Gershon Schtamer, the General Manager of HaEdah HaCharedit. Ruth later discovered that it was Sheinberger who had contacted the supreme court of HaEdah HaCharedit asking for the injunction.

While Ruth was in New York, Schtamer was also there, visiting the rebbe. Ruth and Schtamer met, and he also tried to convince Ruth to cancel the engagement. He offered some new arguments: Amram was not very healthy, and they would find an alternative match for her.[21] On this latter point, we already know they had in mind Rabbi Jungreis, a widower of a similar age to Amram.

In a letter Ruth wrote to Yoel Teitelbaum while she was in New York, she explained her agony when she heard the court ordered her not to marry Amram because she was too young for him: "I could not sleep and I threw up all that I ate." Is being young a crime, she bitterly asked. Having said that, she understood that older men do not have the physical powers of young men, and from a sexual point of view, this can be a health danger if an older man cannot control his sexual desires. However, she assured Teitelbaum, her groom was a Torah scholar and a servant of God, and he never lived for material things. She also promised that she could restrain her sexual desires. She has been waiting for such a groom, "a servant of God,"[22] for a long time. Why did the rabbis think that she would not be able to control herself from this point on?

> I have not waited for a man to take his physical strength, I have not desired for a man for only a few minutes, or for a night to get me a child. I know how precious is the life of R. Amram and how this is important to Judaism and Eretz Yisrael.
>
> I do not want a man to take from him but to give him. I will give him all my strength in work so that he could study as in the past.[23]

In New York, Alta Faige Teitelbaum showed Ruth another piece of the puzzle: Three of Amram's children had also sent a letter to the Satmar Rebbe opposing the match. Yosef Sheinberger wrote the letter for them, while they had merely signed it. "My husband never read such a horrible letter," the rebbetzin said, according to Ruth.[24]

We do not know the content of the letter, but in Ruth's letters, there are references to this specific letter, and from her response, we can understand that two more arguments were brought up:

First, Ruth had a Christian daughter; second, she had worked as a stripper in Paris during the Second World War.

I have reviewed many legal French documents in French archives, and in all of them, it is clear that she was a single mother with one son. Thus the claim that she had an unknown daughter somewhere is false.

As I show in chapter 2, Ruth had lived not in Paris but in southern France during the war. She made a living as a teacher and studied at the university. In 1944, she joined the Resistance and assumed a mission that included a sexual component: She was to become the mistress of an SS officer in order to obtain information about prisoners in Nazi jails. None of the internal secret service documents that I reviewed in the archive mention that Ruth worked as a stripper in Paris or anywhere else.

So, where does this story come from? After the Yossele affair ended, journalists reported that Ruth was a stripper in Paris during the war. One journalist even added to his report that an ultra-Orthodox rabbi testified he saw her stripping with his own eyes. Of course, this addition was intended to embarrass the rabbi, implying that he was attending strip joints, but is it really possible to imagine an ultra-Orthodox rabbi attending a strippers' club in Paris under Nazi occupation? The journalists who reported on the Yossele affair received their information from the Mossad, probably from Isser Harel himself, and he was perhaps the source of this piece of information. Ever since then, it became accepted that Ruth had worked as a stripper in her past—a falsehood that journalists and historians have unfortunately repeated.[25]

In her letters, as well as in her book, Ruth made strongly worded statements about Sheinberger. She called him "greedy," while his partner Schtamer was "a false witness" and "a liar."[26] She heard from the Satmar Rebbe that Sheinberger wanted to speak with her, but she refused because "one should not look at the face of an evil person," and she did not believe that a person who had caused so much damage could repent.[27] In a letter to her fiancé, she called Sheinberger a "modern Korah," a reference to Moses's rival Korah, who made the golden calf with his followers. In that letter, she identified the source of the problem. The opposition to their marriage by the top leadership of HaEdah HaCharedit was a political maneuver intended to remove Amram from his leadership role. She portrays the situation as similar to the Second Temple period of Judaism, when the Pharisees (whom she compared to Neturei Karta) were blended with the Apikorsim (the nonbelievers, represented in her analogy by Gershon Schtamer), and this brought them all down. She spoke poorly of Aaron Katzenelbogen, Amram's partner, and said he was not a warrior: "he shakes like a girl from Morocco when he thinks there is danger, and when he shakes his head spins around and his head speaks unclearly."

She recommended that her fiancé separate himself from evil and fight impurity with all his might, by which she meant to fight HaEdah HaCharedit. She said she was not afraid of the battle: "They [Sheinberger and Schtamer] have a big mouth, but I am not afraid of them. When I was in the hands of the Mossad, alone in front of ten men, I did not shake. I slammed the table and I spoke, and my head was working, and I called them Nazis and idiots and all kinds of names, and I saw them shaking. We need to do the same with our enemies today, they are a new kind of *erev rav* [satanic forces]. We need to fight them without fear."

Erev rav (literally translated as the "mixed multitude") is mentioned in the book of Exodus (12:38): "A mixed multitude [*erev rav*] went up with them, and also large droves of livestock, both flocks and herds." The traditional Jewish literature defines the "mixed multitude" as non-Jewish Egyptians who joined the exodus from Egypt, assimilated into the nation, and were later responsible for various problems, particularly incitement against Moses and God. In the Kabbalistic literature, it is often argued that the "mixed multitude" will be eliminated from the world when the messiah comes.[28] In the circles of Neturei Karta and

Satmar, they typically label "erev rav" any Jew who does not accept their ultra-Orthodox anti-Zionist ideology.[29]

Her recommendation was also to ignore Rabbi Teitelbaum,
because "as a worrier, he is finished," he does not have physical
strength, and all he cares about is peace.[30] From this letter, we
can see that Ruth was trying to push Amram to divide the community in response to weakening his authority. She speculated
that Aaron Katzenelbogen would not join the fight, as well as
Rabbi Teitelbaum.

While Ruth was waiting in New York, she received a letter
from Amram, who had spoken with his children and persuaded
them to withdraw their accusations. They later sent a letter to Yoel
Teitelbaum declaring that they accept his verdict, but no longer
oppose the marriage. In Ruth's archive, there is a letter from Amram to Ruth saying that he had indeed made comments to them
about their immodest dress, thus showing that he accepted her
comments on this matter.

However, another letter arrived in New York. Ruth could not
tell who wrote it and its content, but she felt that the rabbi and
his wife suddenly changed their attitude toward her. The severe
winter of 1964–1965 was starting to hit New York; the city looked
ugly, and Ruth felt suffocated. Over the winters, Teitelbaum took
his vacations in Florida, thus the Hasidic courts went into "hi-
bernation." At that point, Ruth felt there was nothing else for her
to do in New York, so she decided to travel back to France and
spend the winter in Aix-les-Bains. In the summer, Rabbi Teitelbaum was expected to visit Jerusalem, and a decision regarding
the marriage would be determined.

Just before boarding the ship that would take her to France,
she wrote a letter to Dov Sokolovsky, her trusted friend. She told
him she was giving up:

> It is not enough to wish me well; you have to ensure that the per-
> son is not sick. I am now physically and mentally sick. My fiancé is
> letting people throw dirt at me . . . They humiliated me very much.

He wanted to marry me when he thought it would go smoothly but now, he is tired, and I am also tired.

My fiancé allows people to continue slandering me, but I disagree. Enough. Enough. Enough. I am maybe "a little dirty convert," but I am also a human being, flesh and blood. I will not continue it anymore. The Rabbis and scholars who write slander are not Zadikim but wicked. My fiancé believes their words and can stay with them, but this is not for me.

I, myself, believe in no one, not even my groom. He caused a lot of blasphemy. I am staying alone with God.

With all due respect and a broken heart, Ruth Ben David.[31]

"THE GOD OF ISRAEL UNDER WHOSE WINGS YOU HAVE SOUGHT REFUGE"—AMRAM'S RESPONSE

While Ruth was fighting in New York, Amram was fighting in Jerusalem. He was able to quell the opposition of his children, and he also responded to the court. Blau composed a pamphlet, printed in just ten copies in order to prevent its widespread distribution. He also sent a letter adding further arguments to those presented in the pamphlet.

On the basis of both these sources, we may divide Blau's response into two types of arguments: spiritual and halachic, on the one hand, and mundane and practical, on the other. It seems that the court's main concern was the issue of public gossip, since Blau devoted most of his response to this aspect. The court said that the marriage is a "desecration of God's name," Amram responded that the desecration should be determined by the essence of action and not by how the public perceives it. Accordingly, he sought to inquire whether marriage to a convert constitutes a prohibition. Since he said that there is no halachic impediment to marriage to a convert, it follows that no attention should be paid to public gossip.

Amram continued by mentioning various figures from tradition who were married to converts: Joshua married Rahab, Boaz took Ruth, and King David also married a convert (whose name is unknown).[32] According to the traditional principle that each generation is less worthy than its predecessor, Blau argued that if the early generations were greater in Torah, the concern of desecration of God's name in their marrying converts must have been even greater. Despite this, these marriages went ahead and were not canceled due to public gossip.

Moreover, Amram argues that it is God's wish that Jews should love the convert, who for all purposes is to be considered equal to a Jew by birth—"the alien living with you must be treated as one of your native-born" (Leviticus 19:34)—and must not be separated from the general public. Accordingly, it is gossip about converts that desecrates God's name. Those who oppose the convert's wish to marry him are opposing God's will. Meeting the desires of a convert is even greater since there is the additional commandment to "love the stranger."[33] Those who consider the convert less worthy violate explicit commandments from the Torah, and Blau comments "certainly no consideration is to be paid to those with such opinions and to such gossip."[34]

The court said that marrying her would be a deception toward her. Regarding the question of "deceiving the convert," Amram chose a different interpretation to that of the court. He argues that "deceiving the convert" means she must not be considered flawed or less worthy. He emphasizes that Jews by birth have no superiority over converts.[35]

Blau, therefore, asked whether consideration should be given to those with a "foolish and delinquent" opinion who regard the convert as less worthy and gossip about a man who is great in Torah. He asked whether a distinction should be made between converts and those born Jewish based on the foolishness of those who transgress against the Torah. "Is this thinkable?!" he asked, with an overtone of challenge.[36]

Amram noted that had he chosen a "born Jew" as his wife the court would not have intervened in the match. This creates a situation in which there is one law for born Jews and one for converts—in contradiction to the provision in the Torah that "There shall be one standard for you; it shall be for the stranger as well as the native, for I am the Lord your God" (Leviticus 24:22).

Amram also found support from scriptures in response to the claim regarding the age gap between himself and Ruth. According to the biblical story and the traditional exegesis of the book of Ruth, Boaz married Ruth when he was eighty years old and she was just forty.[37] He claimed that the book of Ruth reflects the approach of the Torah to the commandment to love strangers, showing that the decision to take a convert as a wife is great sanctification of God's name.[38]

As for the question of his sexual abilities, Amram's answer is unclear and elusive. As a reminder, the court said that he was deceiving her because she thinks they can have a child together. However, his response casts doubts on the integrity of his halachic argument concerning the requirement to love and refrain from misleading converts. Amram begins his pamphlet with the ruling from the halachic compilation Shulhan Arukh stating that the Torah requires that he marry a woman who will bear him children. As explained earlier, the court argued that since he was sterile, he had no need to marry, and indeed this would be tantamount to deception. Amram hinted obliquely that since his intended bride was a convert, this problem was resolved: "Though my heart hesitates [about the marriage], it is interesting that my body (as two of the members of the *Beit Din Tzedek* have known for some years) frees me of these hesitations."[39] He later repeats this argument: "If a Jew like myself had the opportunity of such a marriage and the intended wife were a Jew by birth, this would certainly be a desirable match for him, but since I have hesitations, as I have mentioned, there is actually an advantage in this match, as distinct from a match with a Jew by birth."[40] In my opinion, his comments imply that since he is impotent, his

marriage to a convert solves the problem created by the fact that
the marriage will not produce any children. In other words, his
argument was based on the concept that a convert has a lesser
status than a Jew by birth. In responsa literature, rabbis often add
considerations that are technically incorrect to make a "stronger
case" to justify their position, and it seems like Amram has used
such a technique.[41] Since he argued that he was "defective" and
unable to have children, he should only marry a "defective" wife;
thus, Ruth's status as a convert is convenient. This leads one to
conclude that Blau's halachic arguments were merely a cloak for
his desire to marry the young and attractive woman, since these
later arguments contradict his earlier claim that converts are in
no way inferior to Jews by birth.

After Amram's death, Ruth attempted to refute the rumors of
her late husband's impotence. In her autobiography, she claimed
that five years after they married, when she was around fifty years
old, she indeed became pregnant. However she fasted on Yom
Kippur, against her physician's orders, and the fetus was lost.[42] I
learned more from her family about this claim. At that time, as
she was indeed reaching the age of fifty, Ruth began her meno-
pause, and this was probably the reason for her irregular periods
that led her to believe that she had had a miscarriage.

Ruth also addressed Amram's infertility in a letter to the Satmar Rebbe from January 1965. She was shocked to learn that the
rebbe had shared a personal letter Amram wrote to him about his
medical issues with someone else (it is unclear who) who then
spoke to Ruth on the subject. That other person discussed her
fiancé's sexual condition with Ruth to break her. Ruth said: "I
lived in spiritual exile among gentiles for thirty years, but this is
the first time that somebody has spoken to me so bluntly on these
matters. The Vilna Gaon [a famous rabbi] said that until the coming of the messiah there would be five types of erev rav [satanic
forces among Jews]. I feel like I already met these five types."[43]

"WHAT A FINE WOMAN YOU
ARE"—THE MARRIAGE

Summer arrived. The Satmar Rebbe and his wife, together with many supporters, came to Israel and received a glowing welcome. Many secular journalists also covered the visit, during which the rebbe would have to decide on the proposed marriage between Ruth and Amram. Throughout the visit, the rebbe refused to meet Ruth; on his last day in Jerusalem, Ruth decided to write him another letter. She asked Uriel to deliver the letter, and at the end of the day, Uriel came back with good news. The rebbe would not oppose the marriage, but he added two conditions: the wedding would have to take place outside of Jerusalem, and the couple would have to live outside of Jerusalem for a while.[44]

Amram quickly seized the moment, sent two of his daughters to Ruth, and asked her to change her mode of dress as agreed in the engagement. Ruth agreed, of course, but she had her doubts. The agreement was that she would change her appearance to meet the modesty rules of HaEdah HaCharedit only after the wedding. If she were seen in the streets of Meah Shearim with a new look, all would understand that the marriage was forthcoming—a fact she was hoping to keep quiet.

They scheduled the wedding for Wednesday 4 Elul in Bnei Brak, but the information was leaked to the press, so they decided to postpone it for twenty-four hours, notifying only their closest circles.

Three days before the wedding, Ruth moved to Bnei Brak, and one of Amram's daughters shaved her head: "I cannot say frankly that this change has left me indifferent, although I was preparing for it for a long time."[45] Shaving a woman's hair before her marriage is part of Hungarian Orthodox tradition and is considered an extreme act of piety. Many ultra-Orthodox circles do not follow this rule, including Satmar women in New York. However, this is the rule in Jerusalem among the followers of HaEdah HaCharedit.[46]

The following day the wedding took place at the Or HaTorah Yeshiva. Although they had hoped for a small and secret wedding, all the press was already waiting outside by the time Ruth arrived at the yeshiva. Dov Sokolovsky performed the service.

Amram's insistence on marrying Ruth, in contradiction to the instruction of the court of HaEdah HaCharedit, forced him to leave Jerusalem and move to Bnei Brak. The wedding took place on September 2, 1965. A week later, Amram received a letter of excommunication from his synagogue for disobeying the court's orders and forbade him to come and pray at the synagogue. The signatories stated that they were signing the letter "with tears in our eyes."[47]

Amram Blau paid a heavy price. He was rejected by the community he had led and with whom he had spent his entire life. Seven months later, however, Amram managed to placate his community and was able to return to his home in Jerusalem. Amram's return was conditioned on his relinquishing his leadership role in Neturei Karta.

During the time in Bnei Brak, Ruth's son, Uriel, was matched to Gittel Fuchs, the daughter of the *shochet* (ritual butcher) of Copenhagen. Gittel's sister, who was associated with circles close to HaEdah HaCharedit's, spoke with Sheinberger about the proposed match, and he again strongly objected. The sister tried to use her influence to cancel the match, which raised Ruth's anxiety level. She sent a strongly worded letter to the Satmar Rebbe demanding her son be left alone. She even insisted that the 25,000 Israeli pounds offered to her to cancel the engagement would be given to Uriel as a wedding gift.[48] The wedding eventually took place on August 22, 1966.

Figure 7.1 Ruth and Amram. Courtesy of Nechama Davidson.

"BETTER TO YOU THAN SEVEN SONS"—
TROUBLES IN THE MARRIAGE

Fairy tales end when the couple lives happily ever after. Indeed, Ruth describes her marriage as a never-ending honeymoon. However, the writer Menashe Darash has revealed several personal letters between Ruth and Amram that suggest that the two had a stormy relationship that included both passionate love and bitter arguments.[49] The marriage saga wounded Ruth,

and the main outstanding issue was Ruth's desire to have a
baby.

While Ruth was visiting France to sell her apartment, she
wrote to her husband: "My beloved, may you live a long life—
Amen—pray for me and us, also on the Sabbath my beloved by
the Torah, pray for me for I long to be by your side in Jerusalem
as speedily as possibly. I am very sad without you my beloved."

Ruth uses the biblical Hebrew word *dod* (beloved) to address
her husband, creating echoes of the Song of Songs, where the beloved is depicted as perfect and flawless. In Jewish tradition, the
character of the beloved is an allegory for God, while the wife is
likened to the Jewish people. The wife's love for her beloved in the
Song of Songs is tempestuous and full of erotic language. Ruth's
choice of this term and the tone of her letter reflect her profound
affection for Amram.

After the couple came back to Jerusalem, Yoel Teitelbaum
and the leadership of HaEdah HaChardit tried to make Amram
sign a statement that he "was forced into the marriage due to
the circumstances," and that he accepted the leadership of the
court. Amram negotiated this request with his rivals.[50] In the
letter quoted previously, however, Ruth addressed their problem
of the rejection of the marriage by the Haredi community. Ruth
continues: "I hope you will not bring me into disgrace and will
not bring such people into our home. As I have told you, they
should not be in our home as long as they fail to repent." In her
book, she said that she expelled the negotiating team from her
home, and these were probably the people she was referring to.

In Ruth's archive, there is an undated letter she wrote to Dov
Sokolovsky after the marriage, where she informs him that
she and Amram plan to meet Dr. Falk Schlesinger, an ultra-
Orthodox physician and the director of Shaarei Tzedek hospital
in Jerusalem regarding Amram's impotence. In the letter, she
wrote that she married Amram not only to have a child with
him but because she loves him. For her, this was like winning

the lottery: "Even before the wedding, I realized he was the dearest in my heart and I understand I sinned before God for daring we would have a child," she said. She was hoping the appointment results would be positive and that Amram could fix his medical issues, but if not, she still wanted to be with him in this world and in the world to come.[51] We do not have the results of the medical checks, but from Ruth's behavior, it seems like the results came back positive, meaning that Amram could fix his condition; however, Amram remained nonresponsive.

Apparently, Ruth left her husband two years after their marriage. She traveled to France to get medical treatment for her stomach problems, and she also wished to undergo treatment for infertility (she was forty-seven years old at that time). However, she used the trip as an excuse not to return to her husband; his reply asking her to change her mind suggests that the reason she left was his impotence, which he refers to obliquely as "a defect" in his body. The correspondence shows that Ruth was aware of the arguments her husband had presented to the supreme court in order to justify his marriage to a convert, who was considered a second-class wife. Her departure from Jerusalem, and apparently a conversation with a woman referred to as "Mrs. Ratterbart," reopened the wound and Ruth decided to leave Amram. He attempted to dissuade her from this course of action:

> I do not claim that this defect or disadvantage is not present in me, or that you are incorrect, but while I did not particularly sense this defect, you came to me on that Sabbath and told me in such a drastic manner that you cannot stand me because of my defect and that for this reason, you would remain in France. Yet you know that even then I promised you that I would correct this defect. Thus you left me when you departed—in peace and tranquility, yet now you are suddenly reopening the wound in such a provocative manner.
>
> I know of no other matters in which I have embittered your life to the point that you state that you no longer wish to be an "embittered rag." . . .

You are already not so angry with me, and surely you will
change your decision, for I miss you very much. . . . Greetings from
your longing husband, Amram Blau.[52]

As is clear from the letter, Amram had promised to attend to
his medical issues. Ruth's accusation that he was self-centered
may be connected to his failure to deal with this issue, which he
emphasizes is not his fault. The impression is that Amram was not
in a rush to treat his condition, maybe he had in mind his promise
to the supreme court that he would not have children with Ruth.

Ruth was not placated and evidently continued to accuse Amram of various offenses and improprieties toward her. She demanded that he mend his ways and punished him by remaining
in France during the High Holidays. Amram sent a further letter
proclaiming his love for her, quoting from Proverbs 10:12: "After
all, Scripture says 'Love covers all wrongs.'"[53]

Amram's pleadings failed to soften his wife's rage. She refused
to return, declaring that she did not wish to do so in a state of
mental anguish. She claimed that Amram had disrespected their
marriage: "Now I understand what will happen on the eve of this
Yom Kippur. You will be with your children like a widow who has
lost his precious wife—like a husband without a wife. You will
tell them, or you will allow them to understand, that you are still
their mother's husband, while I am nothing."[54]

In Ruth's archive, there is an urgent note written by Dov Sokolovsky to Amram, from almost six years after the marriage,
showing that Ruth was still furious that her husband had not
sought treatment for his impotence. Ruth had responded with an
unacceptable protest: she removed her head cover while walking
on the streets of Meah Shearim. Sokolovsky rushed to speak with
her, and she responded that "since she is still a virgin, the rules
of a married woman do not apply to her." By saying that she was
still a virgin, she meant that she still had not had sex with Amram,
and hence their marriage was invalid. Sokolovsky ordered her
to put her head cover back on immediately and told her that she

was entirely in the wrong.[55] As a reminder, she has been asked to cover her hair as a divorced woman after her Orthodox conversion, which she accepted with protest. Removing the head cover completely was thus a rebellious act.

The exchange of letters reveals something of the relationship between Amram and Ruth. Although they had already been married for several years, it is clear that their relationship was clouded by the cold response to the marriage among Amram's supporters. Amram was forced to maneuver between his wife on the one hand and his followers on the other. This balancing process infuriated Ruth to the point that she considered leaving her husband, and threatened not to return after she traveled to France. Amram's infertility was a further source of concern. Although it is clear from the letters that Ruth had been aware of this problem, she nevertheless decided at the age of forty-seven to travel to France to seek treatment at a gynecological clinic. She informed him that she had once again begun to get her period. Accordingly, she was furious at him for failing to address his own problem. Clearly, Ruth was determined to have children with him, perhaps in part to put an end to the gossiping in Haredi circles. Since Amram had emphasized that he did not wish to have children with Ruth during his proposal, he was disappointed by the aggressive tone of her letters. Her demand that he "repent" suggests that he deceived her. As will be recalled, the claim of deception was one of the grounds quoted by the court for opposing the marriage.

One may ask why Amram went ahead with the marriage in spite of all the opposition, even at the price of excommunication. Why did he not just give up? Amram's replies to Ruth's outrageous letters show that he indeed loved and missed her and was doing his best to placate her. The letters explain why he insisted on marrying her even at the cost of disobeying the court: He was in love with her, and she apparently loved him back. However, she was mortally wounded by the insults, gossiping, and giggling of children behind her back as she walked through the streets of Meah Shearim.[56]

Amram Blau passed away in 1974 (his year of birth is unclear). Thousands of mourners participated in his funeral procession. Ruth was in Australia when her husband died, and his sons quickly buried their father alongside his first wife, Hinde. Ruth was unable to attend the funeral and was left helpless and angry as her beloved husband was buried alongside his previous wife.

CONCLUSION

The marriage saga showed how unwelcoming the ultra-Orthodox community was to newcomers. Jewish tradition commands respect and even reverence toward converts, but the social attitudes often deviate from these explicit laws. This is the gap Ruth experienced. The tension between the law and the practice can explain why she was excluded and how she was able to argue her own case and fight back successfully. This is an example of how a marginal actor uses cultural capital to their advantage.

Her life before conversion remained an obstacle that hung over her and did not allow her to integrate and become a true insider. This prejudice against her, based on fear of the outsiders, was used to attack and belittle Amram's status as a leader. The community's bias against outsiders, no matter how loyal they were to the community, was the pretext used by the senior leadership of HaEdah HaCharedit to settle its scores with Amram and remove him from power.

Ruth's letters gave us a glimpse into her soul. Ruth said that she felt sick; she could not get out of her bed for weeks and threw up everything she ate. These could be symptoms of mental illness, perhaps depression. Ruth had joined the most radical movement in modern Judaism because she was looking for the purest possible form of Judaism. To her astonishment, she discovered that even a society governed by flawless religious laws can be unjust, sectarian, and divided. The biblical laws demand fairness, including the specific demand to act kindly toward converts. However, the rabbinical supreme court that handled her matters manipulated the facts, justice was not served, and the most pious people proved extremely prejudiced.

Amram Blau was her third candidate for marriage after her engagements with Poliatschek and Harpaz failed. A comparison of Poliatschek and Amram offers a portrait of the type of man Ruth was looking for—someone who was pious and spiritual, but also a leader. She mentioned clearly in her letters that she was looking for stability; this can be understood in the context of her own mental instability. Her correspondence with Amram after their marriage shows that she could not find the peace of mind she desired so much.

Ruth was a beautiful woman, all the commentators agree. Her sexuality became an issue, especially in the ultra-Orthodox society that represses women's sensuality, with modest clothes and shaving of married women's hair. Although she greatly wished for a baby, she never thought of marriage as an opportunity to meet her sexual needs. We know that as a young woman she had several lovers; some of these formed parts of her duties as a spy, and as such, these were not voluntary love affairs. Being the lover of a (potentially) sadistic Gestapo officer could indeed be a traumatizing experience. While this is purely conjecture, Ruth's instability and desire to join the most modest and asexual Jewish movement may have been related to her past traumas and past experiences with men; as mentioned, she commented that "men are like wolves." Perhaps she chose to marry an older man who was known to have problems with his sexual functioning in order to be married while avoiding sexual intimacy. She said that she could marry a young or a rich man but was looking for something else. Amram's power and influence were attractive to her.

Being the wife of a prominent figure, a rebbetzin, opened for her new opportunities to express her talents, as we see in the following chapter.

EIGHT

RUTH BLAU

The Rebbetzin

"I PROMISED TO OBEY MY husband," Ruth assured her readers and all who doubted her.[1] Indeed, some might be suspecting that she could not serve her husband as required of an ultra-Orthodox woman and, moreover, as the wife of a great leader. The suspicion was not groundless: ultra-Orthodox communities teach their daughters from birth that they must be obedient and listen to male authority. This, however, was not a simple task for Ruth. She was independent and free all her life; she had a mind of her own, and she was rebellious.

There are a set of social expectations of ultra-Orthodox women in general, but there are additional social expectations concerning the wife of a rabbi, the rebbetzin. In this chapter, I discuss the institution of the rebbetzin in general terms and examine how this was applied to Ruth's life. I discuss Ruth's roles in the leadership of Neturei Karta as the wife of Rabbi Blau, with a particular focus on her role in fundraising, matchmaking, and institution building. Ruth, as a rebbetzin, also took on herself a special assignment that no other ultra-Orthodox leader had ever imagined: assisting Jews in distress in Muslim countries. I discuss this aspect of her activities in the next chapter.

There is a unique social status in being a rebbetzin, whereby the husband and wife work together to enhance the man's career, and thereby also elevate the spouse's social status. In sociological terms, this is called a "two-person single career." This family model is very different from a more common model of a typical ultra-Orthodox family, known as a "parallel life family," where Haredi husband and wife live their lives along axes that rarely touch—spiritual, social, and spatial.[2] This second model allows Haredi men, who enjoy a relatively carefree daily life, to devote themselves to their religious duties and the study of the Talmud and consequently to gain high social status, while their wives receive almost no credit for their support.

In the "two-person single career" model, however, the gap between the man and the woman (or more precisely: the rabbi and the rebbetzin) narrows; the woman is more involved in community affairs and consequently enjoys a greater sense of fulfillment and much greater public recognition. Nevertheless, this model is virtually impossible to follow, except in rare cases when a rabbi and his wife are willing to challenge the common social pattern. This can be achieved only if the rabbi's reputation is strong enough to allow him to withstand the criticism of his deviation from the standard norms and only if the rebbetzin's qualities are extraordinary.

WOMEN IN JEWISH TRADITION

Many observers argue that Jewish tradition views women as inferior to men. This observation is evident both in biblical texts and in traditional exegetical literature. According to the biblical narrative, there is a clear distinction between a man and a woman, and just as God created binary contrasts such as day and night, heaven and earth, holy and profane, so Genesis 1:27 declares "male and female He created them."[3]

Jewish religious law (Halakhah) is hierarchic, and the society is ordered according to the degree of answerability to God's commandments. As such, there is a sharp distinction between the Jew and the non-Jew, priests (Cohen and Levy) and ordinary members of Israel, and men and women. Since Mishnaic (post-biblical) times, men's superiority over women was explained by the fact that men bear greater obligations in the study of Torah and performing the mitzvoth (divine commandments.) These weightier obligations are translated into greater worth, and accordingly, the Mishna ruled that a learned man's right to life precedes that of a woman's in most life-threatening situations.[4] In addition, women are exempt from the study of Torah and are barred from all positions of authority;[5] they cannot serve as judges or even bear witness in court.[6] Rabbi Judah b. Bezalel Loew, known as the Maharal of Prague (ca. 1525–1609)—Talmudist, kabbalist, and prominent transitional figure between medieval and modern Jewish thought—held that women have passive nature with more significant potential for spiritual growth and, thus, do not need active duties at fixed times to achieve spiritual perfection. According to the Maharal of Prague, women's natural passivity makes them metaphysically closer to the world to come (*Olam Haba*), which he characterized as a pure and blissful state of total rest and tranquility.[7] Orthodox feminist Tamar Ross concludes: "Because of their lack of proficiency in the Oral Law, women have been virtually excluded from any participation in Halakhic discussion and its formulation."[8]

Although Jewish tradition has glorified the role of women in the home, women are accorded no greater halachic status in that realm either. In traditional societies, the men are the official head of the family. They are entitled and obliged to monitor and criticize how their wives conduct themselves in public, run their home, and raise their children. Fathers bear custody of their children until they marry. A woman's earnings belong to her husband in exchange for his support of her.[9] Rachel Elior summarizes the poor status of women as follows:

> The [religious] perspective . . . deprives a woman of sovereignty and independent standing; instead, she is a virgin in her father's possession, as property until she is wed, at which time she passes to the possession of her husband. . . . Only in old age, after her husband's death and the exhaustion of her reproductive potential, can she become independent.[10]

These social norms may restrict women from developing their potential, fulfilling their life goals, and achieving public recognition similar to that of men.

THE PARALLEL LIFE FAMILY MODEL— WOMEN IN HAREDI SOCIETY

Meah Shearim is one of the earliest Jewish settlements outside the walls of the Old City of Jerusalem, established in 1874 by a building society of one hundred shareholders. The name Meah Shearim is derived from a biblical verse: "Isaac sowed in that land, and in that year, he reaped a hundredfold (meah shearim); God had blessed him" (Genesis 26:12). According to tradition, the community initially had one hundred gates, which is the literal meaning of the phrase *meah shearim*. The neighborhood was built to support the Old Yishuv, the traditional Jewish community in Jerusalem.

Meah Shearim is the heart of the ultra-Orthodox world. It was structured as a courtyard neighborhood, where the different courtyards were inhabited by different groups, mainly Hasidic movements from various European backgrounds. The narrow streets of stone brick buildings are like a living and breathing memory of the eastern European shtetl, the small Jewish town of prewar Europe.

Life in Meah Shearim revolves around strict adherence to Jewish law, prayer, and the study of Jewish religious texts. There are many religious institutions in the neighborhood; for men, religious education begins at the age of three and often continues for life. Many men who live in Meah Shearim devote their lives exclusively to Torah study.

Each Hasidic movement is centered on a rebbe (also called the admor).[11] The rebbe is the most important authority of the movement and his disciples consult with him on everything.

Hasidic men wear black frock coats and black hats; the women wear long-sleeved, modest clothing. In some Hasidic groups, the women wear thick black stockings all year long, even in summer. Married women wear a variety of hair coverings, from wigs to scarves, snoods, hats, and berets. The men have beards, and many grow long side-curls, called peyot. Many residents speak Yiddish in their daily lives and use Hebrew only for prayer and religious study. They believe Hebrew to be a sacred language that should be used for only religious purposes.

Every Friday night, after the family finishes its Friday meal, the rebbe conducts a *tish*. All the male Hasidim attend the event, where the rebbe blesses wine and bread and his followers sing and enjoy the time together. This is the main event of the week in the life of the Hasidic community.

At the entrance to Meah Shearim, large posters in Hebrew and English urge women and girls to wear modest clothes; men and boys are asked to avoid wearing shorts and sleeveless shirts; tourists are requested not to arrive in large groups. The walls of the streets are covered with *pashkevils* (wall posters), an essential medium for communication and the transfer of information.

Since most men devote their lives to religious study and the community encourages large families with many children while family income is low, the community operates many charity institutions for the needy.

Neturei Karta views itself as continuing the traditions of the Old Yishuv, the community of traditional Jews in Jerusalem during the nineteenth century. As such, it is vital to review the role of women in the Old Yishuv in Jerusalem, as discussed by scholar Margalit Shilo.[12] The patterns Shilo identified in this community would later become a role model for the inhabitants of Meah Shearim and many other Haredi societies that developed during the twentieth century and flourish to this day.

The family, Shilo argued, was the fundamental institution of the society of the Old Yishuv.[13] Married life was recognized as the best way to preserve society's purity. The Old Yishuv's regulations mention mostly men, tacitly reflecting the view that women are no more than means for men to fulfill their social and religious obligations.[14]

"All glorious is the princess within her chamber" (Psalms 45:14)—Jewish tradition, focusing on the word *within*, interprets this biblical verse as proclaiming the Jewish home as a women's kingdom. The home was indeed essentially dominated by women—mothers, grandmothers, and sisters—while men were exempted from participation in the maintenance of the house. Shilo suggests that men and women lived separate lives: Men left home early in the morning for the synagogue and the study house (*beth midrash*) or work, while the women were left with their domestic duties.[15]

Shilo argues that husband and wife lived their lives on two parallel axes that only rarely met. Men rose early in the morning and were absent from the home until late at night, or sometimes even for a whole night, and dining separately on weekdays did not leave much room for the couple to meet and communicate.[16] The main time they spent together was Friday night and the Sabbath, which was also the recommended time for them to fulfill the first command of procreation.

The husband in the Old Yishuv was responsible for the behavior of his wife and daughters. His duty was to supervise them, and the community imposed heavy penalties for failure to observe the strict modesty rules, including denying financial benefits and social sanctions. According to Shilo, men's utter devotion to studying the Torah appears to have enjoyed the unquestioning support of their wives.[17] In addition, men were raised from infancy to keep their distance from women, who symbolized temptation, profane matters, and impurity. Consequently, in everyday life, the genders essentially lived in mutual isolation.[18]

Since the primary goal of this society was to encourage men to adopt a total scholarly lifestyle, women were required to support them in every possible way. One of Shilo's findings was that many women became involved in commerce to generate income for their household, particularly when their husbands lacked a profession.[19]Another aspect of women's public activity was philanthropy. Women were involved in various charitable and social initiatives, including cooking or providing food for the needy, collecting money for poor brides' weddings, visiting the sick, and volunteering in local orphanages or nursing homes for the elderly.[20] Since these activities needed to be supervised by activists or by rabbis who were men, women who were social entrepreneurs received far less respect and recognition than their male counterparts.

Scholar Immanuel Etkes studied the family unit among Torah scholars in Lithuania during the nineteenth century, which has had an unprecedented number of students and flourishing Torah institutions. According to Etkes, a communal effort was made to combine Torah study with family life, and the family unit was meant to support the young scholar, who in many cases was in his early teens, and permit him to achieve his ambitions. Typically, an affluent father yearned for a scholarly son-in-law and undertook to support the groom's studies. The father would agree to support the couple at his table for several years and also to set aside a considerable sum as a dowry. Etkes said that the new phenomenon of a "scholarly family" included the understanding that the man needs to excel in his studies; thus, he cannot be the sole supporter of the family, and his wife has to carry the burden of breadwinning. The role occupied by the wife as a supporter of the family was not the result of unexpected misfortune but rather her mission, for she was married to a *ben Torah* (scholar).[21]

Haredi society in Israel has continued the path of the Old Yishuv. It has developed into a "learning men society," a phrase coined by the late sociologist Menachem Friedman, where many men became Torah scholars. At the same time, their wives are expected to support them financially by going to work.[22] Therefore, we can conclude that Haredi society observed the sociological model of "a parallel life family."

THE TWO-PERSON SINGLE CAREER MODEL

In 1973, Hanna Papanek published an article in which she described a social phenomenon she called "the two-person single career,"[23] a unique combination of roles whereby wives are welcomed by the institutions employing their husbands into a form of collaboration. The two-person career pattern serves as a social control mechanism that combines the occupational aspirations of the highly educated women with her husband's career.[24]

Papanek claimed that the two-person single career is an American solution to a common American dilemma; however, other scholars have found the model particularly useful in reviewing women's roles in more conservative, male-dominated environments—not only in the United States but also in other parts of the world.

In 1975, For example, Mary G. Taylor and Shirley Foster Hartley explored how the model explains common attitudes among the wives of Protestant ministers. In 1992, Helen J. Mederer and Laurie Weinstein examined the two-person career model in the context of submarine officers' wives, and in 2007, the theory was used to characterize the social construct of families of soldiers in the Israeli military.

Although more career opportunities were opened to observant Jewish women during the nineteenth and twentieth centuries, none enabled them to be fully independent or reach a social status equal to that of men. As they struggled to find socially acceptable ways to create and sustain meaningful lives, many women discovered that marriage was the best way to expand their opportunities. The position of a rabbi's wife was the highest social status a woman could attain in the traditional Jewish world. Becoming a "wife of" a rabbi opened opportunities for influence, authority, and respect.

According to scholar Shuly R. Schwartz, the rabbi's wives in eastern Europe were known for their piety, scrupulous observance, leadership, and concern for the poor. Living in a home where rabbinic affairs were conducted, these women absorbed a tremendous amount of traditional Jewish learning. Such rebbetzins possessed knowledge of rabbinical texts and Jewish law, particularly in such fields as the dietary laws, family purity, and Sabbath and holiday observance.[25] Schwartz concluded that a marriage to a rabbi allowed them to satisfy their religious calling and experience a life of service.[26]

Whereas the agency and empowerment of an ordinary Haredi woman can be found in her domestic lifestyle, like raising children with strict piety, taking care of the household, and allowing her husband to live the life of a Torah scholar, as was observed by Shilo in her parallel lives model, the agency of the more renowned rebbetzins comes from their extraordinary contribution to the whole community. The privilege of these rebbetzins to operate in a field that is considered "out of limits" for ordinary Haredi women, is directly connected with them having a two-person single career family model and the space that her husband allows her to have in communal affairs.

RUTH BLAU—THE REBBETZIN

Not every woman married to a rabbi becomes a great rebbetzin. There are a set of conditions that push only specific women to such leadership roles.[27]

The first factor in the transformation of Ruth Blau into a great rebbetzin is that Ruth and Amram had no children of their own, while their children from their respective previous marriages were old enough not to require intensive motherly supervision. This domestic factor was necessary, as Ruth did not need to raise her own young children or take care of her husband's children and was thus able to devote time and energy to public affairs. When she married Blau in 1965, he was a widower with ten children, but all of them were already adults, and none lived with him; indeed, he was already a grandfather. Ruth had one son, Uriel, an adult, who married a year after his mother. Ruth indeed craved a baby, but if she had conceived, her life could have taken a different course.

Another related factor is that Ruth was a young woman who married a significantly older man. She established a respectable reputation during the lifetime of her marriage, and after her husband's death, she continued to constitute a significant figure in her community. Ruth, who survived her husband by twenty-six years, did not abandon her duties after Amram died. She would never remarry, constantly referencing his greatness and his memory as her reasons not to, and devoted her life to charity, matchmaking, and advising Haredi women in all ways of life.

Amram Blau was not a great Torah scholar; he was a public figure and politician. In the previous chapter, I show how Ruth served as a consultant to Amram, suggesting a split in Neturei Karta and going to war over their marriage. We saw their collaboration and joint conversation on the matter. Neturei Karta was always a small movement; even at its peak, it had no more than a few hundred followers. Ruth joined the leadership of Neturei Karta when the movement declined significantly because of their marriage, and when Amram, the previously unchallenged leader, was dismissed from leadership. Thus, Ruth's potential influence in the leadership of Neturei Karta was small and behind the scenes.

Ruth Blau also supported charity activities, such as educational institutions for the community, soup kitchens, *gemach* frameworks (support for the needy), and others, albeit on a small scale. In her archive, there are several letters regarding her involvement in various organizations: Maon Lezkenim Limited, a retirement home called in English the Old Age Home Limited; Mifal "Or Hachaim," an educational boarding school for girls; and the Beer Yakov Hebrew Institutions Center, a training college for girls.

At the Old Age Home, Ruth was a board member and served as a fundraiser. In a news article, Ruth states that she founded this institution.[28] Nechama Davidson, Ruth's granddaughter, remembers this place, to which her father, Uriel, was called from time to time at his mother's request to fix things. In her recollection, this was actually a homeless shelter, where the residents stayed only temporarily. The head of the institution was Schaye Blau, Amram's son.

Ruth served as a fundraiser for both these educational institutions and had no other duties. The school in Beer Yaakov was a boarding school for new immigrant girls, mainly from North Africa. Ruth's son Uriel studied in the men's section of the same school. According to correspondence in her archive, this school had an ultra-Orthodox orientation, but the girls were trained using modern educational techniques. The fact that Ruth fundraised for this school, although it did not belong to her immediate circle, can be explained by the fact that she supported this institution even before she became part of Neturei Karta, because her son was studying there.

Or Hachaim is a large boarding school for girls of Mizrachi origin, and for many years this had been the only ultra-Orthodox school available for girls of Middle Eastern and North African descent. This school had room for five hundred girls who otherwise would not have chosen ultra-Orthodox schooling and come from underprivileged homes. However, this specific school belonged to the Beit Yaakov girls' school network that was associated with the Agudat Yisrael movement, one of Neturei Karta's sworn rivals. It may be that Ruth's involvement in these two institutions was due to her French background, since many of the girls who attended these institutions spoke French because of their North African origin.

Ruth also helped place Israeli boys who had dropped out of school in yeshiva settings outside of Israel. In a news article from 1972, Ruth said that she helped boys of Middle Eastern and North African descent study in yeshivot abroad. These are school dropouts who were approached by the Christian mission and neglected by the Israeli schooling system. In the interview, she mentioned that she assisted fewer than ten students in finding yeshivot in Europe and the United States, and she was able to finance their education. She said that these kids were neglected in the streets with bad education, leading to bad morals, drug use, and a life of debauchery. According to Ruth, these children were sent abroad to remove them as far as possible from the life they had in Israel; she regarded them as the victims of the Zionist neglect.[29] In her archive, there is a letter from 1976 about forming the Committee for the Help to North African Children that was established to place children in yeshivot in Switzerland, which is probably connected with this enterprise.

Since Ruth was not an Israeli citizen, she was not allowed to stay in Israel for more than ninety days during each visit, and she had to make frequent trips abroad. This schedule served as a pretext for understanding her fundraising activities. According to Nechama Davidson, Ruth had a regular fundraising route. Her archive shows even surprising fundraising destinations, such as the House of Love and Prayer, a hippie colony composed of followers of the singing Rabbi Shlomo Carlebach in San Francisco, where she traveled in 1975. Ruth used to charge a certain percentage of what she raised as her fee, and according to Davidson, this fee could be as high as 75 percent of the collected money.

MATCHMAKING

Her activities to support boarding schools for girls from North Africa's families were complemented by her matchmaking business. This area probably accounted for the main part of her activities as a rebbetzin. Her archive is full of correspondence regarding matchmaking, primarily for girls of North African origin.

According to scholar Yaron Ben-Naeh who studied the matchmaking profession in the Old Yishuv of Jerusalem in the nineteenth century, this institution existed in the premodern Jewish communities in Europe and the Islamic world. Parents, typically, would match their children, who in most cases obeyed their parents' will. Matchmaking was a side occupation of lower-ranking rabbis and community activists, who were very familiar with the social networks in their community. Some matchmakers performed their function for no pay, but in most cases, fees were collected. The matchmaker would identify possible matches, inquire about the candidates, and might also be involved in finalizing all the conditions of the match, such as the dowry, housing, financial responsibilities, wedding date, and fines for canceling the engagements.[30] According to scholar Orit Yael, although matchmakers served an essential role in the community, they suffered from low prestige, since they tended to exaggerate the qualities of their clients.[31] Although matchmaking might be considered an inferior communal profession, it was an important institution in communities where the genders were divided, and it helped rebuild the ultra-Orthodox enclave.

In Ruth's archives, there are hundreds of letters from individuals who reached out to her seeking help in finding a good match. In these letters, the candidates tell about themselves and express the interests and qualities they are looking for in the other sex. In every case she took as a client, there are many follow-up letters in which the candidates tell about their experiences in contacting their prospect matches and their feelings about continuing or discontinuing the match while moving forward. Some candidates sent letters daily. There are not as many examples of Ruth's replies to these letters in her archive, but in one case, she describes the candidate in glowing terms, leading her to conclude that "I am upset that I do not have another son so I could match him to her [the candidate]."[32]

Ruth's clients came from all over the ultra-Orthodox world: Israel, New York, Antwerp, Brazil, London, France, and elsewhere. Many of her clients were women of North African origin. These girls had not grown up in ultra-Orthodox households; there were concerns about their suitability, and Ruth needed to examine them. In New York, she used the assistance of Attorney Rudolf Meyer, who invited some of these girls to his house to spend the weekend with his family so that he could observe them; in some cases, he indeed recommended not to continue with the matchmaking process. This attorney sent Ruth several letters per week with considerable information about even the most minor details. Ruth's husband, Amram, provided her with letters of support and asked people to assist her in any way and to contribute to her charity activities. Sometimes he or his sons intervened on Ruth's behalf, sending personal letters supporting her matching proposals.[33]

It is important to explain that in most cases where Ashkenazi (European origin) ultra-Orthodox men were offered a match with girls from North African or Middle Eastern background, this would mean, in the codes of this community, that there was something wrong with these men; the flaws could be physical or mental. Since most of Ruth's matchmaking energies were devoted to making such matches, we can conclude that she handled the most complicated cases; these were not simple circumstances.

The small enclave of ultra-Orthodoxy needed to expand its size during the 1970s and 1980s, and matchmakers made an important contribution to this end. As noted, Ruth raised funds for Mizrachi girls' boarding schools, and many of her clients presumably came from these schools. This does not necessarily mean that all the girls needed to marry "damaged" Ashkenazi men; many Mizrachi women married Mizrachi men. These patterns of discrimination inside the ultra-Orthodox communities eventually led to the rise of the Shas Party during the 1980s, which was established to fight for the rights of Mizrachi Jews in ultra-Orthodox communities so that they would not be counted as "second class" to the Ashkenazim.

Another role that Ruth took on herself was to advise women in her community. Since many of the women in Meah Shearim had no exposure to the secular world, Ruth's common sense and knowledge of this world were found to be valuable by many women who came to seek help. In her archive, there are letters from individuals who sent her requests for financial aid. Ruth had funds that she could use at her discretion, and Nechama Davidson recalls that people in need came to her and that she gave them money, whether as gifts or loans.

Since she was a famous convert, a handful of other converts reached out to her with questions and requests. The Israeli press reported that Ruth matched another convert like her in 1971 who joined the ranks of Neturei Karta to a newly observant man.[34]

An interesting report in the Israeli press said that Ruth signed a petition calling on the Knesset, the Israeli parliament, to examine the rise of the pornographic industry in Israel.[35] Neturei Karta was known for its fight against pornography, and Amram Blau even expressed in public his support for violent acts against sex shops.[36] However, I found Ruth's engagement in this subject puzzling; I would not have expected Ruth to reach out to the Knesset, a symbol of Israeli statehood and an institution she considered illegitimate, even to combat pornography.

NECHAMA DAVIDSON ON HER GRANDMOTHER

People in Meah Shearim eventually cooled down, and Amram returned to lead his community. Although my grandmother was the wife of a great leader, she was not truly accepted, and people treated her with suspicions. Kids would throw stones at her door and call her names. Behind her back, she was the subject of painful gossip and jealousy. Her personality stood out even behind the modesty walls that she kept so eagerly. The black headkerchief on her shaved head only emphasized her beauty, and her French elegance was clear even with her modest clothes.

You can see the loneliness and alienation in a person's face, but with Grandma, you could not see a thing. Her bright and stretched skin, her deep blue eyes, did not reveal the many difficulties of her life. She stood firm, taking care of her grandchildren, and all that, next to him, active and full of energy, accepting many guests who knocked on their door over the weekends, without judging, and without canceling her dominant personality.

Their joint life continued until he died in the summer of 1974, buried in Har HaMenuchot in Jerusalem.

After Amram died, Ruth stayed at their home, taking care of families in need in the community and other converts who needed someone to speak with and get the advice of a clever woman.

But her best friends were the cats of Meah Shearim. She cared for them with compassion and dedication, and they rewarded her with loyalty, walking next to her when she went shopping in the local markets.

She traveled a lot all over the world. In 1998, she had a stroke while visiting London. She was hospitalized, and later, she was transferred to a Haredi nursing home in Stamford Hill (London). I stayed by her bed for two years and cared for her until she died in January 2000. My grandmother was born Lucette Ferraille in 1920 and was buried as Ruth Blau in Har HaMenuchot in Jerusalem in 2000.

An outsider and lonely. Like a wildflower.[37]

Ruth died on January 10, 2000, and was buried in Jerusalem on the following day. She had a small funeral attended by family and friends. HaEdah HaCharedit also sent a delegation to the funeral.

CONCLUSION

Ruth was never willing to be satisfied with an ultra-Orthodox woman's "regular" life, with a day job as a teacher or a secretary while devoting herself to raising children and grandchildren. She wanted to be a leader and she knew she could expect more because she was talented, intelligent, and desirable. She directed herself toward the leadership of her community, and eventually, she got what she wanted.

Ruth and Amram's partnership seemed deep. Although they had difficulties in marriage, whether because of Amram's infertility or Ruth's moods, it seems that he appreciated her and respected her talent. Amram allowed his wife to assume the role of a community leader and as his right-hand person. Ruth took upon herself the traditional rebbetzin's roles in charity and matchmaking, and they worked together to advance the religious enclave, thus elevating Amram's reputation.

As we know, Amram was not wealthy, and Ruth committed to supporting him financially. Ruth had lost all of her wealth before the marriage, which might have been a strain on her activities, for she could not selflessly devote all of her life to charity and helping the needy; she also needed to make an income. Her financial sources were a pension she received from the French government for her participation in the Resistance, her fundraising activities that sponsored her many travels, and her business as a matchmaker. Her legal issues in France consumed all her wealth, but she also inherited some property from her father. During her lifetime, she sold all her properties and when she died, she left her son only a small inheritance and her personal archive, according to her granddaughter Nechama Davidson.

Ruth was part of an international network of ultra-Orthodox anti-Zionist Jews, and she was in touch with her connections by constantly visiting them in the United States, Belgium, the United Kingdom, France, and Switzerland, among other locations. She was able to fundraise from her various trips, and in that regard, she was considered an insider. Her role in that network was to take care of matches, deliver funds for her activists in Israel, and be a powerful spokesperson for the ultra-Orthodox anti-Zionist ideological position to the Israeli and international press. Her ultra-Orthodox contacts welcomed her into her homes when she came for her visits. Thus, for example, when she had her stroke, she was staying at a friend's home in London, which was her address whenever she got to the city. She died inside her network, buried in the Old Yishuv cemetery in Jerusalem not too far away from Amram's grave, but not many people attended her funeral. Nechama Davidson attributes the low attendance at the funeral to an expression of her marginality.

Her relationship with her son was stormy and complex. As a child, he always wanted to make her happy and was willing to obey his mother's request and attend ultra-Orthodox educational institutions that were not a good fit for him. Ruth, however, never forgave Uriel for betraying her to the Mossad, and afterward, Uriel became more critical toward her.

Uriel married Gittel in 1966, and Ruth disconnected from him immediately after the wedding because she disapproved of the level of modesty of her new daughter-in-law. Uriel and Gittel lived and raised their children according to a strict Orthodox lifestyle but not according to Neturei Karta's extreme views. She boycotted Uriel for two and half years until they met by chance in Jerusalem's Machane Yehuda Market, while Uriel held his first-born daughter, Nechama, in his hands. During the disconnection, Uriel changed his last name to Davidson, which is a literal translation of "Ben David" to create a disconnection from her and so that people would not associate him with his famous mother. Uriel and Gittel had eight children, and over the years, both the parents and the grandchildren had occasional fights with the grandmother over their lifestyle and education. The grandchildren spoke English with Ruth, who was not fluent in modern Hebrew. Nechama recalls that her father had a strong argument with his mother over the publication of her manuscript in 1977 and he also tried to prevent her from publishing it. Uriel is a Zionist, while his mother was an anti-Zionist, and he felt her narrative of the Yossele affair was inaccurate.

Ruth was well educated in Jewish sources. She had acquired substantial religious education before getting into the world of ultra-Orthodoxy from her academic training and her two conversions. She studied from great scholars like Dov Rappel, a Jewish studies professor at Bar-Ilan University, or Rabbi Leon Ashkenazi "Manitu." The ultra-Orthodox community did not offer formal education at that time in Jewish sources for women, and the community prevented religious education for girls.[38] But from her correspondence with rabbis found in her personal archive, she quoted rabbinical and mystical sources, which suggests she must have studied these sources by herself. Another aspect of her piety was her attraction to mysticism. It is true that there is a branch of Jewish mysticism called kabbalah, but Orthodox circles would not allow women to be engaged in kabbalah, so she might have studied these sources by herself. Nechama Davidson recalls that Ruth prayed fervently, and when the Soviet bloc opened in 1991, she traveled with Gittel, her daughter-in-law, to Ukraine and Poland to pray at the graves of famous Tzadikim (Hasidic rabbis).

As long as her husband was alive, Ruth stayed in his shadow. After his death, however, she made a name for herself. While Amram was alive, Ruth did not publish her autobiography, respecting her husband's wishes. After his death, she felt no need to remain under this prohibition, and she published her book in 1979, five years after his death. The publication served her well, and I will discuss it in the next chapter. She also gave many interviews to the Israeli press. Ruth's constant presence in the spotlight of the Israeli media began after the resolution of the Yossele affair and her scandalous marriage affair. With her travels to the Muslim world, which I will discuss in the next chapter, she kept herself in the news through the 1980s.

Her main concentration as a rebbetzin was in assisting girls of North African background, whether by fundraising for the institutions they attended or matchmaking for them in Israel or overseas. Mizrachi girls are on the periphery of the Haredi enclave, and this might be a projection of how the ultra-Orthodox community viewed Ruth as well. Although she spent half her life in the ultra-Orthodox world, she was never truly accepted as an equal. No matter how much devotion and even risk she took for the well-being of this sector, she was always "the convert," an outsider viewed with fear and suspicion.

Still, devoting her energies to the well-being of women of North African origin was an expression of her lifelong pursuit of the advancement of underprivileged women, even if this was manifested in surprising ways.

NINE

"FIERCE WOMAN!"

Traveling in Muslim Countries

ON JANUARY 16, 1979, THE shah of Iran Mohammad Reza Pahlavi and his family left Teheran for good, fleeing to Egypt. Two weeks later, Ayatollah Ruhollah Khomeini was welcomed back to Iran after fifteen years in exile. Millions of people celebrated his return and the end of the shah's regime. Ayatollah Khomeini would become the founder of the Islamic Republic of Iran and the leader of the Iranian Revolution.

On January 18, 1979, Khomeini was preparing his return to Iran at the villa Neauphle-le-Château in France, which granted him asylum. He had a long day with many visitors. After two and a half hours of waiting, Ruth Blau, whom he had finally agreed to meet, walked into the room. Ruth was accompanied by Lucian Bitterlin, a pro-Palestinian French journalist, who later reported on the encounter. At the end of the meeting, Ruth got what she came for: a declaration from Khomeini that he would protect the Jews of Iran. Bitterlin could not believe his eyes; the meeting seemed so surreal. He concluded his report with the following words: "A fierce woman! Such strength of conviction!" The next time the ayatollah would accept Ruth for a meeting would be several months later, at his residence in Teheran. The leader of the Islamic revolution even gave her a small gift that she would hang on the wall of her living room in Jerusalem.

From 1974, records show that Ruth traveled to Muslim countries to assist Jews in distress. She sought to aid local Jewish communities in Lebanon and Iran, basing her activities on her reputation as an Orthodox Jew, an anti-Marxist, and a fierce anti-Zionist. Helping Jews in distress also included attempting to aid Israeli soldiers who fell into captivity during Israel's wars in Lebanon in the 1980s. Some observers suggest that her missions received the blessing of the Mossad, Israel's secret service. In some of her activities, she served as a hostage negotiator. As far as I was able to ascertain, none of her efforts were successful, and all the hostages involved were eventually executed.

Collecting materials for this chapter was difficult as I could not find a paper trail in Ruth's archives on these activities. The information that I collected came mainly from the Israeli and French press, supported by additional testimonies. Ruth's grandson Itzhak Davidson found in his parents' apartment a phonebook that belonged to Ruth from 1982, which included personal phone numbers of the top leadership of the Palestinian Liberation Organization (PLO), at that time still located in Beirut, Lebanon. The names and phone numbers in the phonebook included Abu Jihad and Hani Al-Hassan, senior leaders of Fatah. He also found her Belgian passport from the 1980s, which shows she visited Jordan, Lebanon, Iran, Syria, Cyprus, the United States, Panama, and Venezuela.[1] These are the only piece of written evidence we have regarding her connections with Arab leaders. There may be a paper trail of her visits, but she may have kept these documents hidden, possibly outside Israel.

This chapter discusses Ruth's two meetings with Khomeini, the reasons for these meetings, and their outcomes. The chapter continues to describe her attempt to gain a pardon for Albert

Figure 9.1 Albert Danialpour. Courtesy of Davar Danialpour.

Danielpour, a prominent member of the Iranian-Jewish community. He was tried as a Mossad and CIA agent in 1980 in Teheran and sentenced to death by the Revolutionary Guard. In 1985,
the Organization of the Oppressed on Earth, a pseudonym of
Hezbollah, kidnapped six members of the Jewish community in
Lebanon. After Ruth's interference, the kidnappers offered a deal

to trade the hostages for Shi'ite prisoners in Israeli jails. Israel declined, and eventually, the Oppressed executed all prisoners. Ruth also played a small part in trying to find information about three Israeli soldiers who were missing after the Battle of Sultan Yacoub in Lebanon in 1982.

TEHERAN

The first evidence of Ruth's engagement in helping Jews in captivity in Muslim countries came in December 1973, about a month after the ceasefire ending the Yom Kippur War. In that war, Syria and Egypt launched a surprise attack on Israel. Israel was eventually able to repel the invading armies, but the Israeli military performed weakly during the first few days of the war and sustained significant losses. By the end of the war, Israel had lost more than 2,500 soldiers and around 300 had been captured, including 65 who were being held in Syrian prisons.

A newspaper article from December 6, 1973, reports that "the convert Ruth Ben-David," the wife of Amram Blau (the leader of Neturei Karta) traveled to the United States to engage in actions intended to secure the release of the Israeli soldiers in Syria. The article adds that before she left, she told her family members that "I have to travel and to do the best possible to save these wonderful young men. I cannot just sit here doing nothing while these boys are rotting in Syria." The article continues that Ruth commented that she knew whom to reach out to; if necessary, sources in Neturei Karta told the reporter, she would continue her travels to France and even Syria to engage with the Syrian government to release the prisoners of war.[2]

We cannot accept this article at face value. It is difficult to believe that Ruth would call Israeli soldiers "wonderful young men"—after all, the military was a central branch of the state she detested. "Wonderful young men" is a classic Israeli expression used to refer to soldiers, and I would not be surprised if the reporter put these words in her mouth. Based on her life actions, I believe she tried to do something to help Israeli soldiers in captivity in Syrian prisons, where prisoners were treated poorly and tortured in many cases. Securing their release was a national priority, and Ruth might have had a plan. But what could she have done in such circumstances? There is no follow-up in the newspapers regarding this initiative, which appears to have failed. Eventually, there was an exchange of prisoners and the Israeli soldiers were all released, but it is unlikely that this had anything to do with Ruth's initiatives. Nevertheless, this incident highlights some early traits that would be repeated later: concern for Jews in distress in Muslim lands, even if they were Israeli soldiers, would inspire Ruth to attempt to offer her assistance. Her efforts included reaching out to the highest levels of leadership, as we will see in the following cases.

The next time she acted in this sphere was in 1979. Her initiatives led her to meet Ayatollah Ruhollah Khomeini, probably twice. I have found two separate reports concerning the first meeting in France in 1979, and she probably met the ayatollah a second time in Teheran in 1980.

Lucien Bitterlin, who was the secretary general and then president of the Association de solidarité franco-arabe (ASFA) (French-Arab Solidarity Association), founded in 1967, provided the most detailed report of the meeting that took place in France.

Bitterlin wrote in his autobiography that he was amazed when Ruth Blau asked him to help secure an appointment with Ayatollah Khomeini. He remembers that Ruth was very determined to meet the ayatollah, who, she told him, was preparing "the greatest act of Islamic revolution in the name of God." This is the same God, Bitterlin cited Ruth, who had entrusted the Jews with a purely spiritual mission on earth, and not with "a major comeback" in Palestine. Ruth's emphasis on the Jews' spiritual mission to the world, and her rejection of any national or territorial dimension, are consistent with the ideology of Neturei Karta, according to which the Jews should not have a national homeland before the coming of the messiah.

Bitterlin reported that he was skeptical toward her line of argument, but he was willing to introduce her to his Iranian friends. By the time the two met, Ruth's book about her kidnapping of Yossele Schumacher, together with her anti-Israeli opinions, had made her something of an iconic figure in France. The prestigious newspaper *Le Monde* had reviewed her book favorably.[3] Nevertheless, Bitterlin felt that her request to meet with the ayatollah was excessive.

On Monday, January 15, 1979, he organized a lunch meeting with two Iranians at a restaurant in the École militaire square in Paris. The simple restaurant with a panoramic view was one of his regular venues for such meetings. One of the guests was Imam Musa el Musawi, an Iranian cleric exiled in the United States who had a doctorate and was a learned scholar in Islamic law at the rank of ayatollah (the highest ranking of Shi'a clergy). El Musawi wore traditional Muslim garb, while Ruth also wore the traditional headscarf of an Orthodox woman. Since the restaurant did not serve kosher food, Ruth brought crackers with her.

The imam was interested in learning about Ruth's worldview and was pleased to hear that she was anti-Zionist and anti-Marxist. During the meeting, she expressed her hope that the religion of Islam would play a more prominent role in the Middle East after the revolution. She displayed knowledge of Islamic law and familiarity with the principle of tolerance emphasized in the Quran toward the "People of the Book," which promises protection to practitioners of other monotheistic faiths under Islamic rule. The fact that Ruth was familiar with Islamic law should not be a surprise—as will be recalled, she had been a doctoral candidate in theological studies at the Sorbonne. Ruth told Musawi that practicing Jews should be allowed to live in Palestine no matter

what. She also told the imam that her late husband, although
the descendant of a family who had lived in Jerusalem for generations, had refused to accept Israeli citizenship. The imam was
surprised to hear that the followers of Neturei Karta refused to
use Israeli money, read the Israeli press, or listen to Kol Israel,
Israel's national radio. Bitterlin said: "In my opinion, all of this
was a bit surreal. But why not?"

Three days later, Bitterlin and Ruth were sitting in Khomeini's
waiting room in Neauphle-le-Château. An assistant led them into
a room where the ayatollah was sitting in a corner. The interpreter
requested that the guests ask only one question, for Khomeini
was very tired. Since he arrived in France, many people had been
coming to meet him.

The guests took off their shoes and walked into the "hearing
room" covered with rugs. Bitterlin walked into the room first, as
the tradition is that women walk behind men. They stopped two
or three meters before the ayatollah, and Bitterlin spoke first. He
introduced himself and the association he led and added some
formulaic wishes for peace and justice. After the translation, the
ayatollah nodded without raising his eyes, and Bitterlin introduced Ruth. She took the lead and mentioned that her late husband was a religious authority in Jerusalem respected by Jews and
Muslims. She continued that the two religions worship the same
God, and that she was very sensitive to the holy words of the ayatollah, who spoke like her late husband. After this introduction,
she got straight to the point: she asked Khomeini to ensure that
after Iran "regained its independence," Jews would not be victims
of the mistakes committed by the Zionists. In other words, Jews
should be safe in Iran and not be persecuted: "I am asking you,
because you are a man of God, to preserve the future of the Jews
in the Middle East," she said. Khomeini nodded several times.
Bitterlin, meanwhile, was asking himself what exactly he had
sought to achieve through the meeting.

After Ruth finished her monologue, Khomeini looked at Bitter-lin and said, "Go in peace, salaam. May your woman worry not," concluding with "We will not harm the Jews." The leader of the revolution spoke to Bitterlin, not to Ruth, since his standards of modesty meant he could not address a woman. Bitterlin was as-tonished: "What an exchange!" He did not know that only a few days later Khomeini would once again walk along the streets of Teheran. He felt that a written document was needed to confirm the statement, and Ruth duly issued a press release declaring that Khomeini confirmed that "as long as the Jews were not seeking their supremacy over the Arab people by force, they could live in peace in the Muslim world."[4]

Bitterlin's uncertainty about the purpose of the meeting sug-gests that he may not have been familiar with its broader context. His account offers no reason why the ayatollah would devote time during his final days in France to meeting a fringe figure like Ruth Blau. A separate report of the meeting by Ari Ben-Menashe adds some vital information and may solve the mystery.

Ben-Menashe was an Iranian-born Israeli spy who became famous after giving the international press several tips on the intelligence work of Israel, the United States, and Iran. He later published his memories in the book *Profits of War* (1992), which included some remarkable revelations concerning the American hostage crisis in Iran and the Iran-Iraq War. Some of Ben-Menashe's accounts are considered questionable. His rev-elations embarrassed many important figures in the intelligence world in Israel and the United States, who tried to undermine them. The US Senate investigated his report that George Bush coordinated the release of fifty-two American hostages in Iran to help the Republican Party and Ronald Regan, who was cam-paigning against Jimmy Carter for the presidency in 1981. The hostages were released on the day Regan was sworn as president, and Ben-Menashe argued this was not a coincidence. He wrote that he saw with his own eyes that Bush met senior Iranian figures in Paris before the election and coordinated with them to prevent the release of the hostages before election day—something that could have increased popular support for Carter. The House October Surprise Task Force investigated these allegations and determined that they constituted a baseless conspiracy theory.[5] Some of Ben-Menashe's descriptions of Ruth's biography are incorrect, further undermining his report. Nevertheless, I am inclined to accept his versions of Ruth's actions since they make sense and answer some important questions. He might not have known Ruth's biography so well, but the meeting he described in his book did take place, as Bitterlin also reported.

Iran under the shah was a dominant force in the Persian Gulf and was both pro-American and pro-Israeli. Ben-Menashe recalls that he, together with the leadership of the Israeli intelligence forces, predicted the downfall of the shah of Iran, but the American intelligence community dismissed these warnings. Only toward the end of Carter's presidency did his administration realize that the shah's time was limited. In December 1978, the CIA, the Mossad, and the SAVAK (Iranian secret service) started considering a plan to assassinate Ayatollah Khomeini in France. Israel put together a team that would carry out the assassination, headed by Colonel Assaf Hefetz, who later became chief of the Israel police. The assassination plan was abandoned, and according to Ben-Menashe, it was the shah's idea to drop the plan.

Israel sought a new strategy for confronting the revolutionaries in Iran. Israel's Prime Minister Menachem Begin agreed with the intelligence departments that there was no harm in talking to Khomeini. But who was going to do the talking on Israel's behalf, asked Ben-Menashe: "The task fell on the shoulders of an unlikely person—Ruth Ben-David."

Ben-Menashe provided some incorrect facts about Ruth's conversion and marriage. He went on to reveal that before Amram Blau died, Ruth accompanied him to Turkey to attend seminars at which Jewish rabbis and Shi'ite Mullas entered into religious debates trying to establish a path for theology to return to earthly governments. During those meetings, Ben-Menashe continued, Ruth met the exiled cleric.[6]

Ben-Menashe made some mistakes in his report: Ruth indeed traveled a lot and had connections in Turkey, but she never traveled with her husband, who never left Israel and did not even have a passport. However, his report offers two essential details. First, it seems possible that Ruth may have had a prior acquaintance with Khomeini before their meeting in Paris. Second, her visit to the ayatollah was with the blessings of Israel's intelligence services. This fact answers the question posed earlier: although she officially came to him on behalf of Neturei Karta, the leader of the Iranian revolution might have accepted her as a backchannel to Israel.

Ben-Menashe continued that Khomeini accepted the emissary, "his old friend," and speculated that she might have been the only woman he would sit with alone in a closed room—though we know that she did not come alone. Ben-Menashe continued that Ruth reported directly and personally to Prime Minister Begin after the meeting. According to an intelligence report issued after the meeting by the Prime Minister's Office, Khomeini made it clear that Iranian Jews were Iranian citizens and that Islam respects Judaism and all other religions that were not regarded as heresy. The report adds that Khomeini mentioned Baha'is as heretics who would not be permitted to practice their faith in Iran. Islamic law states that prophets who came before Prophet Mohamad, including Moses and Jesus, were true ones, but anyone who came after him claiming to carry the word of God was a heretic, and heretics should be put to death. Khomeini was thus referring to the Baha'i belief that the Bab and the Baha'u'allah, who lived in the nineteenth and twentieth centuries, were new prophets, a view that all Muslims reject. Khomeini added that the State of Israel was also heresy and should not exist. However, the

first interest of the Islamic revolution was to bring Islam and Islamic rule to Muslim populations in the Arab countries and to rid
the Muslim world of heretic governments. He also emphasized
that Mecca and Medina must be liberated from the Saudis—an
early manifestation of his feud with Saudi Arabia. Indeed, the
Iranian Revolutionary Guard actively worked to expedite the
revolution to other areas with a Shi'ite population, including
Lebanon (which we will discuss later). Ben-Menashe continued
that Khomeini's message to Begin was clear: "Don't worry Israel.
First, my agenda is to deal with my Arab enemies. Then, I will deal
with Israel." He concluded his report by saying that Khomeini's
message was well received in Israel: "It seemed fortunate that the
plan to assassinate Khomeini had not gone forward."[7]

Ben-Menashe and Bitterlin reported a similar narrative: Ruth
met Khomeini in France before his return to Iran to ask the leader's opinion on the fate of Iranian Jews after the revolution. We
saw a similar response in both testimonies, based on the Islamic
concept of the People of the Book and including a promise not
to harm loyal Jews. There was no logical reason for Khomeini
to waste his time meeting a representative of a powerless fringe
group, and in this case to bend the Islamic rules of modesty by
meeting with a woman, unless she came on behalf of a much
larger entity. Ben-Menashe argued that she came on behalf of the
State of Israel, and bizarre as this sounds, it makes sense. Another
possibility, though this is pure speculation on my part, is that the
French intelligence services sent her. As we can recall, Lucette/
Ruth was employed by the French secret service after World
War II, and agents can sometimes spring back into action after a
very long period of inactivity.

The Iranian hostage crisis, from November 4, 1979, to January
20, 1981, was a major diplomatic incident. Fifty-two American
diplomats and citizens were held hostage for 444 days after a
group of Iranian revolutionary college students stormed the US
Embassy in Tehran.

The crisis reached a climax after diplomatic negotiations failed to win the release of the hostages. Carter ordered the US military to rescue the hostages, but the attempt on April 24, 1980, failed after one of the helicopters crashed into a transport aircraft.

In September 1980, Iraq invaded Iran, beginning the Iran-Iraq War. Saddam Hussein, the Iraqi president, wanted to take advantage of the revolutionary phase in Iran and invaded Iranian oil fields in the Persian Gulf. Iran struggled to defend its border against the Iraqi attack and was left with limited military equipment from the shah's period. Iran could not purchase new weapons to protect itself as the United States had imposed sanctions that crippled its financial abilities and confiscated Iranian assets abroad.

From the Israeli perspective, the Iraqi incursion caused great alarm, Ben-Menashe reported. It would be in Israel's interest to flood Iran with military equipment, but Israel had to be careful. Much of the military equipment held by Israel originated in the United States, and as long as the hostage crisis persisted, there could be severe repercussions for Israel if it sold American arms to Iran. Iran wanted to end the hostages' crisis so that it could purchase military supplies.[8]

The Israeli intelligence community was extremely worried about the Iraqi threat to Iran. If Iraq won, and the Iranian oil reserves came under Saddam's hands, this would create serious problems for Israel. Ben-Menashe said that Israel was looking for ways to help Iran. This led to the suggestion that Israel would broker a hostage deal and present it to America as a fait accompli. Thus, the Iranians would not have to deal directly with Carter's representatives or those of Reagan, who was running for the presidency. Ben-Menashe claimed that the talks were led by George Bush; again, it must be emphasized that the Senate Special Committee investigated and refuted any involvement on Bush's part in the affair.

Ben-Menashe claims that in mid-September, Begin sent Khomeini's "old friend" Ruth Blau to meet with him again. Her

mission was to secure Khomeini's agreement to a plan under
which Iran would release the hostages and Israel would guarantee
arms for Iran. Ben-Menashe reported that the details of the plan
were to be worked out by others at another meeting that took
place a few days later in Amsterdam. According to Ben-Menashe,
at the follow-up meeting, attended by top Israeli intelligence figures and senior Iranian negotiators, among them Khomeini's son,
it was agreed that Iran would release the hostages in Pakistan in
October in exchange for $52 million in cash, while Israel would
be allowed to supply Iran with military equipment. After the
elections, it was agreed, the United States would also unfreeze
Iranian funds in American banks. Ben-Menashe said that the
deal was presented to an American delegation in Washington on
October 2, but it was rejected.[9]

I cannot judge whether Ben-Menashe's accounts are correct,
and I have no other major corroboration for his narrative. I can
only offer three indirect reports. Ruth's grandchildren told me
that she had an Iranian silver plate on the wall of her house in
Jerusalem, which she told them she had received as a present
from Khomeini himself when she met him in Teheran. The family
memories confirm the meeting between the two. Further confirmation comes from an Israeli news report. On December 9, 1979,
journalist Baruch Meiri reported that "the convert" Ruth Ben
David was in Iran and was trying to meet with Khomeini. The report claimed that she had already been in Teheran for two weeks,
and that her objective was to convince Khomeini to release the
American hostages. The report also mentioned that the Jerusalem ultra-Orthodox community had held special prayers for the
success of her mission.[10] The problem with Meiri's report is that
it is dated nine months before the dates Ben-Menashe mentions;
however, it is a further indication of Ruth's involvement in the
affair. A different news report in Israel confirmed that Ruth met
Khomeini but the report is unclear regarding the purpose or timing of the meeting.[11]

This incident teaches us that Ruth indeed tried to use her connections and influence in the hostage crisis. I believe she attempted to intervene in the situation and even coordinated her moves with the Mossad, perhaps visiting Iran with an Israeli proposal. Her goal was to resolve the hostage crisis, and to this end, she was willing to collaborate with anyone, including Israel. Ruth opened the doors in Teheran, and the shocking revelations in Ben-Menashe's book suggest that arms dealers walked through these open doors. Her interest was the well-being of the hostages: she had nothing to do with arms deals and did not profit from them in any way. Saving human lives was her motivation, and she did not shy away from extreme measures to pursue this goal.

THE EXECUTION OF ALBERT DANIELPOUR

With the ayatollah returning to his old country, a new phase began for Iranian Jews. On February 13, 1979, almost two weeks after Khomeini's return to Iran and two days after the revolution's victory, the Jewish leadership showed support en masse for the revolution and welcomed the country's new leader. On February 27, 1979, the keys of the former Israeli embassy on Kakh Street were handed over to the Palestine Liberation Organization representative, Hani al-Hassan.

Just a few months after the revolution, on May 9, 1979, one of the Jewish community's philanthropists and leaders, Habib Elqaniyan, was executed after being accused of spying for Israel and acting against Islam and the revolution. Many Iranian Jews suspected that the revolutionary court and the new government had framed Elqaniyan, and they feared a new era of persecution against Iran's Jewish population. Three days later, a small delegation of Iranian Jews traveled to Qom to meet with Ayatollah Khomeini. The Iranian media widely reported the meeting, which successfully established ground rules regarding the relationship between the Muslim majority and the Jewish minority.

At the meeting, Khomeini distinguished between Judaism and Zionism, allegedly rejecting the widespread speculation that all the Jews were undercover Zionist agents. In his proclamation, Khomeini acknowledged the deep roots of the Jewish community in Iran, underscored the elements of monotheism present in both Judaism and Islam, and distinguished between Zionism and Judaism: "We know that the Iranian Jews are not Zionist. We [and the Jews] together are against Zionism. . . . They [the Zionists] are not Jews! They are politicians that claim to work in the name of Judaism, but they hate Jews. . . . The Jews, like the other communities, are part of Iran, and Islam treats them all fairly."[12]

Despite Khomeini's conciliatory remarks toward Iranian Jews, the persecutions continued. On June 5, 1980, Albert Danielpour was found guilty on charges of selling heroin, sabotaging the revolution, and committing treason by having contacts with the Mossad and the CIA. Danielpour was tortured and executed in Hamadan, Iran. He was first detained in February 1979 and held for questioning by the authorities for five months at Evin Prison in Teheran. No formal charges were brought up against him. He was released after he "donated" all of his property to the Workers Committees, which essentially meant the Revolutionary Guards and the Islamic regime. The true purpose of his imprisonment was intended to confiscate all of his wealth. In a phone interview, Danielpour's son, Davar, who now lives in the United States, estimated the total value of the assets confiscated from the family at about $300 million, including property, factories, bank accounts, and farmland.[13] In mid-January, Danielpour was again arrested on charges of creating an "Israeli Zionist Government," working with Israel "to suppress the Palestinian revolution," and spying for the CIA. On April 16 he was convicted and sentenced to death, together with his two brothers, who had managed to escape and were convicted in their absence. At that point, some seventy Jews were being held in Iranian prisons.

Under Iranian law, no death sentence can be carried out without ratification by the Supreme Court in Teheran. On June 4, Danielpour's wife and an international humanitarian organization were notified that his death sentence had been commuted to three years in prison and that he would be transferred to a prison in Teheran. In reality, the Hamdam prison authorities called in Ayatollah Khakhali, also known as the "Judge Blood," who traveled around the country executing "counterrevolutionaries" by falsely accusing them of being drug dealers. He sentenced Danielpour on a new charge—dealing in heroin—and at 6:00 a.m., he stood in front of a firing squad.[14]

On June 10, the Islamic courts ordered the execution of Yousef Sohbani for aiding Zionism. The three executions raised the level of anxiety among the Jewish community. Many Iranian Jews had family ties to people living in Israel, and bogus charges could easily be concocted based on that fact alone. At the time of the revolution, some eighty thousand Jews were living in Iran. A year later, the number had fallen to fifty thousand. The majority of Iranian Jews have since left the country, and the official census of 2012 showed that only some nine thousand Jews are still living in Iran.[15]

Ruth Blau tried to help Albert Danielpour, and I constructed her actions from several sources who reported on it and from my interview with his son, Davar. The French daily *Le Monde* reported on July 21, 1980, that Ruth Blau traveled to Iran three times after the revolution, in February, April, and May, and was disappointed that Ayatollah Khomeini had not kept his promise and that the situation of the Jews was deteriorating.[16] The Israeli daily *Yediot Ahronot* added that before traveling to Iran in May, Ruth secured a letter of recommendation from the leader of the PLO, Yasser Arafat, and she flew to Iran on her Belgian passport in a mission to reduce Danielpour's sentence. *Le Monde* also reported that she approached Austrian chancellor Bruno Kreisky on the matter. To plea for Danielpour's life, Ruth traveled to the city of Qom to meet with Ayatollah Makarem Shirazi, the president of the Iranian Revolutionary Court. The journalist Noah Zevuluni asked Ruth about these journeys, and unsurprisingly, she claimed that she had visited Iran solely on her own behalf. After the execution, Ruth told an Israeli reporter that Yasser Arafat had sent her a condolence letter.[17]

An interesting corroboration of Ruth's narrative comes from Albert's son, Davar Danielpour, who was six years old when his father was executed. Davar now lives in Los Angeles. At my request, he asked his mother whether she remembers Ruth. Indeed, Hilda Hay confirmed that she recalled that Ruth came to her house with a delegation of Neturei Karta members and begged her to accompany her to Ayatollah Khomeini to ask for mercy. Hilda refused to join Ruth because she was petrified of the Islamists and feared for her life. Hilda told the *Forward*: "She came to my home acting very strangely and said she could help my husband get released by arranging a meeting with Khomeini. I thought she was odd and I never took her seriously."[18] After the husband was executed, the family left Iran and settled in Los Angeles, rebuilding their lives.

BEIRUT

Lebanon descended into turmoil during the 1970s and 1980s. Torn by deep ethnic and religious divisions, and battered by the competing interference of Syrian, Israeli, and Palestinian forces, the country experienced long periods of unrest and civil war. In June 1982, Israel invaded Lebanon to eliminate the PLO's presence in the south.

One of the underrepresented forces in Lebanese society was the Shi'ite community, concentrated mainly in southern Lebanon, along the border with Israel. Fakhr Ruhani, the new Iranian ambassador to Beirut, was convinced that the Iranian revolution would fail unless it was exported, and he viewed Lebanon as an excellent place to begin this process. Young Shi'ite clerics received attractive financial offers to attend seminaries in Qom, Iran.

In November 1982, after the summer's chaos, Syria allowed 1,500 Iranian Revolutionary Guard soldiers to open a training base in the Bekaa valley, with the goal that the forces would fight Israel. It is assumed that in early 1983, Hezbollah was founded to promote Khomeini's agenda to bring a revolutionary struggle to Lebanon. Its top priority was to fight a military jihad against the Israeli occupier and foreign intervention in Lebanon.[19]

The Hezbollah developed several combat tactics: they used martyr operations when they orchestrated a suicide attack on the Israeli headquarters in Tyre on November 11, 1982, killing seventy-five Israeli soldiers. On April 18, 1983, a suicide bomber rammed his explosive-packed vehicle into the US embassy, killing sixty-three. On October 23, 1983, another suicide attack against the Multinational Force in Lebanon killed 239 Americans and 58 French civilians.

Another tactic of Hezbollah was kidnapping. The first person to be hijacked was David Dodge, the president of the American University of Beirut. Between 1982 and 1991, the Hezbollah kidnapped 110 Western hostages: Lebanese, European, American, and Israeli. Typically, the Hezbollah would not take responsibility for the kidnappings and used different names, such as Islamic Jihad, the Revolutionary Justice Organization, and the Movement of the Oppressed on Earth. According to scholars Avon and Khatchadourian, the language these groups use in their ransom demands is consistent with Khomeinist jargon. Most experts believe that these names were merely covers for Hezbollah.

The hostages were pawns in negotiations with several different aims: to buy weapons at less disadvantageous conditions than those proposed indirectly in Tehran, within the context of the Iran-Iraq War; to put pressure on Israel to provide information about the fate of four kidnapped Iranian diplomats, and to secure the release of Shi'ite prisoners.

The Jewish community of Lebanon numbered around six thousand members in 1967, but only some three thousand Jews remained when Israel invaded Lebanon in June 1982; by 1985, only one hundred Jews still lived in Lebanon, mainly in Beirut. On March 30, 1985, four Jews were kidnapped from their homes, and later more were taken. The hostages were Dr. Elie Hallack, Isaac Sasson, Yehuda Benisti, Elie Srour, Haim Cohen, Salim Jammous, and Henri Mann.

For months there was silence about their whereabouts. Based on two articles in Le Monde, we can piece together Ruth's actions on behalf of the kidnapped. Ruth traveled to Beirut during the first two weeks of November 1985. She visited the head of the Hezbollah, Sheikh Mohammad Hussein Fadlalla, and also met with Fakhr Rouhani, the Iranian ambassador to Lebanon, and Nabih Berri, the leader of Shiite militia Amal. After this set of meetings, she confirmed that three hostages—Elie Hallack, Elie Srour, and Haim Cohen—were still alive. As a result of Ruth's negotiations, an unknown movement called the Organization of the Oppressed on Earth proposed to release four of the hostages in exchange for three hundred prisoners held by Israel at Khiam Prison, situated in the "Security Zone" established by Israel in southern Lebanon.[20]

After no progress was made in the negotiations, the Oppressed executed Haim Cohen on December 24, 1985. On December 30, they murdered three other hostages: Yehuda Benisti, Elie Srour, and Henri Mann. On January 1, 1986, they assassinated Isaac Tarrab, and on February 1986, they kidnapped and murdered Yehuda Benisti's sons Ibrahim and Yousuf. In February, they murdered Elie Hallak.[21] Israeli Journalist Shefi Gabbai from the daily Maariv reported that those Jews who decided to remain in Beirut had all paid the special protection tax mandated by Islamic law for People of the Book.[22] Accordingly, Muslims who follow Islamic law, as Hezbollah claims to, could not kidnap and kill Jews per se. To overcome this obstacle, bogus claims were leveled against them that they were Israeli spies.

Israeli prime minister Itzhak Shamir refused to accept the conditions of the kidnappers and said that Israel would punish those responsible for the murders: "Again these barbarians used defenseless Jews as a means of hitting at Israel. We will not engage in contacts or conduct negotiations with anyone who regards Jews as hostages."[23] Israeli public opinion was outraged by the executions, which were reported on the front pages of the newspapers. An editorial article in *Maariv*, the newspaper with the largest circulation in Israel at the time, regretted that these Jews had chosen to remain in Lebanon and had not taken the opportunity to escape to Israel when they could. The editorial said that Jews and Israelis should not be bystanders and should recruit the help of the world to put an end to these horrors.[24]

Ruth's involvement in this sad affair was not reported by the Israeli press and only appeared in *Le Monde*, perhaps due to the military censorship imposed in the Israeli media at that time. In terms of her involvement in this affair, I would make several comments. First, she had excellent connections in Lebanon, especially with the Shi'ite leadership—relationships she had established in Iran. Second, she found a calling in trying to save Jewish lives. This can explain her engagement in the Danielpour case and the case of the kidnapped Lebanese Jews. Third, the local Jews under Shi'ite rule were used as scapegoats and were not protected as required by Islamic law and their leaders' declarations. In the case of the Lebanese hostages, there was really no reason to kidnap them. They were not Israeli citizens and Israel had no reason to surrender to blackmail. Their kidnapping and murder were no more than acts of sadism. One point worth mentioning is that in both cases Ruth's missions were unsuccessful; it is not unreasonable to wonder whether they had any chance from the outset.

THE BATTLE OF SULTAN YACOUB

On June 11, 1982, just a few hours before a ceasefire was due, an Israeli tank unit became embroiled in a confrontation with the Syrian army near the village of Sultan Yacoub in the Bekaa valley in Lebanon, close to the border with Syria. The Israeli unit was ambushed and defeated, with thirty soldiers killed and ten tanks lost. During the aftermath of the battle, three Israeli soldiers went missing. Eyewitnesses testified that the three Israeli soldiers were paraded through Damascus in a victory march. Their names were Zachary Baumel, Yehuda Katz, and Zvi Feldman. The three soldiers were declared missing. On April 3, 2019, Russian president Vladimir Putin announced that the Russian army, in coordination with the Syrian military, had found Zachary Baumel's remains.

Again, Ruth Blau attempted to help in the case of the missing soldiers. After Ruth's death, Yona Baumel, Zachary's father, gave an interview for *Maariv* and said that in 1984 he reached out to Ruth. After a few months of persuasion, Baumel convinced her to act on behalf of the missing soldiers. "At first," he said, "it was a dialogue of the deaf. She asked me to curse the Israeli government, but I refused. Eventually, she agreed to help. She traveled to Jordan with her French passport, and from there she reached Damascus, the capital of Syria." She agreed to help based on the halachic commandment to rescue prisoners but did not want anyone to think she was working for the State of Israel or assisting the IDF in any way.

Her meetings in Syria lasted several days. When she returned, she reported that she had been unable to reach the highest-ranking figures she had hoped to meet. "The fact that she traveled and made a great effort for a woman her age meant a lot to us," Baumel concluded, adding that Ruth asked them to keep this effort a secret; they respected her wish and never discussed the matter until after her death.[25]

Nechama Davidson, Ruth's granddaughter, was a teenager when she saw Yona Baumel coming to her parents' apartment in Jerusalem and receiving a report from Ruth on her activities. Nechama does not remember much of the meeting. She only remembers her grandmother saying that Yasser Arafat, the head of the PLO, was a bad guy who did not care for his people.

CONCLUSION

It was difficult to construct Ruth's activities in Muslim countries with limited information, but a few points can be made. What stands out is her bravery. The assignments she took on herself are not for the faint of heart. It is also apparent that she was a skillful talker and negotiator, equipped with an appealing style and charm. The fact that her book was released in 1979, translated into Arabic and published in Lebanon surely helped build her reputation and her public relations.

Why would Ayatollah Khomeini, Abu Jihad, and Sheikh Fadlallah even bother meeting such a figure? I can think of several possible explanations. As mentioned above, Ruth may have served as a backchannel to Israel; she may even have collaborated with the Mossad, as Ben-Menashe claimed. Second, Lebanon was a place where France still had influence, due to its long colonization of the country. It is not impossible that she acted as a French agent, and the same could apply to her meeting with Khomeini in France. A third possibility is that these contacts were no more than a mutually beneficial publicity stunt. The Muslim side could have used this relationship to show that Iran, the PLO, and Hezbollah are not antisemitic but anti-Zionist, and to claim that they are willing to sit with Jews and respect their rights as long as they are not pro-Israel. Indeed, Neturei Karta developed a relationship with the PLO during the 1990s and enjoyed an open door in Iran as well. In 2006, a Neturei Karta delegation even participated in a Holocaust denial conference in Teheran, and in 2008, Iranian president Mahmoud Ahmadinejad met them again.[26] Thus, Ruth's meetings might have been the first phase of this connection. The fact that these high-ranking figures never allowed her to secure any concrete success in her missions strengthens the view that these meetings were more a series of publicity stunts than serious negotiations.

Ruth used these connections to advance her own reputation; the newspapers reported on her travels and she became a well-known figure in the Israeli and French press. Regardless of this, however, I am convinced that Ruth's goal was to save Jewish life by whatever means possible. Traveling to Lebanon and Iran was dangerous, she would not do so merely for the sake of a few news-paper headlines.

TEN

―᭱―

RUTH BLAU, ULTRA-ORTHODOX SOCIETY, AND ISRAELI PUBLIC OPINION

RUTH BLAU HAD A RICH life, full of thrills and drama. She was anything but ordinary, and she would never satisfy herself with the mundane. "Every aspect of her life was melodramatic; even when she sneezed, it was so full of passion," Nechama Davidson, Ruth's granddaughter, commented in a private conversation.

Ruth lived a very colorful life, and her story is also important, embodying and combining several dramatic events. Her story represents how women participated in the war effort to fight the Nazis in France. It is also an interesting conversion story, part of a larger wave of converts to Judaism in Europe after the Second World War. Ruth was also one of the most controversial figures in Israel during the 1960s and 1970s in the ongoing debate over the role of Orthodox Judaism in Israel's public life. Her joining the Neturei Karta movement certainly raised the profile of this movement in the Israeli public sphere. Her marriage saga opens the window onto the sectarian politics of the Haredi community in Israel. Ruth's role as a rebbetzin in the last decades of her life is an example of the notable place rabbis' wives hold in Haredi society. Her associations with Shi'ite leaders in Iran and Lebanon are fascinating.

UNIQUE OUTSIDERS

Although Haredi society demands conformity and is suspicious toward outsiders, it still allowed some room for Ruth Blau to operate and found her unique talents useful. Even after entering this male-dominated society, Ruth remained stubbornly individualistic and took on herself roles that are typically allowed only for men. While women are expected to take care of the home, raise children, and support their husbands who dedicate their lives to Torah study, Ruth was a fighter, a fundraiser, and a hostage negotiator.

It is helpful to compare Ruth's story to that of Jacob-Israël de Haan (1881–1924), the so-called foreign minister of the Ashkenazi City Council, the main religious and political organization of the Old Yishuv—namely, the ultra-Orthodox and anti-Zionist community of Jewish religious scholars living mainly in Jerusalem. The story of de Haan's life and death is a fascinating episode that I will only be able to touch on briefly here. He was born into a traditional Jewish family in Smilde, Netherlands. At an early age, de Haan left the religious lifestyle and joined various Communist groups. De Haan was a man of outstanding intellectual capabilities. He was considered one of the greatest Dutch poets of his time and authored two novels that were the subject of considerable attention. He found time to gain a PhD in law and went on to teach law at Amsterdam University. He wrote an important report on the prisons of the Russian empire, drawing global attention to the appalling conditions in these institutions. His books and poems openly raised themes reflecting his homosexual orientation, and in response, the Social Democratic party began to distance itself from de Haan.

Despite being gay, he married a Christian woman, Johanna Van Maarseveen, who was nine years his senior and provided him with financial support. He was profoundly influenced by the antisemitism that was rife in upper-class social circles in the

Netherlands. During the First World War, he responded to anti-semitism by returning to Orthodox Judaism and joining the Miz-rahi Religious-Zionist Party. In 1919, he immigrated to Palestine, earning a living as a reporter for the Dutch newspaper *Algemeen Handelsblad* and working as a lecturer at the British Mandate School of Law and Economics. He initially hoped to find his place in the Zionist leadership, but his services were declined. The Miz-rahi movement also responded coolly to his advances, and he failed to secure a place in the faculty of the Hebrew University. De Haan led a covert homosexual lifestyle in Palestine and tes-timony suggests that he had sexual relations with Arab youths.[1]

Shortly after migrating to Palestine, de Haan became pro-foundly disappointed, disillusioned by what he viewed as the bureaucratic and corrupt conduct of the Zionist leadership in Palestine.[2] De Haan met Rabbi Yosef Sonnenfeld (1849–1932), the leader of the Old Yishuv, during his journalistic work and was enchanted by the rabbi. In March 1920, he decided to change his allegiance and became a member of the Ashkenazi City Council. He then began to provide services as a legal counsel and "for-eign minister" to that organization. Its hitherto Haredi activists lacked the necessary political and cultural skills to compete with the Zionists for the sympathy of the British rulers. De Haan, by contrast, was a recognized writer and sophisticated cosmopolitan who spoke numerous languages and enjoyed access to promi-nent figures around the world. His newspaper articles, written in multiple languages, including English, brought the opinion of the Old Yishuv to the readers in Europe, forcing the Zionist establishment to cease ignoring him. De Haan suggested that in order to establish its unique, independent political identity, the Old Yishuv should adopt a pro-Arab policy.[3] At one point, he even attempted to persuade the Hashemite dynasty to sign a political agreement undermining the Balfour Declaration. He met his end in 1924 when a Zionist assassin fired three bullets directly at his heart.[4]

Both Ruth Blau and de Haan were outsiders who could offer unique services to the ultra-Orthodox community in Jerusalem because of the experience they acquired during their non-Haredi life. Those born and raised inside the closed and antimodern ultra-Orthodox enclave often do not have the communication, language, and social skills necessary to negotiate with the outside world. Thus, talented outsiders are welcomed to represent and offer service to the community. The fact that Ruth Blau and de Haan lived in both worlds gave them unique powers. They were extremely loyal to the ideology of HaEdah HaCharedit and the Old Yishuv, and their services were viewed as essential, whether they were to represent the community's interests to the British authorities or to smuggle a child outside Israel in an escalating ideological conflict.

It should be noted that both Ruth Blau and de Haan were belittled by their communities and had to struggle for recognition. Ruth tells us in her letters that people call her "a dirty little convert," and after his death, Haredi leadership distanced itself from de Haan's legacy, likely due to his homosexual orientation.[5]

Most newcomers who join the ultra-Orthodox enclave but do not have such capital that de-Hann and Blau could offer are typically pushed to the bottom of society; their status as newcomers never ends, scholar Shlomi Doron observed.[6] But with their unique abilities, de Haan and Blau stood out and were able to break the glass ceiling. However, the number of cases like these are small, and typically ultra-Orthodox leadership prefers to avoid the services of newcomers.

HAREDI WOMEN AND REBBETZINS

Another aspect of breaking the glass ceiling is the position of the rebbetzin. Despite tremendous social pressure to maintain a low profile, a handful of Haredi women have managed to achieve remarkable status and influence. Ruth's example is not the only one. Other examples of rebbetzins who have attained powerful positions include the late Haya Mushka (wife of Menachem Mendel Schneersohn, the Lubavitcher Rebbe), Alta Faige (wife of Yoel Teitelbaum, the Satmar Rebbe), Lea Esther (wife of Moshe Yehoshua Hager, the Vizhnitzer Rebbe), and others.[7]

Unlike outstanding Haredi rabbis, whose fame and success are explained only by their extraordinary learning capabilities, character, and devotion to the world of Torah, rebbetzins' social status is limited by that of their husbands, and they cannot elevate it without their active support. In fact, part of the reason some rebbitzins obtain a high social status is because of their extraordinary contribution to their husbands' success. Thus, great Haredi rebbetzins must be extremely talented and ambitious, be married to well-known rabbis, and have an intrafamilial relationship with their husbands that is of the two-person single career type whereby both the man and the women join forces to promote the husband's social position. Their significant involvement in their husbands' careers is the only social mechanism that allows the rabbis to disregard certain social norms and offer their wives greater leeway for social activism. Their actions, in turn, promote not merely their status but also that of their husbands. The rabbis' elevated status allows them to grant their wives more options to demonstrate their capabilities, and so the positive feedback mechanism continues.

Whereas the agency and empowerment of ordinary Haredi woman can be found in her domestic lifestyle, like raising children with strict piety, taking care of the household, and allowing her husband to live the life of a Torah scholar,[8] the agency of the more renowned rebbetzins comes from their extraordinary contribution to the whole community. The privilege of these rebbetzins to operate in a field that is considered "out of limits" for ordinary Haredi women is directly connected with them having a two-person single career family model.

In recent decades, following the example set by outstanding rabbinical couples, such as Ruth and Amram, lay Haredi couples have also begun to reject the concept of "parallel life" which is typical to most Haredi households, and to embrace either the "dual-career families" model or that of "two-person single career," which results in more Haredi women making it to the front row. In 2012, Saki Dodelson, cofounder, president, and CEO of the multimillion-dollar company Achieve3000®, was named Private Company CEO of the Year by the New Jersey Technology Council (NJTC). She attended the first Jewish Women's Entrepreneur Conference a year later, organized by Chaya Fishman, another successful Haredi businesswoman. In 2014, Adina Bar-Shalom, daughter of Rabbi Ovadia Yosef and leader of Shas, the Haredi Sephardi movement, was awarded Israel's most prestigious prize for establishing the first Haredi advanced education college. In 2016, Rachel Freier, a Hasidic woman, was elected a civil court judge in New York and was followed by Hava Toker, who later became Israel's first Haredi judge.[9]

These examples represent a larger social phenomenon. Thus, there is more than one model to characterize the social status of ultra-Orthodox women and their intramarital relations. While most ultra-Orthodox families still follow the more traditional "parallel life" model, some families prefer a more egalitarian model such as the dual career or the two-person single career. Therefore, while in the past marrying a rabbi and following the two-person single career model was the only way a woman could attain public influence and recognition, nowadays Haredi couples who adopt the dual career model enable Haredi women to develop an independent career.[10]

Figuratively speaking, it seems like those individualistic figures like Ruth Blau, who considered themselves devoted to Jewish tradition and costumes but insisted on leadership roles and were supported by their husbands, paved the way for new intramarital patterns that today are present in an increasing number of Haredi families, allowing more women to live their life to the fullest extent.

MARRIAGE, LOVE, AND MUTUAL BENEFITS—
THE CASE OF RUTH BLAU

Amram Blau was the founder and leader of the Modesty Patrols. This semipolice group monitored, controlled, and raised the modesty bars inside the ultra-Orthodox enclave in Jerusalem. The large wall posters at the entrance of Meah Shearim demand that women do not walk in their community with immodest clothes, and the Modesty Patrols enforce these demands still today.[11]

Although from the outside, it may seem that Haredi society is asexual, with high bars of modesty with vigorous societal enforcement, Ruth and Amram's story shows how expressions of physical attraction can work in this society when a strong man wishes to marry a young and attractive woman.

A somewhat similar case occurred in 1937. At the age of twenty-five, Alta Faige married Rabbi Yoel Teitelbaum, who was then the chief rabbi of Satmar (Satu Mare), Romania.[12] Rabbi Yoel was twenty-five years older than her. His first wife, who had died a year earlier, had not borne him a son to inherit the Hasidic dynasty he sought to establish. Moreover, two of his three daughters had died at an early age. His only surviving daughter, Royza, who was slightly older than Alta Faige, approved the match, hoping that her father would be blessed with more children, especially with a son to succeed him. Oral traditions suggest that Alta Faige was divorced and had suffered a miscarriage. This may partially explain the unusually high age at which she married and that she agreed to marry a widower who was twenty-five years her senior. Whether or not this is the case, the twenty-five-year-old Alta Faige had much to gain both in economic and social terms from taking a chief rabbi of a large community, who was also the head of an established prominent yeshiva and a Hasidic leader.

However, it is unclear why Rabbi Yoel agreed to marry a woman whose social status and *yichus* (rabbinical genealogy) were much lower than his. No clue to this mystery can be found in any of the many biographies written about him. The only reasonable explanation was that the intended bride was young, pretty, and childless yet known to be fertile.[13]

Alta Faige eventually was proven to be barren, but Yoel Te-itelbaum did not divorce her, although he was expected to do so in accordance with Jewish law. Alta Faige turned out to be a significant figure in the Satmar Hasidic court, established in America after the Holocaust. She raised money for her husband's institutions and dedicated her life to establishing educational or-ganizations for Haredi girls, some of which were later named after her. She also founded charitable institutions, the most important of which was an organization of women who visited and assisted sick Jews in New York's hospitals. At the same time, she advised her husband on all matters regarding the court's daily manage-ment and helped him plan his political future.[14]

Comparing and contrasting the two couples (Ruth and Amram Blau and Alta Faige and Yoel Teitelbaum) shows some similarities: Old and powerful men marry much younger and attractive looking wives. In both cases, there are no mutual children in the picture, and the wives turned into an engine of activism and promotion of their husbands' careers. But there is also a difference: While Teit-elbaum rationalized his marriage to Alta Faige by hoping she could bring him a son, Amram Blau had no such expectations, although Ruth did have such hope. The excuse of marrying a young woman so that she could bear children doesn't exist in Amram's case.

Amram Blau, who was the front man in charge of curtailing women's advancement in the Haredi enclave of Jerusalem with his Modesty Patrols, was not immune to being attracted to a younger woman, and this marriage can be regarded as his sym-bol of status and seniority. From these cases, we can observe that when it comes to the second marriage of senior rabbis, Haredi society allows them to desire beautiful young women.

When it comes to the first marriage of young men and women, Haredi society is much more controlling, and expressions of physical attractiveness are less allowed. The young men and women are connected by a matchmaker based on their requests and social status, and are allowed to meet a handful of times before deciding whether they are to be married or not.

In Ruth's archive, there are many letters addressed to her about requests for matches, but almost no responses from Ruth, with one exception: a letter found in the archive to the mother of a potential groom. Ruth describes the girl as "not only the ideal daughter, but she is also pretty, smart, sweet, modest, Haredi, and above all, she is very gracious," proving how she prioritized her beauty. Whereas the bride is described by her merits and looks, the groom was described as a member of "an important family and a *talmid chacham* [a Torah student]." From this, we can understand that *yichus* (family status) and education were the most important for the two sides. Ruth did not mention his physical looks at all.

In describing the family of the groom, Ruth condemned the mother: "From what I have learned about you . . . you hold from you honor too much, and none of the girls you met were good enough for you." History taught us, she continued, that "many people who were [excessively] proud were fools and also insane!" From Ruth's response, we see that the family has much control over who will marry their son, and the decision is in the mother's hands. Their pickiness allowed the potential groom to meet many potential wives.

In a different letter from a man in a Toronto yeshiva, we learn that the young man met the potential bride's father, and he thinks the interview did not go so well. He did not come out as "frumm [pious] enough" and states, "Near him [the father], I felt very small, and I am also afraid that I didn't strike him as being particularly intelligent."

From this example, we see again that the choice of the *shidduch* was in the hands of the parents, who make inquiries on the candidates, interview the potential matches, and seek a bright Torah student for their girls.

These two cases show that a woman's physical appearance is important in the matching process, whether with senior rabbis or young men. Still, the highest quality of the men in this process would be his level of education and piety. It also appears that parents have a decisive say in their children's matches. There is room for more research and scholarly insights on this interesting subject.

ISRAELI VIEWS ON ULTRA-ORTHODOXY— THE CASE OF RUTH BLAU

Ruth played the role of a villain in Israeli public opinion during the 1960s and 1970s due to being in charge of hiding and smuggling Yossele Schumacher and her strong anti-Zionist opinion. Still, the media developed a fascination with her, and during the 1980s and 1990s, she received multiple cover stories in the leading press.[15] It seems like although there were substantial ideological disagreements, the Israeli public learned to accept Ruth as unique and eccentric and a legitimate part of Israeli society.

The transitions in the image of Ruth Blau teaches a more important lesson on Neturei Karta and ultra-Orthodox Judaism in Israel. Many Israelis strongly criticize Haredi Jews. Many Israelis accuse them of avoiding the expected duties of military services without penalties, exploiting and maneuvering the Israeli political system to their advantage with state budgets and social securities, and using their political power for religious cohesion. At times, criticism of ultra-Orthodoxy turns to ugly stereotypes. In many cases, the objection to ultra-Orthodox Judaism has specific reasons. Neturei Karta, for example, sometimes disrupted everyday life in Jerusalem with their constant demonstrations, which sometimes even slipped into violence. Known for throwing stones on cars driving on the Sabbath, Neturei Karta has made many non-ultra-Orthodox Jews upset about their disruptive behavior.

Still, it seems like many Israeli Jews agree that all segments of the Jewish society—secular, Orthodox, or ultra-Orthodox—want what is best for the Jews; thus, these ideological disagreements are like disputes "inside the family." These political quarrels, which do not only limit themselves to debates over religion and state, all stem from a shared desire for a better present and future. Thus, different movements might be polarized rivals, but they are not each other's enemies. There is a sense of Jewish solidarity that surpasses the ideological disagreements. Unlike de Haan, who was actively working to cancel the Balfour Declaration and was viewed as a traitor whom the Zionist movement needed to eliminate, none of the other ultra-Orthodox leaders seriously engaged in attempts to undermine Israeli statehood. This view, for example, is much different from the image that many Israeli Jews might hold of Israeli-Palestinians, that are perceived as people who wish to harm Jews and thus should be considered with suspicion and exclusion.

In this context, we can understand the surprising comment that Ben-Gurion made about his respect for Neturei Karta because they are driven by their ideology. In a Knesset session gathering in 1960, Ben-Gurion said: "I am full of respect toward the anti-Zionist Neturei Karta from my old town from 60 years ago . . . I can understand them. I disagreed with them, but I can understand them."[16] From this comment, we can see why his government was so tolerant toward everyone responsible for the abduction of Yossele Schumacher a few years later.

Seeing all Jews as responsible for one another can also explain why Ruth tried to save the lives of Israeli soldiers—because it was her understanding that when it comes to Jews in distress, she needed to help with no regard to their political views. She also might have hoped her initiatives would show that Neturei Karta cares for all Jews. Ruth articulated her position to the greater Israeli public with the publication of her book, in which she explained why she assisted in kidnapping Yossele Schumacher, and her interviews with the press, which helped make many Israelis feel more inclusive toward her and the movement she represented.[17] Like Ben-Gurion, even if many Israelis disagreed with her politics, they could at least understand where she was coming from. Her desire that outsiders of her enclave would know her motivations and see her good actions toward Jews in distress showed how desperately she wanted the approval of this world. This can teach us a greater lesson: Although she was much opposed to the secular world, she too wanted to be included in the larger Israeli story. Although she and her husband Amram much opposed the State of Israel, they considered themselves to be an essential part of *Am Israel*—the Jewish people, and of *Eretz Israel*—the holy land.

Another aspect that may explain the forgiving Israeli attitudes toward Neturei Karta and Ruth Blau is with a famous statement that secular Israelis often quote: "The synagogue I do not go to is an Orthodox synagogue." What lies behind this statement is the common view that even nonpracticing and even total secular Israelis regard Orthodox Judaism as the authentic expression of the Jewish religious tradition. The uncompromising path of Neturei Karta and its willingness to pay communal and personal prices for its way of life causes its members to be viewed as true zealots. They are respected as people who are faithful to absolute truths and do not surrender to pragmatic considerations or compromise on their religious principles. For many, they represent the pure ideal and a perfect manifestation of the Jewish religion. With that in mind, many secular Israelis may disagree but also to some extent respect ultra-Orthodox Jews in general, with Neturei Karta and Ruth Blau in particular. In that regard, in the last two decades of her life, Ruth served as a bridge between the two worlds.

EPILOGUE

"WHO ARE YOU, RUTH BEN David?" was the question famously posed by Isser Harel, head of the Mossad, after he was charged with the task of locating the missing child Yossele Schumacher. I would try to offer some points that would help answer it.

Ruth had a deep spirituality. Over her life, she had gone through several stages that eventually brought her to the most pious movement in contemporary Judaism. Ruth joined the world of Neturei Karta and became one of its most vocal and well-known representatives. This is not just personal piety gone extreme; it was a political aspect of religion gone extreme. Ruth's struggles and polemics that made her famous were primarily political. Her anti-Zionism was a blend of religious and political motivations. Even her attempt to save the lives of Israeli prisoners of war was rationalized by her desire to fulfill the biblical commandment of releasing hostages. Although she despised modern political ideologies, she was very political herself. Just as her husband Amram Blau was a political figure, Ruth assumed a similar role.

An interesting observation concerns her attraction to martyrdom. She took dangerous actions while risking her life and freedoms in the name of higher goals, and it is possible that her Christian upbringing may have influenced this aspect of her character. Early Christianity was molded by men and women who were willing to die for their faith in the first centuries, and it seems that this ideal influenced Ruth.

Ruth was a courageous woman. From an early age, Ruth assumed life-threatening challenges. For the liberty and well-being of France, she joined the fight against the Nazis by penetrating the Gestapo headquarters, saving the life of Jews in southern France, and even joining the French secret services. Her thrill of danger was met again in 1960–1962 in the Yossele affair, where she assumed the highly dangerous challenge of hiding Yossele from his parents and the State of Israel. The fact that she traveled to Muslim countries to meet the top leadership of Iran and Hezbollah was also an expression of her courage in her commitment to the well-being of Jews.

Ruth was a fighter. She went to war against the most difficult challenges and refused to abandon her principles and positions. On her side, she had her looks, intellect, and charms. She knew how to manipulate the men around her.

Ruth admired strict men. A careful reading of her autobiography shows that Ruth was not particularly fond of men in general, often describing them in unflattering terms. She offered the opinion that Isser Harel looked like a Nazi, while her father reminded her of Charlie Chaplin. She described her fiancé Rabbi Poliatschek as mentally ill, and the list goes on. Her descriptions of women were far more positive. However, a series of unusual men are excluded from this generalization: Rabbi Avraham Maizes, Nahman Starks, Amram Blau, and Rabbi Yoel Teitelbaum. Their common denominator is a tough character, combining strict piety with a combative personality. All four men spent time in prison: Maizes and Starks were incarcerated in the Soviet Union and fought for their right to observe their religion; Ruth described them as modern-day martyrs. Amram Blau was imprisoned in Israeli jails many times for his violent conduct as leader of Neturei Karta. Amram also headed the "Modesty

Patrols" in Jerusalem, which used physical force to impose the Haredi modesty code. Yoel Teitelbaum spent five months in the Bergen-Belsen concentration camp during the Holocaust. Thus, the profile of her preferred Haredi man, for whom she was will-ing to embark on a dangerous operation to kidnap and smuggle a child, was very different from the stereotypical image of the Haredi man pouring over the religious texts—a character Daniel Boyarin has referred to as a "feminine man."[1] She admired men who were strong and tough, like her father: the father she hated so much that she was unable even to bring herself to mention him by name in her autobiography; whom she claimed to pity; and who, according to her own descriptions, was rigid and cold but who was also the fearless recipient of a medal for his heroism in fighting the Nazi occupiers. We can therefore suggest that the qualities she attributes to her father also describe herself as well as the men she liked. Yet while she maintained a fierce hatred of her father, she showed unconditional loyalty to these Haredi men, to the point that she was willing to forego her liberty for them—since kidnapping is a serious offense that could have led to her protracted imprisonment.

Ruth was an outsider. Her life journey is a story of transition intended to find a port. She could not fit into any of the places she explored, forcing her to continue her search. Eventually, she landed in Neturei Karta, the most extreme of all the options she could have chosen. Yet this community never really accepted her or welcomed her as an equal. General Israeli society, too, saw her as an outsider, "the convert."

Ruth was moody and she suffered from depression. She kept moving from one place to another to find the inner peace she wanted so much, but she could never find comfort. She even ran away from her husband because of her bad moods.

Ruth lost her moral compass. She acted by what she believed was the right thing to do all her life. With the Yossele affair, this compass spun out of control, to the point that Ruth remained one of only a handful of ultra-Orthodox people who refused to relinquish and return the boy to his parents, including the Satmar Rebbe who wished to have nothing with this abduction. Ruth was a woman who changed all her life, but with the Yossele affair she refused to change her behavior and never apologized. Ruth said that it was the role of converts to offer their help to Jews in times of distress; Isser Harel responded that Jews do not need converts who, like her, just bring strife and distress. Clearly, there was something flawed in her compass if she never saw the wrongdoing of her actions. Her son, for example, decided to end the Yossele affair, and although he adhered to a strict Orthodox lifestyle, he and his large family never joined the Neturei Karta circles. When it comes to raising her son, Ruth never dedicated herself fully to this task, and throughout her life, she always had a complicated relationship with him. Her mistreatment of Yossele and her own son is an example of her flawed personality. However, overall, she atoned for her sins in the way she came to the help of Jewish prisoners in Lebanon and Iran.

Who are you Ruth Ben David? Ruth was a living contradiction with a life full of paradox and purpose.

NOTES

INTRODUCTION

1. Yossi Schumacher, interview with the author, on April 1, 2020.

1. CHILDHOOD

1. Ruth Blau, *The History of Yossele Schumacher* (Brooklyn: Copy Corner, 1993), 9.
2. Ibid., 9–10.
3. Ibid., 10.
4. Ibid., 12.
5. Ibid., 14.
6. Henie Persitz, phone interview with the author, August 6, 2018.
7. Blau, *History*, 15.
8. Ibid., 15–17.
9. Greer F. Cashman, "No Stranger to Controversy," *Jerusalem Post*, May 24, 2000, https://web.archive.org/web/20010119125400/http://www02.jpost.com/Editions/2000/03/05/Features/Features.3576.html.
10. Blau, *History*, 18.
11. Ibid.
12. Ibid., 18–19.
13. Ibid., 20.
14. Ibid., 21–23.
15. Ibid., 24.

2. RESISTANCE

1. Quoted in Max Hastings, *Das Reich: Resistance and the March of the 2nd SS Panzer Division through France, June 1944* (London: Michael Joseph, 1981), 9.

2. Gordon Williamson, *The Waffen-SS (1): 1 to 5 Divisions* (Oxford: Osprey Publishing, 2003), 3.

3. Hasting, *Das Reich*, 10–11.

4. Paul Mons, *Afin que nul n'oblie: En France la Das Reich fit la guerre aux civils* (Brive, France: Ecritures, 2004), 16–24.

5. Williamson, *Waffen-SS*, 19–20.

6. Lynne Olson, *Madame Fourcede's Secret War: The Daring Young Woman Who Led France's Largest Spy Network against Hitler* (New York: Random House, 2019), 21–22.

7. Ibid.

8. Olivier Wieviorka, *The French Resistance* (Cambridge, MA: Harvard University Press, 2016).

9. Olson, *Madame Fourcede's Secret War*, xx–xxi.

10. Ruth Blau, "To Our Righteous Genius Rebbe," n.d. (1965), Ruth Blau's Folder, Itzhak Davidson's 'Eretz Israel' Private Collection.

11. Ruth Blau, *The History of Yossele Schumacher* (Brooklyn: Copy Corner, 1993), 29–30.

12. Margaret C. Weitz, *Sisters in the Resistance: How French Women Fought to Free France 1940–1945* (New York: John Wiley & Sons, 1995), 44–57.

13. Ibid.

14. I hold a copy of her graduation diploma from the University of Toulouse.

15. Asher Cohen, *The Shoah in France* (Jerusalem: Yad Vashem, 1996).

16. Blau, *History*, 32–33.

17. File 3213–423, Service Historique de la Defense, Paris, France.

18. N.2146/SM in file 3213–423, Service Historique de la Defense, Paris, France.

19. File 3213–423.

20. Blau, *History*, 43–44.

21. Ibid., 40.

22. Her interview is dated December 7, 1946, file 3213–423.

23. I learned this from Nechama Davidson, Ruth's granddaughter, in a private conversation. Nechama recalls her father telling her of it.

3. "YOUR GOD IS MY GOD": LUCETTE'S
QUEST FOR SPIRITUALITY

1. I found her educational records at the Sorbonne's archive.

2. Ruth Blau, *The History of Yossele Schumacher* (Brooklyn: Copy Corner, 1993), 46.

3. In her archive she kept Claude's school reports from Geneva.

4. Blau, *History*, 49.

5. Ibid.

6. Ibid., 50.

7. Ibid.

8. Ibid., 52.

9. Ruth Blau, *Les Gardiens de la Cité: Histoire d'une Guerre Saint* (Paris: Lammarion, 1978), 23–24.

10. Blau, *History*, 53.

11. Ibid., 54.

12. Ibid., 55.

13. Ibid., 56.

14. Ibid., 57.

15. Ibid., 50.

16. Edouard Schuré, *The Great Initiates: A Study of the Secret History of Religions* (San Francisco: Harper & Row, 1980), 19–22.

17. Blau, *History*, 60.

18. Ibid., 59–62.

19. Ibid., 63.

20. William James, *The Varieties of Religious Experience* (New York: Modern Library, 1902), 126.

21. Ibid., 142.

22. Ibid., 172.

23. Ibid., 236.

24. I quoted from chapters 5–10, on pages 77–253.

25. Charles Taylor, *A Secular Age* (Cambridge, MA: Harvard University Press, 2007), 732.

26. Chana Ullman, *The Transformed Self: The Psychology of Religious Conversion* (New York: Plenum Press, 1989), 1–26.

27. Raymond Paloutzian, James Richardson, and Lewis Rambo, "Religious Conversion and Personality Change," *Journal of Personality* 76, no. 6 (2009): 1047–79.

28. Ibid.

29. Ullman, *Transformed Self*, 1–26.

30. Pehr Granqvist and Lee Kirkpatrick, "Religious Conversion and Perceived Childhood Attachment: A Meta-Analysis," *International Journal for the Psychology of Religion* 14, no. 4 (2004): 223–50.

31. Mark D. Baer, "History and Religious Conversion," in *The Oxford Handbook of Religious Conversion*, ed. Lewis R. Rambo and Charles Farhadian (New York: Oxford University Press, 2004), 25–47.

32. Ullman, *Transformed Self*, 1–26.

4. "YOUR PEOPLE SHALL BE MY PEOPLE":
CONVERSION

1. Ruth Blau, *The History of Yossele Schumacher* (Brooklyn: Copy Corner, 1993), 75.

2. Ibid., 76.

3. Ibid., 76–78.

4. Ibid., 78.

5. Valentin Nikiprowetzky and André Zaoui, *Maimonide: Le livre de la connaissance* (Paris: Presses Universitaires de France, 1961).

6. Menachem Finkelstein, *Conversion, Halakhah, and Practice* (Ramat Gan, Israel: Bar Ilan University Press, 2006).

7. Blau, *History*, 81.

8. Bianca Zaoui, telephone conversation with the author, June 6, 2016. Madame Zaoui remarked that Lucette had a strong personality and was prone to grab everyone's attention, which she described as "immodest behavior."

9. Rabbi Jonas Jaquelin, email correspondence with the author, June 2, 2016.

10. Blau, *History*, 81.

11. Conversion is a postexilic phenomenon in Judaism. It was born in the Persian period and flourished during the Hellenistic period and the Roman period, beginning in 65 BCE. See Alan Segal, "Conversion to Judaism," in *The Oxford Handbook of Religious Conversion*, ed. Lewis Rambo and Charles Farhadian (New York: Oxford University Press, 2004), 578–97.

12. Blau, *History*, 78.

13. Ibid., 82.

14. Ruth Blau, *Les Gardiens de la Cité: Histoire d'une Guerre Saint* (Paris: Lammarion, 1978), 34.

15. Henie Persitz, phone interview with the author, August 6, 2018.

16. Blau, *History*, 90.

17. David Ellenson and Daniel Gordis, *Pledges of Jewish Allegiance* (Stanford: Stanford University Press, 2015), 38–69.

18. Blau, *History*, 90–92.

19. Ibid., 94.

20. Greer Cashman, "No Stranger to Controversy," *Jerusalem Post*, May 24, 2000, https://web.archive.org/web/20010119125400/http://www02 .jpost.com/Editions/2000/03/05/Features/Features.3576.html.

21. "Extradition Agreement Signed with France," *Davar*, November 13, 1958, 2 (in Hebrew).

22. New York Supreme Court, Dutch-American Mercantile Corporation v. Corta Corporation and Leon Swergold, Appellate Division—First Department, file 8432.

23. Moshe Cheshin, "Yossele Was Smuggled Aboard through 'Jordan,'" *Herut*, July 18, 1962, 2 (in Hebrew).

24. Blau, *History*, 95–97.

25. Ibid., 96.

26. Ibid., 98–103.

27. Cheshin, "Yossele."

28. Blau, *History*, 105.

29. Ibid., 107.

30. "Manitou—His Biography," Manitou Institute, accessed January 6, 2022, https://manitou.org.il/page/290.

31. Blau, *History*, 104.

32. Ibid., 104–5.

33. Ibid., 114–15.

34. Cashman, "No Stranger."

35. Blau, *History*, 122.

36. Ibid., 122.

37. Ibid., 123–24.

38. Chana Ullman, *The Transformed Self: The Psychology of Religious Conversion* (New York: Plenum Press, 1989), 59–74.

39. Blau, *History*, 128.

40. Ibid., 130.

41. Ibid., 140–63.

42. Motti Inbari, *Jewish Radical Ultra-Orthodoxy Confronts Modernity, Zionism, and Women's Equality* (New York: Cambridge University Press, 2016), 131–72.

43. Blau, *History*, 167.

44. Ibid., 173.

45. Ibid., 175–76.

46. Yosef Fund, *Separation or Integration: Agudat Yisrael Confronts Zionism and the State of Israel* (Jerusalem: Magnes Press, 1999) (in Hebrew).

47. Susan Cohen-Weitz, "Joining the Jewish Fold: The Changing Conversion Policies in Austria and Germany since 1945," in *Becoming Jewish: New Jews and Emerging Jewish Communities in Globalized World*, ed. Tudor Parfitt and Netanel Fisher (Newcastle, UK: Cambridge Scholars Publishing, 2016), 138–55.

48. Barbara J. Steiner, "Between Guilt and Repression—Conversion to Judaism after the Shoah," in *Contemporary Jewish Reality in Germany and Its Reflection in Film*, ed. Claudia S. Dorchain and Felice N. Wonnenberg (Berlin: De Gruyter, 2013), 124.

49. Barbara Steiner, "'The German Desire to be Jewish': Conversions of Non-Jewish Germans to Judaism after 1945," in *Becoming Jewish: New Jews and Emerging Jewish Communities in Globalized World*, ed. Tudor Parfitt and Netanel Fisher (Newcastle, UK: Cambridge Scholars Publishing, 2016), 156–66.

50. Ibid.

51. Menachem Friedman, *Society and Religion: Non-Zionist Orthodoxy in the Land of Israel* (Jerusalem: Ben-Zvi Institute, 1978); Aviezer Ravitzky, *Messianism, Zionism, and Religious Radicalism* (Chicago: University of Chicago Press, 1993), 40–78; Inbari, *Jewish*, 173–202.

5. WHERE IS YOSSELE?

1. The biographical information is taken from Shlomo Cohen-Sidon, *Where's Yossele? The Story of Yossele Schumacher* (Tel Aviv: Haolam Hazeh, 1963), 1–30 (in Hebrew).

2. Samuel Heilman and Menachem Friedman, "Religious Fundamentalism and Religious Jews: The Case of the Haredim," in *Fundamentalism Observed*, ed. Martin E. Marty and Scott Appleby (Chicago: University of Chicago Press, 1991), 197–264.

3. Cohen-Sidon, *Where's Yossele?* 30–35.

4. Ibid.

5. Ibid., 12.

6. Ibid., 16–22.

7. On the difficulties of Polish immigrants in Israel, see Marcos Silber, "'Immigrants from Poland Want to Go Back': The Politics of Return

Migration and Nation Building in 1950s Israel," *Journal of Israeli History* 27, no. 2 (2008): 201–19.

8. Yossi Schumacher, interview with the author, April 1, 2020.

9. Isser Harel, *The Yossele Campaign* (Tel Aviv: Yediot Aharonot, 1982), 31–39 (in Hebrew).

10. Cohen-Sidon, *Where's Yossele?* 73–101.

11. Ibid., 102–3.

12. Harel, *Yossele*, 30.

13. Cohen-Sidon, *Where's Yossele?* 143–44.

14. Harel, *Yossele*, 26–28.

15. "Kanievsky, Jacob Israel," in *Encyclopedia Judaica*, 2nd ed., ed. Michael Berenbaum and Fred Skolnik (Detroit: Macmillan Reference USA, 2007), 11:762–63.

16. Ruth Blau, *The History of Yossele Schumacher* (Brooklyn: Copy Corner, 1993), 193–98.

17. Ibid., 201–2.

18. Collection of articles *Mishmeret Chomatenu*, from members of Neturei Karta, vol. 14, 6 Iyar 5722–1962, Blau Archive, Box 1, Itzhak Davidson's 'Eretz Israel' Private Collection.

19. Blau, *History*, 203.

20. Harel, *Yossele*, 11–13.

21. Blau, *History*, 214.

22. Ibid., 220.

23. Ibid., 216–28.

24. Ibid., 250.

25. Menachem Keren-Kratz, *The Zealot: The Satmar Rabbe, Rabbi Yoel Teitelbaum* (Jerusalem: Shazar Center, 2020), 193–200 (in Hebrew).

26. Blau, *History*, 258–60.

27. Harel, *Yossele*, 106.

28. Her Immigrant Declaration, dated September 1, 1961, was found in Ruth Blau's Archives, Jerusalem, Israel. A letter from the Israeli Consulate dated May 6, 1963, and signed by Consul Shlomo Nahmias confirms her request to renounce her citizenship, Ruth Blau's Archives, Jerusalem, Israel.

29. Blau, *History*, 269.

30. Cohen-Sidon, *Where's Yossele?* 168.

31. Blau, *History*, 269.

32. Cohen-Sidon, *Where's Yossele?* 155.

33. Ibid., 158–59.

34. Ibid., 158.

35. Blau, *History*, 297–99. Harel reached a similar conclusion in *Yossele*, 77.

36. Michael Wolf, "The Halakhic Attitude to Din Rodef and Din Moser," in *Delinquency and Social Deviation: Theory and Practice*, ed. Moshe Arad and Yuval Wolf (Ramat Gan, Israel: Bar Ilan University Press, 2002), 215–49 (in Hebrew).

37. Chabad sources claim that the rebbe supported the resolution of the affair and the child's return to his parents only toward the end of the stage, when it was clear that the Mossad was about to discover Yossele's location. He did so after ensuring that all those involved would be pardoned, including several Chabad Hasidim who had been involved from the beginning, including the child's uncle. See Schneeor Zalman Berger, "The House of the Messiah: The Tract of Exposures in the Yossele Affair Continues," Chabad Info, accessed January 6, 2022, https://chabad.info/magazine /117361/.

38. Blau, *History*, 302.

39. Ibid.

40. Harel, *Yossele*, 121.

41. Ibid., 80.

42. The copy of Uriel Davidson's unpublished autobiography is in the possession of his daughter Nechama Davidson.

43. A. Ben David, "The Malochim Sect Hid Yossele," *Maariv*, July 3, 1962, 3 (in Hebrew).

44. Blau, *History*, 312.

45. According to Uriel's testimony in his unpublished manuscript.

46. Cohen-Sidon, *Where's Yossele?* 163.

47. Ibid.

48. Ibid., 164.

49. Ibid., 165.

50. Blau, *History*, 350–51.

51. Cohen-Sidon, *Where's Yossele?* 167.

52. Ibid., 169.

6. THE HUNT (1962)

1. Isser Harel, *The Yossele Campaign* (Tel Aviv: Yediot Aharonot, 1982), 48 (in Hebrew).

2. Ibid., 48–49.

3. Ibid., 53–54.

4. Ibid., 53–55.

5. Ibid., 55.

6. Ibid., 77.

7. Ibid., 80.

8. Ibid., 80–81.

9. Uriel described this chain of events in his unpublished autobiography. His daughter, Nechama Davidson, holds a copy of the manuscript.

10. Harel, *Yossele*, 85.

11. Ibid., 89–90.

12. "Infractions à la réglementation des changes," no. 006520, May 25, 1962, Ruth Blau's Archives, Jerusalem, Israel.

13. Ruth Blau, *The History of Yossele Schumacher* (Brooklyn: Copy Corner, 1993), 374–75.

14. Harel, *Yossele*, 89–95.

15. Blau, *History*, 378.

16. Harel, *Yossele*, 100.

17. Ibid., 100–101.

18. Ibid., 102–5.

19. Ibid., 105–6.

20. Ibid., 107.

21. Ibid.

22. Blau, *History*, 409.

23. Ibid., 424.

24. Ibid., 429.

25. Greer F. Cashman, "No Stranger to Controversy," *Jerusalem Post*, May 24, 2000, https://web.archive.org/web/20010119125400/http://www02.jpost.com/Editions/2000/03/05/Features/Features.3576.html.

26. Blau, *History*, 432.

27. Harel, *Yossele*, 107–9.

28. John Earl Haynes and Harvey Klehr, *Early Cold War Spies: The Espionage Trials That Shaped American Politics* (Cambridge: Cambridge University Press, 2006), 208–29.

29. Shlomo Cohen-Sidon, *Where's Yossele? The Story of Yossele Schumacher* (Tel Aviv: Haolam Hazeh, 1963), 169–71.

30. Harel, *Yossele*, 262.

31. Yossele Schumacher, interview with the author, April 2020.

32. Israel A. Gruvis and Aaron Kluger, "Here Is Yossele," *Hamishpacha*, Tishrei 11, 5782 (September 17, 2021), 244–60 (in Hebrew).

33. Harel, *Yossele*, 372.

34. Ibid., 370–72.

35. Ibid., 106.

36. Blau, *History*, 245–51.

37. On the efforts of Ruth to find Simone, see "The Convert Ruth Ben David Penetrated Several Missionary Centers in Arab States," *Maariv*, December 13, 1972, 1, 2 (in Hebrew).

38. Blau, *History*, 245.

39. Harel, *Yossele*, 111.

40. The offer is described in Blau, *History*, 456.

41. During the meeting, the Mossad representative again offered to purchase her house, and also suggested that the Mossad would fund a vacation for her in Europe (Blau, *History*, 461–63).

42. J. S. Markowits, Imperial Crystals & China Co. June 13, 1962; Gottfried Neuburger, International Trade Show, June 25, 1964, Ruth Blau's Archives, Jerusalem, Israel.

43. Shlomo Nahmias, Consulat D'Israel, Paris May 6, 1963; Albert de Bonfils, Ambassade de France, October 31, 1963, Ruth Blau's Archives, Jerusalem, Israel.

44. The libraries that hold a copy are Harvard, Princeton, Hebrew Union College, Jewish Theological Seminary, and Yeshiva University. New York Public Library holds a copy and so does the National Library of Israel.

45. Blau Archives, Box 1, letter on behalf of Avraham Stenmann, 29 Tevet 5724 (January 14, 1964), Itzhak Davidson's 'Eretz Israel' Private Collection.

46. Yerachmiel Domb, n.d., Ruth Blau's folder, Itzhak Davidson's 'Eretz Israel' Private Collection.

47. Ruth Blau, *Guardians of the City* (Jerusalem: Idanim, 1979) (in Hebrew).

48. Gittel Davidson, Uriel Davidson, and Nechama Davidson, interview with the author, Jerusalem, July 3, 2019.

49. Unclear signature, Ministère des Affaires Étrangères, December 12, 1962, Ruth Blau's Archives, Jerusalem, Israel.

50. Yehezkel Adiram, "The Convert Who Kidnapped Yossele Will Be Indicted in France," *Yediot Aharonot*, September 30, 1964, 16 (in Hebrew).

51. Blau, *History*, 468.

52. As Yossi Schumacher clarified to me by email correspondence on May 15, 2020. See also Adiram, "Convert."

53. Eyal Kafkafi, "The Dismantling of the Palmach According to the Rules of Mamlakhtiyut," *Zemanim* 33 (1990): 86–100 (in Hebrew).

54. Jarold Auerbach, *Brothers at War: Israel and the Tragedy of Altalena* (New Orleans: Quid Pro Books, 2011).

55. Nir Kedar, "Jewish Republicanism," *Journal of Israeli History* 26, no. 2 (2007): 179–99. See also Adam Raz, *The Iron Fist Regime: David Ben-Gurion, the Statism Controversy and the Political Debate on Israel's Nuclear Program* (Jerusalem: Karmel, 2019) (in Hebrew).

56. Eliezer Don-Yehiya, "Mamlakhtiyut and Judaism in the Teachings and Policies of David Ben Gurion," *Hatziyonut* 14 (1989): 51–88.

57. "Ben-Gurion Met the Hazon Ish," *Maariv*, October 20, 1952, 1 (in Hebrew).

58. Nir Kedar, "Ben Gurion's View of the Place of Judaism in Israel," *Journal of Israeli History* 32, no. 2 (2013): 157–74.

59. Minutes of Government Meeting, February 25, 1962.

60. Minutes of the Knesset Meeting, "The Disappearance of Yossele Schumacher," Meeting no. 121, April 3, 1962.

61. Minutes of Government Meeting, July 8, 1962.

62. Minutes of Government Meeting, July 15, 1962.

7. "I AM ALSO ACQUIRING RUTH AS MY WIFE": THE MARRIAGE OF RUTH BEN DAVID AND RABBI AMRAM BLAU

1. Amram Blau's personal archive was stored in Boston University's archives between 2008 and 2020. Ruth's grandson, Itzhak Davidson, demanded the collection back to the family, and eventually, in 2020 his request was approved. Itzhak Davidson owns a personal collection called the Eretz Israel Collection stored at his home in Israel, which now also includes Amram's and Ruth's personal archives. In addition, some of Ruth's documents are stored at her son's apartment in Jerusalem. Therefore, in the notes, I have distinguished between the two collections.

2. Menachem Keren-Kratz, "HaEdah HaCharedit in Jerusalem and Its Attitude toward the State of Israel, 1948–1973," *Cathedra* 161 (2017): 140 (in Hebrew).

3. Ibid., 156–57.

4. Ibid., 164.

5. Shlomi Doron, *Shuttling between Two Worlds: Coming to and Defecting from Ultra-Orthodox Judaism in Israeli Society* (Tel Aviv: Hakibbutz Hameuchad Publishing House, 2013) (in Hebrew).

6. Ruth Blau, *Guardians of the City* (Jerusalem: Idanim, 1979), 169 (in Hebrew).

7. Ruth Ben David, "17 Tevet," January 2, 1964, Ruth Ben David Folder, Itzhak Davidson's 'Eretz Israel' Private Collection.

8. In her book, she mentioned that in addition to Sokolovsky, the son-in-law of "Rabbi Levi" was accompanying, who was also the husband of one of her closest friends in Meah Shearim; thus, we can conclude the "Rabbi Levi" is Rabbi Aharon Katzenelbogen, and his son-in-law was Avraham Yaakov Epstein (R. Blau, *Guardians*, 170 [in Hebrew]).

9. R. Blau, *Guardians*, 174; Menashe Darash, *Neturei of Meah Shearim* (Jerusalem: Atnahta Publishing House, 2010), 72–73 (in Hebrew).

10. Ruth Blau, "To Rabbi David Jungreis," Sunday Parashat Vayakhel (n.d.), Ruth Ben David Folder, Itzhak Davidson's 'Eretz Israel' Private Collection.

11. Ruth Ben David, no title, n.d., Ruth Ben David Folder, Itzhak Davidson's 'Eretz Israel' Private Collection.

12. Ruth Blau, no title, n.d., Ruth Ben David Folder Itzhak Davidson's 'Eretz Israel' Private Collection.

13. For Neturei Karta's modesty guidelines, see Motti Inbari, *Jewish Radical Ultra-Orthodoxy Confronts Modernity, Zionism and Women's Equality* (New York: Cambridge University Press, 2016), 74–93.

14. Ruth Ben David, "For the Zadik, My Groom for a Few Months, Rabbi Blau Shlita," n.d., Ruth Ben David Folder, Itzhak Davidson's 'Eretz Israel' Private Collection.

15. R. Blau, *Guardians*, 175.

16. *"Wort,"* Ruth Ben David folder, Itzhak Davidson's 'Eretz Israel' Private Collection. See also R. Blau, *Guardians*, 172.

17. Amram Blau, *The Claim of Amram Blau against the Court of HaEdah HaCharedit in Jerusalem* (Jerusalem: self-published, 5725 [1964–1965]) (in Hebrew); found in Blau Archive, Box 3, Ruth Ben David folder, Itzhak Davidson's 'Eretz Israel' Private Collection.

18. The ruling was copied to Amram Blau's response to the court mentioned in A. Blau, *Claim*.

19. Ruth Ben David, "On the Ship," 5 Adar 1 (unclear year, probably 5725) (February 7, 1965), Ruth Ben David Folder, Itzhak Davidson's 'Eretz Israel' Private Collection.

20. Ruth Ben David, no title, n.d. (Address to Yoel Teitelbaum), Ruth Ben David Folder, Itzhak Davidson's 'Eretz Israel' Private Collection.

21. R. Blau, *Guardians*, 181.

22. In her letters, Ruth repeatedly uses the term *servant of God*; this is not currently used among these circles and is probably a remnant of her Catholic background.

23. Ruth Ben David, "To the Tzadik Genius Admor Shlita," n.d., Ruth Ben David Folder, Itzhak Davidson's 'Eretz Israel' Private Collection.

24. R. Blau, *Guardians*, 181.

25. See, for example, Kimmi Caplan, *Amram Blau: The World of Neturei Karta's Leader* (Jerusalem: Yad Yitzhak Ben-Zvi, 2017), 372 (in Hebrew). Caplan made many factual mistakes and errors in his book; on these, see Menachem Keren-Kratz, "Book review: Kimmy Caplan, Amram Blau—The World of Neturei Karta's Leader," *Modern Judaism* 39, no. 2 (2019): 223–29.

26. Ruth Blau, "To Reb David Jungreis," Sunday, Parashat Vayakhel (n.d.), Ruth Ben David Folder, Itzhak Davidson's 'Eretz Israel' Private Collection.

27. Ruth Ben David, "To the Zadik Admor Shlita," 17 Shvat (5725?) (January 20, 1965?), Ruth Ben David Folder, Itzhak Davidson's 'Eretz Israel' Private Collection.

28. Shaul Magid, "The Politics of (un)Conversion: The 'Mixed Multitude' (*Erev Rav*) as Conversos in Rabbi Hayyim Vital's Ets ha–da'at tov," *Jewish Quarterly Review* 95, no. 4 (2005): 625–66; Yitzhak Baer, "The Historical Background of the *Ra'aya Mehemena*," *Zion* 5, no. 1 (1940): 1–44 (in Hebrew); Yeshayahu Tishbi, *The Teaching of the Zohar*, vol. 2 (Jerusalem: Bialik Institute, 1949), 686–92 (in Hebrew). During the Sabbatean controversy in the seventeenth century, both followers and opponents of Shabtai Zvi denigrated each other as the mixed multitude: Pawel Maciejko, *The Mixed Multitude: Jacob Frank and the Frankist Movement, 1755–1816* (Philadelphia: University of Pennsylvania Press, 2011).

29. Inbari, *Jewish*, 173–202.

30. Ruth Ben David, "B"H After Taanit," n.d., Ruth Ben David Folder, Boston University's Archives.

31. Ruth Ben David, "For the Tzadik Rabbi Dov," n.d., Ruth Ben David Folder, Boston University's Archives.

32. A. Blau, *Claim*.

33. Ibid., 8–10.

34. Ibid., 10.

35. Ibid.

36. Ibid., 11.

37. Ibid., 14.

38. Ibid., 16-17.

39. Ibid., 1.

40. Ibid., 6.

41. Mark Washofsky, "Responsa and Rhetoric: On Law, Literature, and the Rabbinic Decision," in *Pursuing the Text: Studies in Honor of Ben Zion Wacholder*, ed. John C. Reeves and John Kampen (Sheffield: Sheffield Academic Press, 1994), 360-409.

42. R. Blau, *Guardians*, 198-99.

43. Ruth Ben David, no title, 14 Shvat (January 17, 1965?), Ruth Ben David Folder, Itzhak Davidson's 'Eretz Israel' Private Collection.

44. R. Blau, *Guardians*, 185-86.

45. Ibid., 188.

46. See Inbari, *Jewish*, 159-60.

47. "Kahal Yereim VeHasidim to A' Blau," 12 Elul 5725 (September 9, 1965), Ruth Ben David Folder, Itzhak Davidson's 'Eretz Israel' Private Collection.

48. Ruth Blau, "Monday Parashat Korah," n.d. (around July 1966), Ruth Ben David Folder, Itzhak Davidson's 'Eretz Israel' Private Collection.

49. Darash, *Neturei*, 85-89.

50. R. Blau, *Guardians*, 196.

51. Ruth Blau, "To My Best Friend the Zadik Rabbi Dov," n.d., Ruth Ben David Folder, Itzhak Davidson's 'Eretz Israel' Private Collection.

52. Darash, *Neturei*, 85-86.

53. Ibid., 86.

54. Ibid., 88.

55. Dov Sokolovsky, "To My Dear Friend Rabbi Amram Blau Shlita," 11 Tamuz 5729 (June 27, 1969), Ruth Ben David Folder, Itzhak Davidson's 'Eretz Israel' Private Collection.

56. In her own book, Ruth emphasizes her desire to have children (R. Blau, *Guardians*, 198).

8. RUTH BLAU: THE REBBETZIN

1. Ruth Blau, *Guardians of the City* (Jerusalem: Idanim, 1979), 187 (in Hebrew).

2. Margalit Shilo, *Princess or Prisoner? Jewish Women in Jerusalem 1840-1914* (Waltham: Brandeis University Press, 2005).

3.　Tamar Ross, *Expending the Place of Torah—Orthodoxy and Feminism* (Waltham: Brandeis University Press, 2004), 14.

4.　Mishna Horayot 3:7.

5.　Deuteronomy 17:14.

6.　*Shulchan Arukh*, Hoshen Mishpat 7:4; BT Shevuot 30a.

7.　Judah b. Bezalel Loew, "Drush al ha-Torah," in *Sifrei Maharal: Beer ha- Golah* (Jerusalem: n.p., 1972), 28 (in Hebrew). The Maharal anchors the passivity of women in the Talmudic interpretation of the term *nashim sha'ananot* (carefree women) (Isaiah 32:9). See BT Barcot 17:1.

8.　Ross, *Expending*, 16.

9.　Ibid., 17.

10.　Rachel Elior, "'Present but Absent,' 'Still Life,' and 'A Pretty Maiden Who Has No Eyes': On the Presence and Absence of Women in the Hebrew Language, in Jewish Culture, and in Israeli Life," *Studies in Spirituality* 20 (2010): 381–455 at 396.

11.　Admor is the title by which Hassidic rabbis are known. The term is an abbreviation of the Hebrew words *adonenu, morenu, ve-rabenu* (our lord, teacher, and master).

12.　Shilo, *Princess*.

13.　Margalit Shilo, "Takanot Yerushalaim Ke-Me'atsvot Migdar," in *A Woman in Jerusalem: Gender, Society and Religion*, ed. Tova Cohen and Joshua Schwartz (Ramat Gan, Israel: Ingeborg Rennert Center for Jerusalem Studies, 2002), 65–77 (in Hebrew).

14.　Shilo, *Princess*, 37.

15.　Ibid., 79.

16.　Ibid., 83.

17.　Ibid., 85.

18.　Ibid., 91.

19.　Ibid., 117.

20.　Ibid., 128–29.

21.　Immanuel Etkes, "Marriage and Torah Study among the Lomdim in Lithuania in the Nineteenth Century," in *The Jewish Family: Metaphor and Memory*, ed. David Charles Kraemer (New York: Oxford University Press, 1989), 153–78.

22.　Samuel Heilman and Menachem Friedman, "Religious Fundamentalism and Religious Jews: The Case of the Haredim," in *Fundamentalism Observed*, ed. Martin E. Marty and Scott Appleby (Chicago: University of Chicago Press, 1991), 227–34.

23.　Hanna Papanek, "Men, Women, and Work: Reflections on the Two-Person Career," *American Journal of Sociology* 78, no. 4 (1973): 852–72.

24. Ibid.

25. Shuly R. Schwartz, *The Rabbi's Wife—The Rebbetzin in American Jewish Life* (New York: New York University, 2006), 9–12.

26. Ibid., 23.

27. Menachem Keren-Kratz and Motti Inbari, "The Sociological Model of Haredi (Ultra-Orthodox) Rebbetzins (Rabbi's Wives): 'Two-Person Single Career' vs. 'Parallel Life Family,'" *AJS Review* 46, no. 2 (2022): 270–90.

28. Yosef Zuriel, "R. Amram's Widow Will Publish Her Memories," *Maariv*, July 16, 1976, 26 (in Hebrew).

29. Yosef Zuriel, "Ruth Ben David Admits She Helps Kids Travel Abroad to Study in Yeshivot," *Maariv*, February 2, 1972, 3 (in Hebrew).

30. Yaron Ben-Naeh, "A Closet and a Mirror, a Sewing Machine with a Leg: Match Making among Sephardi Jews in Mandatory Jerusalem according to the Notebook of a Jerusalemite Match-Maker," *Cathedra* 170 (2019): 81–124 (in Hebrew).

31. Orit Yael, "The Modern Match-Maker: Josef Liber's Hebrew Match Making Revolution," *Kesher* 52 (2019): 49–62 (in Hebrew).

32. The letter is held in her personal archive, Ruth Blau's Archives, Jerusalem, Israel.

33. Kimmy Caplan, *Amram Blau: The World of Neturei Karta's Leader* (Jerusalem: Yad Yitzhak Ben-Zvi, 2017), 502–3 (in Hebrew).

34. Noah Zevuluni, "An American Convert Married a Painter in Meah Shearim," *Maariv*, May 31, 1970, 10 (in Hebrew).

35. "Must Watch Movies for Knesset Members," *Maariv*, July 5, 1971, 10 (in Hebrew).

36. Motti Inbari, *Jewish Radical Ultra-Orthodoxy Confronts Modernity, Zionism, and Women's Equality* (New York: Cambridge University Press, 2016), 88–90.

37. Nechama Davidson, "My Ruth's Scroll," Facebook, May 25, 2020, https://www.facebook.com/groups/1592170434330768/permalink/2689781097903024.

38. Inbari, *Jewish*, 157–58.

9. "FIERCE WOMAN!": TRAVELING IN MUSLIM COUNTRIES

1. It is interesting to note that in that passport, she goes by her Christian name Madelene Lucette Ferraille and her occupation is "professor."

2. Reuven Leib, "The Convert Ruth Ben David Traveled to the US to Act for Our Prisoners in Syria," *Yediot Ahronot*, December 6, 1973, 8 (in Hebrew).

3. E. A. El Maleh, "Le combat singulier d'une néophyte," *Le Monde*, March 30, 1979, https://www.lemonde.fr/archives/article/1979/03/30/le -combat-singulier-d-une-neophyte_2770537_1819218.html.

4. Lucien Bitterlin, *La Flamme et la Soufre* (Paris: VegaPress, 1988), 205–10.

5. Lee H. Hamilton, "Last Word on the October Surprise?; Case Closed," *New York Times*, January 24, 1993, https://www.nytimes .com/1993/01/24/opinion/dialogue-last-word-on-the-october-surprise -case-closed.html.

6. Ari Ben-Menashe, *Profits of War: Inside the Secret US-Israeli Arms Network* (New York: Sheridan Square Press, 1992), 41–42.

7. Ibid.

8. Ibid., 68.

9. Ibid., 67–73.

10. Baruch Meiri, "'The Convert' Stays in Iran to Meet Khomeini," *Maariv*, December 9, 1979, 1 (in Hebrew).

11. Naomi Gal, "Rebbetzin Ruth Blau Returned from Iran; She Tried to Save a Jew That Was Sentenced to Death," *Yediot Ahronot*, July 13, 1980, 1 (in Hebrew).

12. Lior B. Sternfeld, *Between Iran and Zion: Jewish Histories of Twenti-eth-Century Iran* (Stanford: Stanford University Press, 2018), 112–13.

13. Davar Daneilpour, phone interview with the author, April 22, 2019.

14. George E. Gruen, *Iranian Jewry and the Execution of Albert Daniel-pour: A Foreign Affairs Background Memorandum* (New York: American Jewish Committee, June 11, 1980).

15. Karmel Melamed, "Family of Jewish Businessman Executed by the Iranian Regime Speaks Out, 40 Years Later," *Forward*, June 4, 2020, https://forward.com/news/national/448093/family-of-jewish-business -man-executed-by-the-iranian-regime-speaks-out-40/.

16. Francis Cornu, "LES PÉRÉGRINATIONS D'UNE JUIVE D'ISRAËL Mme Ruth Blau a intercédé auprès de l'iman Khomeiny en faveur de juifs jugés par les tribunaux islamiques," *Le Monde*, July 21, 1980, https://www.lemonde.fr/archives/article/1980/07/21/iran-les -peregrinations-d-une-juive-d-israel-mme-ruth-blau-a-intercede-aupres -de-l-iman-khomeiny-en-faveur-de-juifs-juges-par-les-tribunaux -islamiques_3069535_1819218.html.

17. Noah Zevuluni, "A Conversation with Ruth Ben David, the Wife of Amram Blau," unpublished article, accessed June 2, 2016, http://www .ranaz.co.il/notPublished/article47_19930616.asp.

18. Melamed, "Family."

19. Dominique Avon and Anaïs-Trissa Khatchadourian, *Hezbollah: A History of the Party of God* (Cambridge, MA: Harvard University Press, 2012), 26.

20. "Les six juifs enleves a Beyrouth seraient vivants," *Le Monde*, December 6, 1985, https://www.lemonde.fr/archives/article/1985/12/06/les -six-juifs-enleves-a-beyrouth-seraient-vivants_2757457_1819218.html.

21. "Une revendiction de l'Organisation des opprimes sur terre. Trois otages juifs libanais ont ete assaaines a Beyrouth" *Le Monde*, January 1, 1987.

22. Shefi Gabbai, "All the Kidnapped are in the Hands of the Hezbollah," *Maariv*, April 1, 1986, 1, 9 (in Hebrew).

23. Joseph Finklestone, "Lebanese Jews Facing Kidnapping and Death," *Jewish Chronicle*, January 9, 1987, 25.

24. Editorial, "The Horrors in Beirut," *Maariv*, January 2, 1986, 10 (in Hebrew).

25. Shlomo Tzazana, "The Rebbetzin Traveled Secretly to Damascus and Tried to Get Information on Missing Soldiers," *Maariv* January 13, 2000, 12 (in Hebrew).

26. Claudia Parsons, "Accused of anti-Semitism, Ahmadinejad Meets Jews," *Reuters*, September 24, 2008, https://www.reuters.com/article/us -un-assembly-iran-jews/accused-of-anti-semitism-ahmadinejad-meets -jews-idUSTRE48O00220080925.

10. RUTH BLAU, ULTRA-ORTHODOX SOCIETY, AND ISRAELI PUBLIC OPINION

1. Shlomo Nakdimon and Shaul Mayzlish, *De Haan: The First Political Assassination in the Land of Israel* (Tel-Aviv: Modan, 1985) (in Hebrew).

2. Michael Berkovitz, "Rejecting Zion, Embracing the Orient: The Life and Death of Jacob Israel de Haan," in *Orientalism and the Jews*, ed. Evan D. Kalmar and Derek Penslar (Waltham, MA: Brandeis University Press, 2005), 109–24.

3. Menachem Keren-Kratz, "Israel and Ishmael: The Arabs in the Land of Israel in the Eyes of the Haredi Old Yishuv," in *Religion and Nationality: Jewish*

Leadership and Thought and the Arab Question, ed. Ephraim Lavie (Jerusalem: Carmel, 2017), 145–62 (in Hebrew).

4. The Haredi literature relating to de Haan presents a fuller version of his activities on behalf of the community. However, this literature ignores de Haan's personal life and provides a highly selective review of his actions. For further discussion of his legal and political campaigns, see David Halevy, *Murder in Jerusalem: The Affair of the Murder of Prof. de Haan* (Bnai Brak: Tefutza, 1987) (in Hebrew); Zvi Meshi Zahav and Yehuda Meshi Zahav, *The Martyr Rabbi Yaacov Yisrael de Haan, May G-d Avenge His Blood: The First Zionist Murder in the Land of Israel* (Jerusalem: Institute of Haredi Judaism, Sivan 5746 [1986]) (in Hebrew).

5. Nakdimon and Mayzlish, *De Haan,* 207–18.

6. Shlomi Doron, *Shuttling between Two Worlds: Coming to and Defecting from Ultra-Orthodox Judaism in Israeli Society* (Tel Aviv: Hakibbutz Hameuchad Publishing House, 2013) (in Hebrew).

7. Menachem Keren-Kratz and Motti Inbari, "The Sociological Model of Haredi (Ultra-Orthodox) Rebbetzins (Rabbi's Wives): 'Two-Person Single Career' vs. 'Parallel Life Family,'" *AJS Review* 46, no. 2 (2022): 270–90.

8. As was observed by Margalit Shilo in her parallel lives model: Margalit Shilo, *Princess or Prisoner? Jewish Women in Jerusalem 1840–1914* (Waltham, MA: Brandeis University Press, 2005).

9. Menachem Keren-Kratz, "The Quest for Meaning and Fulfillment among Haredi Women," in *The Search for Meaning in the Israeli Scene,* ed. Ofra Mayseless and Pninit Russo-Netzer (London: Oxford University Press, 2022), 275–95.

10. Keren-Kratz and Inbari, "Sociological."

11. Motti Inbari, *Jewish Radical Ultra-Orthodoxy Confronts Modernity, Zionism and Women's Equality* (New York: Cambridge University Press, 2016), 74–93.

12. Menachem Keren-Kratz, *The Zealot: Rabbi Yoel Teitelbaum* (Jerusalem: Shazar Center, 2021) (in Hebrew).

13. Keren-Kratz and Inbari, "Sociological."

14. Ibid.

15. See for example Amos Nevo, "Ruth Blau Is Waiting for the Messiah," *Yediot Ahronot,* December 13, 1985, 16–19 (in Hebrew); Yosef Zuriel, "Ruth Blau Has an Open Door at Arafat's," *Maariv,* July 28, 1980, 19 (in Hebrew); Aaron Bachar, "A Riddle and Her Name Is Ruth Blau," *Yediot Ahronot,* August 13, 1976, Weekend Supplement, 6 (in Hebrew).

16. Knesset Meeting Protocol, May 18, 1960, 1275.

17. Ruth's attempt to help Albert Danielpour was reported on the front page of the newspapers. See Naomi Gal, "Rebbetzin Ruth Blau Returned from Iran; She Tried to Save a Jew That Was Sentenced to Death," *Yediot Ahronot*, July 13, 1980, 1 (in Hebrew).

EPILOGUE

1. Daniel Boyarin, *Unheroic Conduct: The Rise of Heterosexuality and the Invention of the Jewish Man* (Berkeley: University of California Press, 2007), 1–29.

BIBLIOGRAPHY

Adiram, Yehezkel. "The Convert Who Kidnapped Yossele Will Be Indicted in France." *Yediot Aharonot*, September 30, 1964, 16 (in Hebrew).

Auerbach, Jarold. *Brothers at War: Israel and the Tragedy of Altalena*. New Orleans: Quid Pro Books, 2011.

Avon, Dominique, and Anaïs-Trissa Khatchadourian. *Hezbollah: A History of the Party of God*. Cambridge, MA: Harvard University Press, 2012.

Bachar, Aaron. "A Riddle and Her Name Is Ruth Blau." *Yediot Ahronot*, August 13, 1976, Weekend Supplement, 6 (in Hebrew).

Baer, Mark D. "History and Religious Conversion." In *The Oxford Handbook of Religious Conversion*, edited by Lewis R. Rambo and Charles Farhadian, 25–47. New York: Oxford University Press, 2004.

Baer, Yitzhak. "The Historical Background of the *Ra'aya Mehemena*." *Zion* 5, no. 1 (1940): 1–44 (in Hebrew).

Ben David, A. "The Malochim Sect Hid Yossele." *Maariv*, July 3, 1962, 3 (in Hebrew).

Ben David, Ruth. "B'H after Taanit." n.d. Ruth Ben David Folder, Itzhak Davidson's 'Eretz Israel' Private Collection.

Ben David, Ruth. "For the Tzadik Rabbi Dov." n.d. Ruth Ben David Folder, Itzhak Davidson's 'Eretz Israel' Private Collection.

Ben David, Ruth. "For the Zadik, My Groom for a Few Months, Rabbi Blau Shlita." n.d. Ruth Ben David Folder, Itzhak Davidson's 'Eretz Israel' Private Collection.

Ben David, Ruth. 14 Shvat (January 17, 1965?). Ruth Ben David Folder, Itzhak Davidson's 'Eretz Israel' Private Collection.

Ben David, Ruth. "On the Ship." 5 Adar 1 (n.d.) 5725 (February 7, 1965?). Ruth Ben David Folder, Itzhak Davidson's 'Eretz Israel' Private Collection.

Ben David, Ruth. "17 Tevet." January 2, 1964. Ruth Ben David Folder, Itzhak Davidson's 'Eretz Israel' Private Collection.

Ben David, Ruth. "To the Tzadik Genius Admor Shlita." n.d. Ruth Ben David Folder, Itzhak Davidson's 'Eretz Israel' Private Collection.

Ben David, Ruth. "To the Zadik Admor Shlita." 17 Shvat (n.d. 5725?) (January 20, 1965?). Ruth Ben David Folder, Itzhak Davidson's 'Eretz Israel' Private Collection.

Ben-Menashe, Ari. *Profits of War: Inside the Secret US-Israeli Arms Network*. New York: Sheridan Square Press, 1992.

Ben-Naeh, Yaron. "A Closet and a Mirror, a Sewing Machine with a Leg: Match Making among Sephardi Jews in Mandatory Jerusalem according to the Notebook of a Jerusalemite Match-Maker." *Cathedra* 170 (2019): 81–124 (in Hebrew).

Berger, Schneeor Zalman. "The House of the Messiah: The Tract of Exposures in the Yossele Affair Continues." Chabad Info. Accessed January 6, 2022. https://chabad.info/magazine/117361/.

Berkovitz, Michael. "Rejecting Zion, Embracing the Orient: The Life and Death of Jacob Israel de Haan." In *Orientalism and the Jews*, edited by Evan D. Kalmar and Derek Penslar, 109–24. Waltham, MA: Brandeis University Press, 2005.

Bitterlin, Lucien. *La Flamme et la Soufre*. Paris: VegaPress, 1988.

Blau, Amram. *The Claim of Amram Blau against the Court of HaEdah HaCharedit in Jerusalem*. Jerusalem: Self-published, 5725 [1964–1965] (in Hebrew).

Blau, Ruth. *Guardians of the City*. Jerusalem: Idanim, 1979 (in Hebrew).

Blau, Ruth. *The History of Yossele Schumacher*. Brooklyn: Copy Corner, 1993.

Blau, Ruth. *Les Gardiens de la Cité: Histoire d'une Guerre Saint*. Paris: Lammarion, 1978.

Blau, Ruth. "Monday Parashat Korah." n.d. (around July 1966). Ruth Ben David Folder, Itzhak Davidson's 'Eretz Israel' Private Collection.

Blau, Ruth. "To My Best Friend the Zadik Rabbi Dov." n.d. Ruth Ben David Folder, Itzhak Davidson's 'Eretz Israel' Private Collection.

Blau, Ruth. "To Our Righteous Genius Rebbe." n.d. (1965). Ruth Blau's Folder, Itzhak Davidson's 'Eretz Israel' Private Collection.

Blau, Ruth. "To Rabbi David Jungreis." Sunday Parashat Vayakhel (n.d.). Ruth Ben David Folder, Itzhak Davidson's 'Eretz Israel' Private Collection.

Boyarin, Daniel. *Unheroic Conduct: The Rise of Heterosexuality and the Invention of the Jewish Man*. Berkeley: University of California Press, 2007.

Caplan, Kimmi. *Amram Blau: The World of Neturei Karta's Leader*. Jerusalem: Yad Yitzhak Ben-Zvi, 2017 (in Hebrew).

Cashman, Greer F. "No Stranger to Controversy." *Jerusalem Post*, May 24, 2000. https://web.archive.org/web/20010119125400/http://www02.jpost.com/Editions/2000/03/05/Features/Features.3576.html.

Cheshin, Moshe. "Yossele Was Smuggled Aboard through 'Jordan.'" *Herut*, July 18, 1962, 2 (in Hebrew).

Cohen, Asher. *The Shoah in France*. Jerusalem: Yad Vashem, 1996.

Cohen-Sidon, Shlomo. *Where's Yossele? The Story of Yossele Schumacher*. Tel Aviv: Haolam Hazeh, 1963.

Cohen-Weitz, Susan. "Joining the Jewish Fold: The Changing Conversion Policies in Austria and Germany since 1945." In *Becoming Jewish: New Jews and Emerging Jewish Communities in a Globalized World*, edited by Tudor Parfitt and Netanel Fisher, 138–55. Newcastle: Cambridge Scholars Publishing, 2016.

Collection of Articles Mishmeret Chomatenu, from Members of Neturei Karta. Vol. 14. 6 Iyar 5722–1962. Blau Archive, Box 1, Itzhak Davidson's 'Eretz Israel' Private Collection.

Cornu, Francis. "LES PÉRÉGRINATIONS D'UNE JUIVE D'ISRAËL Mme Ruth Blau a intercédé auprès de l'iman Khomeiny en faveur de juifs jugés par les tribunaux islamiques." *Le Monde*, July 21, 1980. https://www.lemonde.fr/archives/article/1980/07/21/iran-les-peregrinations-d-une-juive-d-israel-mme-ruth-blau-a-intercede-aupres-de-l-iman-khomeiny-en-faveur-de-juifs-juges-par-les-tribunaux-islamiques_3069535_1819218.html.

Danielpour, Davar. Phone interview with the author, April 22, 2019.

Darash, Menashe. *Neturei Karta of Meah Shearim*. Jerusalem: Atnahta Publishing House, 2010 (in Hebrew).

Davar. "Extradition Agreement Signed with France." November 13, 1958, 2 (in Hebrew).

Davidson, Gittel, Uriel Davidson, and Nechama Davidson. Interview with the author, July 3, 2018.

Davidson, Nechama. "My Ruth's Scroll." Facebook, May 25, 2020. https://www.facebook.com/groups/1592170434330768/permalink/2689781097903024/.

De Bonfils, Albert. Ambassade de France. October 31, 1963. Ruth Blau's Archives, Jerusalem, Israel.

Domb, Yerachmiel. Untitled, n.d. Ruth Blau's folder, Itzhak Davidson's 'Eretz Israel' Private Collection.

Don-Yehiya, Eliezer. "Mamlakhtiyut and Judaism in the Teachings and Policies of David Ben Gurion." *Hatziyonut* 14 (1989): 51–88.

Doron, Shlomi. *Shuttling between Two Worlds: Coming to and Defecting from Ultra-Orthodox Judaism in Israeli Society.* Tel Aviv: Hakibbutz Hameuchad Publishing House, 2013 (in Hebrew).

Douglas, Mary. *In the Wilderness: The Doctrine of Defilement in the Book of Numbers.* Sheffield, UK: Sheffield Academic Press, 1993.

Editorial. "The Horrors in Beirut." *Maariv*, January 2, 1986, 10 (in Hebrew).

Elior, Rachel. "'Present but Absent,' 'Still Life,' and 'a Pretty Maiden Who Has No Eyes': On the Presence and Absence of Women in the Hebrew Language, in Jewish Culture, and in Israeli Life." *Studies in Spirituality* 20 (2010): 381–455.

Ellenson, David, and Daniel Gordis. *Pledges of Jewish Allegiance.* Stanford, CA: Stanford University Press, 2015.

El Maleh, E. "Le combat singulier d'une neophyte." *Le Monde*, March 30, 1979. https://www.lemonde.fr/archives/article/1979/03/30/le-combat-singulier-d-une-neophyte_2770537_1819218.html.

Etkes, Immanuel. "Marriage and Torah Study among the Lomdim in Lithuania in the Nineteenth Century." In *The Jewish Family: Metaphor and Memory*, edited by David C. Kraemer, 153–78. New York: Oxford University Press, 1989.

Ferziger, Adam. *Exclusion and Hierarchy: Orthodoxy, Nonobservance, and the Emergence of Modern Jewish Identity.* Philadelphia: University of Pennsylvania Press, 2005.

File 3213–423. Service Historique de la Defense. Paris, France.

Finkelstein, Menachem. *Conversion, Halakhah, and Practice.* Ramat Gan, Israel: Bar Ilan University Press, 2006.

Finklestone, Joseph. "Lebanese Jews Facing Kidnapping and Death." *Jewish Chronicle*, January 9, 1987, 25.

Friedman, Menachem. *Society and Religion: Non-Zionist Orthodoxy in the Land of Israel.* Jerusalem: Ben-Zvi Institute, 1978 (in Hebrew).

Fund, Yosef. *Separation or Integration: Agudat Yisrael Confronts Zionism and the State of Israel.* Jerusalem: Magnes Press, 1999 (in Hebrew).

Gabbai, Shefi. "All the Kidnapped Are in the Hands of the Hezbollah." *Maariv*, April 1, 1986, 1, 9 (in Hebrew).

Gal, Naomi. "Rebbetzin Ruth Blau Returned from Iran; She Tried to Save a Jew That Was Sentenced to Death." *Yediot Ahronot*, July 13, 1980, 1 (in Hebrew).

Granqvist, Pehr, and Lee Kirkpatrick. "Religious Conversion and Perceived Childhood Attachment: A Meta-Analysis." *International Journal for the Psychology of Religion* 14, no. 4 (2004): 223–50.

Gruen, George E. *Iranian Jewry and the Execution of Albert Danielpour: A Foreign Affairs Background Memorandum*. New York: American Jewish Committee, 1980.

Gruvis, Israel A., and Aaron Kluger. "Here Is Yossele." *Hamishpacha*, Tishrei 11, no. 5782 (September 17, 2021): 244–60 (in Hebrew).

Halevy, David. *Murder in Jerusalem: The Affair of the Murder of Prof. de Haan*. Bnei Brak, Israel: Tefutza, 1987 (in Hebrew).

Hamilton, Lee H. "Last Word on the October Surprise?; Case Closed." *New York Times*, January 24, 1993. https://www.nytimes.com /1993/01/24/opinion/dialogue-last-word-on-the-october-surprise -case-closed.html.

Harel, Isser. *The Yossele Campaign*. Tel Aviv: Yediot Aharonot, 1982 (in Hebrew).

Hastings, Max. *Das Reich: Resistance and the March of the 2nd SS Panzer Division through France, June 1944*. London: Michael Joseph, 1981.

Haynes, John E., and Harvey Klehr. *Early Cold War Spies: The Espionage Trials That Shaped American Politics*. Cambridge: Cambridge University Press, 2006.

Heilman, Samuel, and Menachem Friedman. "Religious Fundamentalism and Religious Jews: The Case of the Haredim." In *Fundamentalism Observed*, edited by Martin E. Marty and Scott Appleby, 197–264. Chicago: University of Chicago Press, 1991.

Inbari, Motti. *Jewish Radical Ultra-Orthodoxy Confronts Modernity, Zionism, and Women's Equality*. New York: Cambridge University Press, 2016.

"Infractions à la réglementation des changes." No. 006520, May 25, 1962. Ruth Blau's Archives, Jerusalem, Israel.

Jaquelin, Jonas. Email correspondence with author, June 2, 2016.

Kafkafi, Eyal. "The Dismantling of the Palmach According to the Rules of Mamlakhtiyut." *Zemanim* 33 (1990): 86–100 (in Hebrew).

"Kahal Yereim VeHasidim to A. Blau." 12 Elul 5725 (September 9, 1965). Ruth Ben David Folder, Itzhak Davidson's 'Eretz Israel' Private Collection.

"Kanievsky, Jacob Israel." In *Encyclopedia Judaica*, 2nd ed., edited by Michael Berenbaum and Fred Skolnik, 11:762–63. Detroit, MI: Macmillan Reference USA, 2007.

Kedar, Nir. "Ben Gurion's View of the Place of Judaism in Israel." *Journal of Israeli History* 32, no. 2 (2013): 157–74.

Kedar, Nir. "Jewish Republicanism." *Journal of Israeli History* 26, no. 2 (2007): 179–99.

Keren-Kratz, Menachem. "Book review: Kimmy Caplan, Amram Blau—The World of Neturei Karta's Leader." *Modern Judaism* 39, no. 2 (2019): 223–29.

Keren-Kratz, Menachem. "HaEdah HaCharedit in Jerusalem and Its Attitude toward the State of Israel, 1948–1973." *Cathedra* 161 (2017): 139–74 (in Hebrew).

Keren-Kratz, Menachem. "Israel and Ishmael: The Arabs in the Land of Israel in the Eyes of the Haredi Old Yishuv." In *Religion and Nationality: Jewish Leadership and Thought and the Arab Question*, edited by Ephraim Lavie, 145–62. Jerusalem: Carmel, 2017 (in Hebrew).

Keren-Kratz, Menachem. "The Quest for Meaning and Fulfillment Among Haredi Women." In *The Search for Meaning in the Israeli Scene*, edited by Ofra Mayseless and Pninit Russo-Netzer, 275–95. London: Oxford University Press, 2022.

Keren-Kratz, Menachem. *The Zealot: The Satmar Rabbe, Rabbi Yoel Teitelbaum*. Jerusalem: Shazar Center, 2020 (in Hebrew).

Keren-Kratz, Menachem, and Motti Inbari. "The Sociological Model of Haredi (Ultra-Orthodox) Rebbetzins (Rabbi's Wives): 'Two-Person Single Career' vs. 'Parallel Life Family.'" *AJS Review* 46, no. 2 (2022): 270–90.

Leib, Reuven. "The Convert Ruth Ben David Traveled to the US to Act for Our Prisoners in Syria." *Yediot Ahronot*, December 6, 1973, 8 (in Hebrew).

Le Monde. "Les six juifs enleves a Beyrouth seraient vivants." December 6, 1985. https://www.lemonde.fr/archives/article/1985/12/06/les-six-juifs -enleves-a-beyrouth-seraient-vivants_2757457_1819218.html.

Le Monde. "Une revendiction de l'Organisation des opprimes sur terre: Trois otages juifs libanais ont ete assaaines a Beyrouth." January 1, 1987.

Loew, Judah b. Bezalel. "Drush al ha-Torah." In *Sifrei Maharal: Beer ha-Golah*. Jerusalem: n.p., 1972 (in Hebrew).

Maariv. "Ben Gurion Met the Hazon Ish." October 20, 1952, 1 (in Hebrew).

Maariv. "The Convert Ruth Ben David Penetrated Several Missionary Centers in Arab States." December 13, 1972, 1, 2 (in Hebrew).

Maariv. "Must Watch Movies for Knesset Members." July 5, 1971, 10 (in Hebrew).

Maciejko, Pawel. *The Mixed Multitude: Jacob Frank and the Frankist Movement, 1755–1816.* Philadelphia: University of Pennsylvania Press, 2011.

Magid, Shaul. "The Politics of (un)Conversion: The 'Mixed Multitude' (*erev rav*) as Conversos in Rabbi Hayyim Vital's Ets ha–da'at tov." *Jewish Quarterly Review* 95, no.4 (2005): 625–66.

"Manitou—His Biography." Manitou Institute. Accessed January 6, 2022. https://manitou.org.il/page/290.

Markowits, J. S. Imperial Crystals & China Co. June 13, 1962. Ruth Blau's Archives, Jerusalem, Israel.

Meiri, Baruch. "The Convert Stays in Iran to Meet Khomeini." *Maariv*, December 9, 1979, 1 (in Hebrew).

Melamed, Karmel. "Family of Jewish Businessman Executed by the Iranian Regime Speaks Out, 40 Years Later." *Forward*, June 4, 2020. https://forward.com/news/national/448093/family-of-jewish -businessman-executed-by-the-iranian-regime-speaks-out-40/.

Meshi Zahav, Zvi, and Yehuda Meshi Zahav. *The Martyr Rabbi Yaacov Yisrael de Haan, May G-d Avenge His Blood: The First Zionist Murder in the Land of Israel.* Jerusalem: Institute of Haredi Judaism, Sivan 5746–1986 (in Hebrew).

Ministère des Affaires Étrangères. December 12, 1962. Ruth Blau's Archives, Jerusalem, Israel.

Minutes of Government Meeting. February 25, 1962.

Minutes of Government Meeting. July 8, 1962.

Minutes of Government Meeting. July 15, 1962.

Minutes of Knesset Meeting. May 18, 1960, 1275.

Minutes of Knesset Meeting. "The Disappearance of Yossele Schumacher." Meeting no. 121, April 3, 1962.

Mons, Paul. *Afin que nul n'oblie: En France la Das Reich fit la guerre aux civils.* Brive, France: Ecritures, 2004.

Nahmias, Shlomo. Consulat D'Israel. Paris May 6, 1963. Ruth Blau's Archives, Jerusalem, Israel.

Nakdimon, Shlomo, and Shaul Mayzlish. *De Haan: The First Political Assassination in the Land of Israel.* Tel Aviv: Modan, 1985.

Neuburger, Gottfried. International Trade Show. June 25, 1964. Ruth Blau's Archives, Jerusalem, Israel.

Nevo, Amos. "Ruth Blau Is Waiting for the Messiah." *Yediot Ahronot*, December 13, 1985, 16–19 (in Hebrew).

New York Supreme Court. Dutch-American Mercantile Corporation v. Corta Corporation and Leon Swergold. Appellate Division—First Department. File 8432.

Nikiprowetzky, Valentin, and André Zaoui. *Maimonide. Le livre de la connaissance*. Paris: Presses Universitaires de France, 1961.

Olson, Lynne. *Madame Fourcede's Secret War: The Daring Young Woman Who Led France's Largest Spy Network against Hitler*. New York: Random House, 2019.

Paloutzian, Raymond, James Richardson, and Lewis Rambo. "Religious Conversion and Personality Change." *Journal of Personality* 76, no. 6 (2009): 1047–79.

Papanek, Hanna. "Men, Women, and Work: Reflections on the Two-Person Career." *American Journal of Sociology* 78, no. 4 (1973): 852–72.

Parsons, Claudia. "Accused of Anti-Semitism, Ahmadinejad Meets Jews." *Reuters*, September 24, 2008. https://www.reuters.com/article/us-un -assembly-iran-jews/accused-of-anti-semitism-ahmadinejad-meets -jews-idUSTRE48O00220080925.

Persitz, Henie. Phone interview with the author, August 6, 2018.

Ravitzky, Aviezer. *Messianism, Zionism, and Religious Radicalism*. Chicago: University of Chicago Press, 1993.

Raz, Adam. *The Iron Fist Regime: David Ben-Gurion, the Statism Controversy and the Political Debate on Israel's Nuclear Program*. Jerusalem: Karmel, 2019 (in Hebrew).

Ross, Tamar. *Expending the Place of Torah—Orthodoxy and Feminism*. Waltham, MA: Brandeis University Press, 2004.

Schumacher, Yossi. Virtual interview with the author, April 1, 2020.

Schuré, Edouard. *The Great Initiates: A Study of the Secret History of Religions*. San Francisco: Harper & Row, 1980.

Schwartz, Shuly R. *The Rabbi's Wife—The Rebbetzin in American Jewish Life*. New York: New York University, 2006.

Segal, Alan. "Conversion to Judaism." In *The Oxford Handbook of Religious Conversion*, edited by Lewis Rambo and Charles Farhadian, 578–97. New York: Oxford University Press, 2004.

Shilo, Margalit. *Princess or Prisoner? Jewish Women in Jerusalem 1840–1914*. Waltham, MA: Brandeis University Press, 2005.

Shilo, Margalit. "Takanot Yerushalaim Ke-Me'atsvot Migdar." In *A Woman in Jerusalem: Gender, Society and Religion*, edited by Tova Cohen and Joshua Schwartz, 65–77. Ramat Gan: Ingeborg Rennert Center for Jerusalem Studies, 2002 (in Hebrew).

Silber, Marcos. "'Immigrants from Poland Want to Go Back': The Politics of Return Migration and Nation Building in 1950s Israel." *Journal of Israeli History* 27, no. 2 (2008): 201–19.

Silber, Michael. "The Emergence of Ultra-Orthodoxy: The Invention of Tradition." In *The Uses of Tradition: Jewish Continuity in the Modern Era,* edited by Jack Wertheimer, 23–84. New York: JTS, 1992.

Sokolovsky, Dov. "To My Dear Friend Rabbi Amram Blau Shlita." 11 Tamuz 5729 (June 27, 1969). Ruth Ben David Folder, Itzhak Davidson's 'Eretz Israel' Private Collection.

Steiner, Barbara J. "Between Guilt and Repression—Conversion to Judaism after the Shoah." In *Contemporary Jewish Reality in Germany and Its Reflection in Film,* edited by Claudia S. Dorchain and Felice N. Wonnenberg, 123–37. Berlin: De Gruyter, 2013.

Steiner, Barbara J. "'The German Desire to Be Jewish': Conversions of Non-Jewish Germans to Judaism after 1945." In *Becoming Jewish: New Jews and Emerging Jewish Communities in Globalized World,* edited by Tudor Parfitt and Netanel Fisher, 156–66. Newcastle, UK: Cambridge Scholars Publishing, 2016.

Stenmann Avraham. Untitled. 29 Tevet 5724 (January 14, 1964). Blau Archives, Box 1, Itzhak Davidson's 'Eretz Israel' Private Collection.

Sternfeld, Lior B. *Between Iran and Zion: Jewish Histories of Twentieth-Century Iran.* Stanford: Stanford University Press, 2018.

Taylor, Charles. *A Secular Age.* Cambridge, MA: Harvard University Press, 2007.

Tishbi, Yeshayahu. *The Teaching of the Zohar.* Vol. 2. Jerusalem: Bialik Institute, 1949 (in Hebrew).

Tzazana, Shlomo. "The Rebbetzin Traveled Secretly to Damascus and Tried to Get Information on Missing Soldiers." *Maariv,* January 13, 2000, 12 (in Hebrew).

Ullman, Chana. *The Transformed Self: The Psychology of Religious Conversion.* New York: Plenum Press, 1989.

Washofsky, Mark. "Responsa and Rhetoric: On Law, Literature, and the Rabbinic Decision." In *Pursuing the Text: Studies in Honor of Ben Zion Wacholder,* edited by John C. Reeves and John Kampen, 360–409. Sheffield, UK: Sheffield Academic Press, 1994.

Weitz, Margaret C. *Sisters in the Resistance: How French Women Fought to Free France 1940–1945.* New York: John Wiley & Sons, 1995.

Wieviorka, Olivier. *The French Resistance*. Cambridge, MA: Harvard University Press, 2016.

Williamson, Gordon. *The Waffen-SS (1): 1 to 5 Divisions*. Oxford: Osprey Publishing, 2003.

Wolf, Michael. "The Halakhic Attitude to Din Rodef and Din Moser." In *Delinquency and Social Deviation: Theory and Practice*, edited by Moshe Arad and Yuval Wolf, 215–49. Ramat Gan, Israel: Bar Ilan University Press, 2002 (in Hebrew).

"*Wort*." Ruth Ben David folder. Itzhak Davidson's 'Eretz Israel' Private Collection.

Yael, Orit. "The Modern Match-Maker: Josef Liber's Hebrew Match Making Revolution." *Kesher* 52 (2019): 49–62 (in Hebrew).

Zaoui, Bianca. Telephone conversation with the author, June 6, 2016.

Zevuluni, Noah. "An American Convert Married a Painter in Meah Shearim." *Maariv*, May 31, 1970, 10 (in Hebrew).

Zevuluni, Noah. "A Conversation with Ruth Ben David, the Wife of Amram Blau." *Noah Zevuluni*, June 16, 1993. http://www.ranaz.co.il/notPublished/article47_19930616.asp.

Zuriel, Yosef. "R. Amram's Widow Will Publish Her Memories." *Maariv*, July 16, 1976, 26 (Hebrew).

Zuriel, Yosef. "Ruth Ben David Admits She Helps Kids Travel Abroad to Study in Yeshivot." *Maariv*, February 2, 1972, 3 (Hebrew).

Zuriel, Yosef. "Ruth Blau Has an Open Door at Arafat's." *Maariv*, July 28, 1980, 19 (in Hebrew).

INDEX

MOTTI INBARI is Professor of Jewish Studies at the University of North Carolina at Pembroke. Dr. Inbari is author or editor of nine books, including *The Making of Modern Jewish Identity: Ideological Change and Religious Conversion* and *Jewish Radical Ultra-Orthodoxy Confronts Modernity, Zionism and Women's Equality.*

For Indiana University Press

Gary Dunham, Acquisitions Editor and Director
Anna Francis, Assistant Acquisitions Editor
David Miller, Lead Project Manager/Editor
Stephen Williams, Marketing and Publicity Manager